NEW PERSPECTIVES ON ANCIENT JUDAISM

Volume 1

Religion, Literature, and Society
in Ancient Israel, Formative Christianity and Judaism

Number 206
NEW PERSPECTIVES ON ANCIENT JUDAISM

Edited by
Jacob Neusner
Peder Borgen
Ernest S. Frerichs
Richard Horsley

NEW PERSPECTIVES ON ANCIENT JUDAISM

Volume 1

Religion, Literature, and Society
in Ancient Israel, Formative Christianity and Judaism

Second Printing

Edited by

Jacob Neusner
Peder Borgen
Ernest S. Frerichs
Richard Horsley

Scholars Press
Atlanta, Georgia

NEW PERSPECTIVES ON ANCIENT JUDAISM

Library of Congress Cataloging-in-Publication Data

Religion, literature, and society in ancient Israel, formative
      Christianity and Judaism : formative Judaism / edited by Jacob
      Neusner . . . and others.
      p. cm. —(New perspectives on ancient Judaism ; v. 1)
      (Brown Judaic studies ; no. 206)
      Reprint. Originally published: Lanham, MD : University Press of
      America. c 1987. (Studies in Judaism).
      Includes bibliographical references and index.
      ISBN 1-55540-497-9
      1. Judaism—History—Talmudic period, 10–425. 2. Mishnah—
Criticism, interpretation, etc. 3. Sociology, Jewish.
I. Neusner, Jacob, 1932–   . II. Series. III. Series: Brown Judaic studies ;
no. 206.
BM177.R45 1990   90-8810
296'.09'015—dc20   CIP

Paperback edition published 2006 by Brown Judaic Studies
ISBN 1-930675-31-3 (alk. paper : paperback)

Printed in the United States of America
on acid-free paper

∞

To

Howard Clark Kee

In tribute to a definitive voice of this generation's research
into the interplay of religion and society
in the formative history of Christianity and Judaism.

His lessons on the study of Christianity
shape our understanding of our work
in the study of formative Judaism,
its texts, and the textual community represented by them.

'ad me'ah ve'esrim

...to one hundred and twenty years...

CONTENTS

Preface

Professor Howard Clark Kee, whose achievements we celebrate on the occasion of his recent retirement, showed the way for research into the interplay of religion and society in the case of ancient religion, with special emphasis upon Christianity. But what makes his achievement truly remarkable is his genuinely academic commitment. He studied Christianity because he found it interesting and located within its early phases examples of probative interest for an inquiry into principles of general intelligibility. That is what it means to study religion in an academic way. We who honor him here mean to do the same and to follow his example, but in study of a different subject, namely, Judaism of the period studied, for Christianity, by Kee. Each of the papers in this volume takes up the theme and method that have occupied Kee's scholarly program. Within the setting of the Judaism revealed in the documents of the rabbinic movement of late antiquity, down to the seventh century, all of us work on that theme or with that method of inquiry. In this way the authors represented here express their admiration for Kee and propose to carry forward lines of inquiry pioneered by him.

This volume is joined not only by a comprehensive theme and method, but also by a single occasion, a public and well-earned tribute to Howard Clark Kee. The book takes its place as a kind of *Beiheft*, beside the festschrift, *The Social World of Formative Christianity and Judaism. Essays in Tribute to Howard Clark Kee*, edited by Peder Borgen, Ernest S. Frerichs, Richard Horsley, and Jacob Neusner, to be published in 1988 by Fortress Press, Philadelphia. This separate tribute is partly adventitious. Most of the papers here were written for the principal *festschrift*, but because of the unexpectedly large response to the invitation to celebrate Kee and his career in scholarship, these papers, which formed a distinct unit in viewpoint, method, and approach, as well as in theme, were set apart to be published here on their own. In this way a larger number of scholars, particularly among the younger generation, have their opportunity to pay their respects than we could accommodate in the principal volume.

What holds the papers together are commonalities of theme, perspective, method, and critical judgment. All of the contributors have studied or taught in Judaic Studies at Brown University and have framed a common program of inquiry. Each of course pursues questions defined in terms of his or her interests, and results that one finds critically satisfying another may deem somewhat limited. But the scholars in this book do form a community of shared values, specifically, those of the academy. That is why they find it possible to learn from, and also to contribute to the learning of, other academic citizens, working in different areas from their own, such as are represented by Howard Clark Kee. Indeed, the one trait that characterizes all doctoral alumni and other colleagues of Brown University's Program in Judaic Studies is concern to learn from others, both in our own field and also in unfamiliar ones.

That is what sets apart the authors of the papers in this volume and joins them as a group. For a complete and final split has now taken place between Jewish and gentile scholars of Judaic studies in universities and Jewish scholars of Judaic studies (there are no gentiles to speak of) in institutions under Jewish auspices in the USA and Europe as well as most Israeli scholars of Judaic studies in the humanistic mode (as distinct from the social scientific).. A civil war – fought on uncivil terms, of course – has broken out. What unites these papers also distinguishes them from counterparts – and opposites – deriving from scholars of a different sort but working on the same subject-matter, namely, Jews. There is no more a single field of Jewish learning, whether called Jewish or Judaic Studies. Two separate academies have taken shape, the ethnic and the genuinely academic, and discourse between them is becoming increasingly strained. The one side addresses issues of humanistic learning, engages in no special pleading, and treats the Jewish or the Judaic data as exemplary of broader issues. The other side takes for granted the interest and importance of the Jewish and the Judaic data and regards incremental erudition, whether or not formed for a purpose, as self-evidently interesting. Let Howard Clark Kee provide the occasion for our stating explicitly the implicit meaning of current happenings in the academic world.

These are elegantly characterized by Professor William Scott Green, University of Rochester, writing in *Midstream*, October, 1986, p. 39, who states matters as follows:

> From the perspective of ethnic Jewish studies, materials are deemed interesting because they are Jewish. This school of thought is marked by a fundamentally romantic view of all things it defines as Jewish. Ethnic scholarship tends to be avenging and celebratory. Ethnic education at whatever level makes learning into a ritual attachment to the heroic people.

> Ethnic intellectual discourse tends to be restricted...and directed primarily to those within the ethnic group or those who share its romantic suppositions. In short, ethnic Jewish Studies is a self-validating enterprise, designed to preserve Jewish distinctiveness. Ethnic Jewish scholarship serves a powerful communal purpose and therefore is highly charged. It aims to teach the Jews about themselves and thereby to create a usable Jewish past, a workable Jewish present, and a viable Jewish future. Within this framework, reasoned intellectual dissent is all too often ignored or censored, or discounted and dismissed, as a form of disloyalty and disrespect.

I am inclined to think that, in the coming decade, Judaic Studies will break apart into two essentially irreconcilable camps, with little interchange between them. The size of the two camps is roughly the same in numbers, but the distribution is different. The Jewish ethnic scholars of Judaic Studies are concentrated in a few places, the Jewish seminaries, for example, along with the Hebrew teachers colleges, yeshivas, and the like (so far as yeshivas participate in the scholarly world at all), and in the State of Israel and its universities. The academic scholars of Judaic studies, both Jewish and otherwise, are widely distributed among universities, with from one to ten at any one place, but no sizable number anywhere. They are scattered in a second sense. In their universities, they are not assembled in a single department, but they serve in a variety of disciplines and therefore also disciplinary departments, e.g., as at Brown, history, religion, literature, language, sociology, political science, and the like. In some places there may be a program or center or even interdisciplinary department. But it is not the same thing as a yeshiva or a seminary or the Hebrew University of Jerusalem and its confreres, in which dozens of scholars, not differentiated as to discipline, form a unified and large cadre in a single school.

But while widely distributed, the academic and discipline-oriented scholars of Judaic studies are numerous. By definition they want no journals of "their own," since they propose to address the scholarly universe formed by their particular disciplines. They also do not form organizations of Jewish studies, nor do many of them join such organizations. But that is not because the academic scholars of Judaic studies do not concur or constitute a community. They form a vital consensus on the basic issues of learning. They view the Jews as exemplary, and they address a broad audience of interested but neutral scholars, in a variety of fields, on a common and shared agenda of inquiry. They do not treat the Jews as self-evidently interesting, and the data do not validate themselves without analysis.

This volume, which inaugurates a new series of monograph-articles, stands for the perspective of the academic sector of Judaic Studies, as that sector works on the problems of ancient Judaism. The academic scholars of Judaic studies do not concur or constitute a community form a vital consensus on the basic issues of learning. They view the Jews as exemplary, and they address a broad audience of interested but neutral scholars, in a variety of fields, on a common and shared agenda of inquiry. They do not treat the Jews as self-evidently interesting, and the data do not validate themselves without analysis. The academic sector of Judaic studies proves as productive as other parts of the humanities and social sciences; debates go forward; theses are presented and tested; much, for learning, is at stake. Green explains matters in this way:

Disciplinary Jewish Studies...apply to Jewish sources and materials the standardized inquiries, analytical criteria, and...skepticisim of university studies in the humanities and social sciences. These disciplines attempt

to address common questions to various texts, cultures and societies, and
thus deny special privilege to any ofthem.　They reject in principle
private, self-validating worlds of experience whose meaning is pertinent
and can be transmitted only to initiates.　Within a disciplinary
freamework, the study of discrete Jewish materials is shaped by general
questions about human imagination and behavior, questions extrinsic to
particular Jewish needs, concerns, and preoccupations.

The ethnic or theological or Israeli sector, by contrast, which emphasizes other
matters altogether, tends to a certain aridity in both method and result. While –
if not very witty – wonderfully erudite, little is at stake in debates conducted
under the ethnic and theological auspices, and in a broad range of subjects,
publication is limited.　What is more consequential than the absence of
publication is the poverty of a scholarly program characteristic of the ethnics,
since most of the articles in *Tarbiz* and *Zion* – to take two prominent journals of
the ethnics – can – and should – have been written a century ago, so far as
program and problem are concerned.　The range of publication limited, the
volume spare, the ethnic sector of Jewish or Judaic studies finds little to
contribute to common discourse, when work on X's view of Y or on the Jews in
Z in the year 1904 has been placed on display.　We look in vain in the corpus of
Kee's scholarship for articles of that type.　When we want examples of
scholarship as search for what is exemplary and refers to issues beyond the data,
we find them in his writings.　That is why we find it appropriate to conduct the
present project in his honor.

Kee himself has understood events and their meaning.　In his way, he
confronted the ethnic definition of both Christian and Judaic studies.　He
therefore knows in concrete ways what we now make public.　Proof of the
complete break between the two academies may be adduced from the conduct of
the ethnics toward the academics.　The former condemn without reading, receive
with sedulous silence major statements, and violate the accepted norms of
academic debate.　As Professor William Scott Green comments:

> Strong criticism of others' work is an academic commonplace.　It is the
> principal form of public intellectual engagement – the way scholars
> transact their business – and is supposed to promote the understanding of
> ideas, the assessment of theories, and the advancement of knowledge.
> When criticism degenerates into mere condemnation and overt insult, the
> dispute is political or personal, not academic and professional.　When
> criticism aims simply to discredit rather than to discern, the conflicting
> positions are irreconcilable, perhap incommensurable.

The mode of criticism of the ethnics is to point to "mistakes," which may
or may not be mistakes at all, of which much is made.　That is a form of
discrediting.　To prove plausible, however, lists of mistakes should be joined
with lists of non-mistakes.　Otherwise the mistakes may prove – if in fact errors

at all, and the great authorities pass their opinion on the basis of remarkable disinterest in facts – adventitious. Reviews that list errors but do not list correct statements are invidious and present mere innuendo; they do not persuade anyone who is not already persuaded.

In starting this new series, our sector of Judaic Studies signals its acceptance of the new situation. What we have now to accept, in my view, is that the world of Jewish learning has broken in half, with a few strong and segregated centers of the ethnic, and many, diffused and integrated presences of the disciplinary and academic. The two sides can no longer meet and transact business, because there is no business to be done any more, and, if truth be told, there probably never was. As Green says:

> There is a surrealism to the entire dispute. Ethnic and disciplinary Jewish Studies operate in incongruous worlds, have incompatible motivations, and address disparate constituencies. The dispute between them is bitter because it is pointless. Not enough is shared between them to allow the possibility of communication, much less persuasion.

I find the development of the two worlds of Judaic Studies a perfectly natural outcome of that free academy which welcomes Judaic learning on its terms, alongside that Jewish world which nurtures Judaic learning for its purposes. Both are valid terms and purposes. But the absolute and final division between the one and the other has now to be recognized, so that we can get on with the work and see for what it really is the rather overstated and overwrought statement with which the ethnic scholars have dismissed their enemy and competition.

What we see is simply the end of a monopoly and the beginning of competition. Our side has broken the monopoly, which cannot be regained. What can be wrong with that? I see nothing so healthy as the free market place in which ideas compete, as they must compete, and in which people make up their own minds. The disciplinary scholars will learn what the ethnics have to teach, when (and that is often) they come up with new facts. They will not be much affected by the imprecations of the ethnics; they will go on with their work, and they already do. As Green says:

> Ethnic Jewish Studies, which serve communal political needs and have communal support, will continue. But disciplinary Jewish Studies have taken firm root in American universities, and they will endure there. No amount of ethnic resentment, hosility, or anger can change that.

Green is surely right. I am not inclined to regret what has happened. On the contrary, I believe it is healthy for the Jewish people to preserve both kinds of learning, since there is a vital role for each, the one for the inner world, the other for the sheltering academy beyond. So our work begins.

We seize the occasion of honoring a distinguished colleague and good friend, who in his world exemplifies precisely the academic values that animate our work, to inaugurate a series which, we believe, is appropriate to the honoree and to his public career of controversy and enormous accomplishment. It is as it should be. The time has come.

We note support of The Max Richter Foundation of Rhode Island, at the instance of its trustees, in expression of their respect and esteem for the honoree of this volume.

This writer and his colleague, Professor Ernest S. Frerichs, express their thanks to Brown University, which has covered many incidental costs connected with this project, and has always made possible its faculty's unencumbered participation in scholarly ventures. Further thanks are owing to Mrs. Annette Boulay, Administrator of the Program in Judaic Studies at Brown University, for her efficient help in many aspects of the organization of this book.

JACOB NEUSNER
For the editors

Ernest S. Frerichs and Jacob Neusner
Program in Judaic Studies
Brown University
Providence, Rhode Island

Richard Horsley
Department of Religious Studies
University of Massachusetts
Boston, Massachusetts

Peder Borgen
Department of Religious Studies
University of Trondheim
Dragvoll, Trondheim, Norway

Part One

LITERARY PROBLEMS

Chapter One

Rabbi Ishmael and His Thirteen *Middot*

Gary G. Porton

University of Illinois at Urbana-Champaign

I

Many scholars accept the accuracy of the *beraita* in the opening of Sifra which states that Ishmael exegeted Scripture according to thirteen *middot*.[1] This essay will challenge this traditional picture of Ishmael's midrashic activity by examining those *sugyot* in the rabbinic corpus which attribute an exegetical comment and technique to him. Because the document in which Ishmael's sayings appear determines the literary form of the comment[2] and perhaps its content,[3] I have organized the *sugyot* according to the rabbinic collections in which they are found.

---

[1]H. Weiss, *The Generations and Their Exegetes* (Jerusalem: n.d.), II, 91-106. W. Bacher, *The Aggadah of the Tannaim*, translated by A. Z. Rabbinovitz (Jerusalem: 1922), I, 2, 4ff. J. Brull, *Introduction to the Mishnah* (Frankfort aM: 1879), 103-66. Z. Frankel, *The Pathways of the Mishnah* (Leipzig: 1859), I, 105-11. A. J. Heschel, *The Theology of Ancient Judaism* (London: 1962), I, ix-lix. J. D. Eisenstein, *Otzar Yisrael: An Encyclopedia of All Matters Concerning Jews and Judaism* (London: 1933), 328. J. D. Derenbourg, *Essai Sur l'Historie de la Geographie de la Palestine* (Paris: 1868), 389-91. M. Petuchowski, *Der Tanna Rabbi Ismael* (Frankfort aM: 1894), 81ff. E. Schurer, *The History of the Jewish People in the Age of Jesus Christ (175B.C.-A.D. 135)*, a new English version revised and edited by G. Vermes, F. Millar, and M. Black (Edinburg: 1979), 376-377. L. Finkelstein, *Akiba: Scholar, Saint and Martyr* (New York: 1975), 308-312. M. Margalioth, *Encyclopedia of Talmudic and Geonic Literature* (Tel Aviv: 1962), II, 599-605. A. Hyman, *A History of the Tannaim and Amoraim* (Jerusalem: 1964), II, 819-824. S. Safrai, "Ishmael ben Elisha," C. Roth and G. Widoger (eds.), *Encyclopaedia Judaica* (Jerusalem: 1973), IX, 83-86. S. Mendelssohn, "Ishmael b. Elisha," I. Singer (ed.), *The Jewish Encyclopedia* (New York: n.d.), VI, 648-650. S. Baron, *A Social and Religious History of the Jews* (New York and Philadelphia: 1957), V, 213, 218. This is only a sampling of the scholars who accept this view of Ishmael's activity in relationship to biblical interpretation.

[2]Porton, *The Traditions of Rabbi Ishmael, Part Four: The Material As a Whole* (Leiden: 1982), 18-56; especially 53-54.

[3]Porton, 94-159.

II

Before reviewing those pericopae in which Ishmael employs an identifiable exegetical method, we need to take a close look a Sifra's opening *beraita*.

A. Rabbi Ishmael says: "By thirteen methods the Torah is expounded."

B. [It is expounded] (1) by means of an *a fortiori* argument *(mql whwmr)*, (2) by means of a *gezarah shavah (mgzrh swh)*, (3) by means of a prototype based on one passage *(mbnyn 'b mktwb 'hd)*, (4) by means of a prototype based on two passages *(mbnyn 'b msny ktwbym)*, (5) by means of a general statement and a specific statement *(mkll wprt)*, (6) by means of a specific statement and a general statement *(mprt wkll)*, (7) by means of a general statement and a specific statement and a general statement *(mkll wprt wkll)*,

C. you only decide according to the subject of the specific statement.

D. [Scripture is expounded] (8) by means of a general statement which requires a specific statement *(mkll shw' sryk lprt)*, (9) and by means of a specific statement which requires a general statement *(wmprt shw' sryk lkll)*.

E. (10) Anything which is included in the general statement and which is specified in order to teach [something] teaches not only about itself but also about everything included in the general statement *(kl dbr shyh bkll wys' mn hkll llmd l' llmd 'l 'smw ys' 'l' llmd 'l hkll klw ys')*. (11) Anything which is included in the general statement and which is specifically mentioned as a requirement concerning another requirement which is in keeping with the general statement is specifically mentioned in order to make [the second requirement] less stringent and not more stringent *(kl dbr shyh bkll wys' mn hkll lyt'wn t'n 'hr shw' k'nynw ys' lhql wl' lhhmyr)*. (12) Anything which is included in the general statement and which is specifically   mentioned as a requirement concerning another requirement which is not in keeping with the general statement is specifically mentioned either to make less or more stringent *(kl dbr shyh bkll wys' mn hkll lyt'n 'hr sl' k'nynw ys' lhql wlhhmyr)*. (13) Anything which is included in the general statement and which is exempted from it by an entirely new [provision], you may not return it to [the provisions] of its [original] general statement unless Scripture expressly indicates that you may do so *(kl dbr shyh bkll wys' mn hkll lydwn bdbr hds 'y 'th ykwl lhhzyrw lkllw 'd syhzyrnw hktwb lkllw bpyrws)*.

F. (14) A thing is to be explained from its context *(dbr hmld m'nyynw*, (15) and a thing is to be explained from what follows it *(wdbr hmld mswpw)*.

G. (16)   And thus two passages which contradict each other [cannot be reconciled] unless a third passage comes and decides between them *(wkn sny ktwbyn hmkhysyn zh 't zh 'd wyb' hktwb hslysy wyry' bynyhm)*.[4]

A is a simple declarative sentence attributed to Ishmael: "By thirteen methods the Torah is expounded." The context suggests that the midrashic principles

---

[4] There are slight variations among the various Hebrew editions; however, these are unimportant. G. Porton, *The Traditions of Rabbi Ishmael, Part Two: Exegetical Comments in Tannaitic Collections* (Leiden: 1977), 63-64.

which follow are those to which the opening statement refers. However, the list, B-G, contains sixteen, not thirteen, rules.[5]

A careful analysis of B-G suggests that they were compiled from different sources and that they probably do not reflect the work of one person other than the sage who first redacted the list. In B and D, rules 1-9, the particle *mem,* m, introduces each rule. In addition, the methods are merely stated; we are not told how one should apply them. C, which explains 7, interrupts the flow of the passage and appears to be an editorial addition. Rules 10-13 are set in a different literary pattern, for each opens with *kl dbr shyh bkll wys' mn hkll.* The techniques are longer than 1-9, and they include explanations of how the rules should be employed. The two exegetical methods in F, 14 and 15, appear in yet another formulation, *dbr hmld;* again the statement of the rule indicates the manner of its use. Rule 16, G, is stylistically different from the other principles.

The discrepancy between the number of *middot* mentioned in A and the number of items contained in the list and the different literary forms which appear in B-G argue against connecting the list with the Ishmael of A. However, one could theorize that in fact Ishmael employed a set of thirteen or sixteen exegetical techniques and that those listed in Sifra were the ones he actually used. In order to test this theory, we shall quickly review the midrashic methods which Ishmael employed in the *sugyot* found in the various rabbinic collections.

III

Mishnah: Ishmael appears in eight exegetical pericopae in Mishnah. In Yoma 6:8 he takes Isa. 1:18 as a simile. In Shebu. 2:4 his comment rests on the appearance of the same phrase in Lev. 5:2 and Lev. 5:3. In Bekh. 7:5 Ishmael employs a pun to interpret Lev. 21:20, and in Arak. 8:7 he attempts to solve the apparent contradiction between Deut. 15:19 and Lev. 27:26 by claiming that the two verses do not actually discuss the same issue; he does not use rule 16 in Sifra. The most important mishnaic passage for our purpose is Shebu. 3:5:

    A. Rabbi Ishmael says: "One is liable only [for an oath sworn] about the future, for it is said: *To do evil or to do good* (Lev. 5:4)."

    B. Said Rabbi Aqiba to him: "If so, I [can] only [learn about oaths] which contain matters of good and evil [from Lev. 5:4]. From where [can I learn about oaths] which do not contain matters of good and evil?"

    C. [Ishmael] said to him: "[You can learn about these oaths] from an extension of Scripture *(mrbwy hktwb)* [in Lev. 5:4]."

---

[5]The number thirteen is achieved by combining some of the rules; for example, see D. De Sola Pool, *The Traditional Prayer Book for Sabbaths and Festivals* (New York: 1960), 127-129. 3 and 4 are combined; 8 and 9 are combined; and 14 and 15 are combined.

D. [Aqiba] said to him: "If Scripture can be extended to include this [oaths which do not contain matters of good and evil], Scripture can be extended to include this [oaths which do not deal with the future]."

In A Ishmael seems to take Lev. 5:4 literally: One is liable for only those oaths which speak about the future because the verb, *tsb'*, is in the imperfect. Aqiba's response, B, ignores the issue raised by Ishmael, for Aqiba discusses the *content* of the oath, not the *time-element*. Aqiba suggests that if one takes the verse literally, one can be held liable for only those oaths which are concerned with matters of good and evil, for these are the only topics which Lev. 5:4 mentions. Ishmael responds, C, that one may "extend," *rbwy*, the meaning of Lev. 5:4 to include oaths which treat matters other than good and evil, and Aqiba retorts, D, that if Ishmael is willing to "extend" the meaning of Scripture with regard to the oath's content, he also must be willing to "extend" Scripture's meaning with respect to the time-element of the oaths. The result of the debate is that Ishmael must now reject his original statement concerning the oath's time-element because he has employed the principle of rbwy, a method usually attributed to Aqiba and his followers.[6] We have a carefully designed *sugya* in which Ishmael's use of an "Aqiban" exegetical technique forces the former to reject his original interpretation of Lev. 5:4. The point of the *sugya* is that Ishmael unwittingly rejected his own opinion in favor of Aqiba's because he used one of the latter's midrashic methods.

Tosefta: There are twenty exegetical *sugyot* in which Ishmael appears in Tosefta; however, an exegetical principle can be assigned to him in only a few of these passages. In Sanh. 3:6 he uses an argument by analogy. In Sot. 6:6 Ishmael makes use of a *gezarah shavah,* and in B.Q. 6:18 Yosi states that Ishmael employed a *heqqes.* In Shab. 7:14 Ishmael seems to interpret Deut. 18:10 by means of a pun. In Shebu. 3:1 he interprets Lev. 5:1 in light of its context. In the rest of the *sugyot* in Tosefta Ishmael's midrashic techniques are unstated or unclear, although often he seems to follow the plain meaning of the verse he cites. Shebu. 1:7, although awkward, is an important pericope for our purposes; its relevant sections follow:[7]

A. Rabbi Nathan says: "*[Thing* in Lev. 5:2 was said] to include vessels, for uncleanness only goes down upon them by means of intention."

B. Said [Aqiba] to him: "Why do they consider vessels according to intention?"

C. For Rabbi Ishmael used to expound [Scripture] by means of "extensions" and "limitations." And he used to expound [Scripture by means of] a general statement, a specific statement, and a general statement.

D. *Or if anyone touches any unclean thing* (Lev. 5:2); [this] is a general statement. *Or touches the uncleanness of a man* (Lev. 5:3); [this] is a

---

[6]See the discussions of Aqiba in the works cited in note 1 and Y. Schechter, *Otzar HaTalmud* (Tel-Aviv: 1965), 337.

[7]For a fuller discussion of tShebu. 1:7 see Porton, II, 46-48.

specific statement. [If] there is a general statement, specific statement, and a general statement, you rule only according to the specific statement.

E. When it says: *Of whatever sort the uncleanness may be with which one becomes unclean* (Lev. 5:3), it returns and makes [another] general statement. Or [perhaps this] general statement [is included] in the first general statement. You say, "No!"

F. [Concerning a case in which there is] a general statement, a specific statement, and a general statement, you rule according to the specific statement.

The *sugya* is an exegetical dispute between Nathan and Aqiba concerning Lev. 5:2; the reference to Ishmael in C is an intrusion into the pericope. The passage changes direction at this point from a discussion of "intention," mentioned in B, to Ishmael's exegetical techniques. Therefore, there is no logical reason for C to follow B; however, the treatment of Ishmael's exegetical methods does parallel the discussion of Aqiba's exegetical practices which appears earlier in this *sugya*, in a section which I did not reproduce. There we read that Aqiba employs the principles of "extension" and "limitation," but does not use the techniques of a specific statement-general statement-specific statement. Thus, the discussions of Ishmael and Aqiba are parallel.

It is unfortunate that this section is in such poor condition, for it seems to contain an important piece of information, viz., Ishmael exegeted Scripture by means of the methods of "limitation" and "extension" as well as by the principle of a general statement, specific statement, and a general statement. The problem is that D mentions the specific statement-general statement-specific statement, while only giving a general statement and a specific statement. E-F realize this and awkwardly solve the problem. While Hasde David emends the text to read "Rabbi Ishmael did *not* expound [Scripture by means of the principles of] extension and limitation,"[8] I am inclinded to follow the text as we have it, especially because in mShebu. 3:5 both Ishmael and Aqiba used the principle of "extension."

Ishmael appears pretty much the same in Mishnah and Tosefta. In both texts he makes use of puns, and in both we find evidence that he employed the principle of "extension." Tosefta does indicate that he also used a *gezarah shavah* and a *heqqes*. It also *attributes* to him the use of the rule of the general statement-specific statement-general statement; Tosefta *does not provide* us with an example of his actual use of this technique.

Sifra: In addition to the opening *beraita* of Sifra, there are thirty exegetical pericope in this collection. Four of these appeared in Mishnah,[9] one is also

---

[8] See Hasde David on bkl tm' and S. Lieberman, *Tosefeth Rishonim* (Jerusalem: 1938), II, 174-175.

[9] All references to Sifra are from the edition of I. H. Weiss, *Torah Cohanim* (New York: reprint 1946). Sifra 23b = mShebu. 2:5; Sifra 23c = mShebu. 3:5; Sifra 95c = mBekh. 7:5; Sifra 114c = mArak. 8:7.

found in Tosefta,[10] and one appears twice in our collection.[11] With the exception of the opening of Sifra, this text does not offer us a new view of Ishmael's exegetical activity.

In five *sugyot* Ishmael employs a *gezarah shavah: Vayiqra' parsheta* 4:10; *Shemini pereq* 5:3-8; *Masora' parasha* 7:11; *'Aharei Mot pereq* 7:4; *'Emor pereq* 4:18. Ishmael makes use of an *a fortiori* argument in *Vayiqra' pereq* 9:2. The most interesting fact about the exegetical passages in Sifra is that they do not picture Ishmael's conforming to the opening *beraita* of the text. Although we are told that Ishmael exegeted Scripture according to thirteen exegetical techniques, and a supposed list of these rules appears, Sifra contains many passages in which we cannot discover Ishmael's midrashic principles. Furthermore, the examples of Ishmael's exegetical activity in Sifra do not have him using many of those methods which are attributed to him in the opening section of this collection. In fact, of those items mentioned in the list, Ishmael employs only two: a *gezarah shavah* (five times) and an *a fortiori* argument (one time).

Mekhilta Ishmael: Mekhilta contains sixty-six *sugyot* in which we find an exegetical statement attributed to Ishmael. In five instances he uses an *a fortiori* argument: *Pisha' Bo'* 3, 6; *Neziqin* 3, 10; *Shabta' Ki Tisa'* 1. He uses a *gezarah shavah* in *Pisha' Bo'* 6; *Vayehi BeShallah* 2; *Neziqin* 17, 18. Ishmael makes use of a *heqqes* in *Neziqin* 8, and in *Neziqin* 6 he interprets Scripture by means of a prototype. He uses an argument by analogy in *BaHodesh* 7, *Neziqin* 2, and 7. In *Neziqin* 9 Ishmael solves a contradiction between two verses by bringing a third verse; however, in *Pisha' Bo* 4 he does not bring a third verse to solve a contradiction between two other verses. In *BaHodesh* 11 Ishmael states that "all but three 'ifs' in the Bible indicate a voluntary act," and in *Neziqin* 1 he employs this principle. In *Neziqin* 6 he states that three verses in the Bible should be interpreted figuratively. In *Neziqin* 7 Ishmael seems to rely on the context to interpret Ex. 21:20.

In brief, the passages from Mekhilta do not differ significantly from those analyzed to this point. Ishmael may or may not apply a clearly recognizable exegetical technique to a verse. He most frequently uses the *a fortiori* argument and the *gezarah shavah*. We do find two *new* general principles attributed to him: 1) All but three "ifs" in the Bible indicate a voluntary action; and 2) three biblical verses are to be taken figuratively.

Mekhilta Simeon: There are eight exegetical pericopae in Mekhilta Simeon which are part of the Ishmaelean corpus. Ishmael employs one *a fortiori* argument, *Bo'* 12:45, one *gezarah shavah*, *Mishpatim* 21;2, and one argument by analogy, *Mishpatim* 22:16.

---

[10]Sifra 90c = tShab. 7:14.

[11]Sifra 6c = Sifra 81d.

Sifre Numbers: Ishmael appears in forty-five exegetical *sugyot* in Sifre Numbers. In this text we find that he employs a wide variety of exegetical techniques, some of which he has not used before. In *Naso'* 1 he uses a prototype based on two verses, and in *Shelah* 107 he employs a prototype based on one verse. In *Qorah* 118 he lays down the general rule that one cannot use something itself derived by an analogy as the basis of a second analogy,[12] and in *Huqat* 124 he states that "an extending particle follows an extending particle only to limit." In *Huqat* 124 and 125 Ishmael again employs the technical language of "extending" and "limiting;" in the former he uses the term *lrbwt*, while in the latter he makes use of the term *lhwsy'*. In *Naso* 44 he applies the principle of interpreting a verse from its context, and in *Naso'* 32 he states that three *'ts* in the Bible make their verbs reflexive. Also, *Naso'* 8 provides us with the first example of Ishmael's *using* the principle of a general statement and a specific statement, although the use of this principle was *attributed* to him in Tosefta, as well as in the opening *beraita* of Sifra. While Sifre Numbers provides us with those *sugyot* in which Ishmael has recourse to exegetical methods not yet encountered in his corpus, it also provides us with evidence of his use of the same principles he employed in the Tannaitic documents we have examined so far: He uses an analogy in *Naso'* 1, 6, and *Huqat* 124; an *a fortiori* argument in *Naso'* 7; a *gezarah shavah* in Qorah 116, and a pun in *Shelah* 112. Thus, while Sifre Numbers draws a much broader picture of Ishmael's exegetical activity than we have encountered in other Tannaitic collections we have investigated so far, we still notice that he fails to use many of the exegetical principles attributed to him in the opening of Sifra.

Sifre Deuteronomy: Ishmael appears in eighteen exegetical *sugyot* in Sifre Deuteronomy; five of these occur in other Tannaitic collections as well.[13] In the thirteen pericopae which appear only in this document, Ishmael uses a pun in *Re'ah* 107 and an *a fortiori* argument in *Shoftim* 203.

Midrash Tannaim: Thirty-eight exegetical *sugyot* from the Ishmaelean corpus appear in Hoffmann's edition of Midrash Tannaim.[14] Fifteen of these pericopae appear in other Tannaitic collections and need not concern us here.[15] In the remaining passages, Ishmael makes use of the term *lhws'y* on p. 69, a pun on p. 168, a *gezarah shavah* on p. 148, and the context of a verse on p. 144. Twice he states that an "extending" term follows an "extending" term only to "limit," pp. 93 and 163.

---

[12]He violates this rule on yQid. 1:2.

[13]The references to Sifre Deuteronomy are from L. Finkelstein, *Siphre ad Deuteronomium* (New York: 1969). 79 = tSheq. 2:2; 106 = tSanh. 3:6; 124 = mArak. 8:7 = Sifra 114c; 171 = tShab. 7:14; 237 = Mekh. Ish. *Mishpatim* 6.

[14]D. Hoffmann, *Midrash Tannaim* (Tel Aviv and New York: n.d.).

[15]Porton, IV, 180-183.

To this point we have reviewed those pericopae in the Tannaitic documents in which a specific exegetical rule can be attributed to Ishmael. In these texts Ishmael employs nine *a fortiori* arguments, thirteen *gezarot shavot*, three prototypes, one general statement-specific statement, eleven arguments by analogy, and four puns. Once he brings a third verse to solve a contradiction between two other verses, twice he employs a *heqqes*, five times he makes use of either the principle of "extension" or "limitation," twice he interprets the "ifs" in the Bible to indicate voluntary or required actions, three times he states that an "extending" term follows an "extending" term only to "limit," and once he argues that one cannot illustrate a case by something which is itself derived by analogy. Four times he relies on the context of verse in order to interpret it. In the Tannaitic corpus Ishmael made use of a limited number of exegetical rules, many of which are not attributed to him in the list at the opening of Sifra and some of which are usually associated with Aqiba and his students. Furthermore, we discover that he *does not use* many of those rules attributed to him in the *beraita* with which Sifra opens.

IV

When we move to the two *gemarot* our evidence does not change drastically. The most interesting new fact we discover is that the Palestinian Talmud contains a comparatively large number of references to Ishmael's use of the general statement-specific statement or its variations.[16] Three times in the Palestinian *gemara* Ishmael interprets a verse by means of a general statement-specific statement-general statement: Sot. 9:5; Qid. 1:2, M.S. 3:5. Three times he refers to or employs the principle of a general statement and a specific statement: Ter. 11:3, Pes. 9:3, Naz. 6:2. In Shab. 7:2 Ishmael states that two things specified in a general statement multiply its teachings. His use of these principles in the Palestinian Talmud is all the more striking when we remember that Ishmael does not employ this principle at all in the Babylonian *gemara* and that he used it only once in the entire Tannaitic corpus, although its use was attributed to him in Tosefta.[17]

The rest of the evidence from the Palestinian Talmud agrees with the data we have collected from the Tannaitic stratum in that both bodies of traditions

---

[16]In general, the Palestinian Talmud contains information about Ishmael which is not found elsewhere. See Porton, IV, especially 223-224.

[17]The fact that Ishmael seldom employs these principles and that the Palestinian Talmud contains the majority of those *sugyot* in which he does employ them is surprising in light of bShebu. 26a. On this page we find the following: "Said Rabbi Yohanan: 'Rabbi Ishmael served Rabbi Nehunia b. Haqanah who used to expound the whole Torah [by the principle of] a general statement and a specific statement. [Ishmael] likewise expounds [the whole Torah by the principle of] a general statement and a specific statement.'" Given Yohanan's remark, we would expect to find many more pericopae in which Ishmael employed the general statement-specific statement or one of its variations. Furthermore, we would expect to find some of these passages in the Babylonian Talmud.

attribute to Ishmael the use of the *gezarah shavah* more often than any other exegetical method: Hal. 1:1, Shab. 7:2, Suk. 2:7, Hag. 1:6, Yeb. 6:2, Yeb. 8:1, Yeb. 11:1, Sot. 2:1, Sot. 5:6, Git. 8:1, Qid. 1:2, Qid. 4:6, Ket. 3:6, and Sanh. 3:9. He uses one argument by analogy, Yoma 1:1, one *heqqes*, Yoma 8:3, and one *a fortiori* argument, Shebu. 8:1. He employs the principle of "extension" in Shebu. 8:1 and the term *'rbh* in Pes. 9:1. In Qid. 1:2 he violates the rules which he laid down in Sifre Numbers, of which the Palestinian Talmud's *sugya* takes note, and does illustrate a case by something which itself was derived by an analogy. Ishmael makes use of two puns, one in Shab. 2:1 and one in Qid. 1:7. In short, with the exception of the information about Ishmael's use of the general statement-specific statement and its variations, admittedly an important point, the Ishmael of the Palestinian Talmud looks much like the Ishmael of the Tannaitic stratum.

The evidence from the Babylonian Talmud agrees exactly with what we have found in the Tannaitic documents and with the major thrust of the Palestinian *gemara*. Like in the Tannaitic stratum, Ishmael does not rely on the general statement-specific statement, although Yohanan attributes its use to him on bShebu. 26a. Ishmael makes use of the *gezarah shavah* six times: Ber. 48b, Hag. 9a, Yeb. 6a, Sanh. 51b, Sanh. 84a, and Shebu. 86a. He uses two arguments by analogy, Zeb. 103b and Nid. 30b and three *a fortiori* arguments, Zeb. 40b and two on Zeb. 52a. Once, Naz. 25a, he uses the word *rq* as a limiting particle, and once, Sanh. 34b, he utilizes the word *lrbwt* in his comment. In addition, Ned. 32b contains the only pun attributed to Ishmael in the Babylonian Talmud.

It is striking that the picture of Ishmael which emerges from the Amoraic stratum is so close to the image of him we have from the Tannaitic sources. Throughout, he uses virtually the same limited number of exegetical techniques in about the same frequency.

V

Genesis Rabbah contains three highly stylized passages in which the use of the principle of extension is attributed to Ishmael:

Genesis Rabbah 1:

A. *The heavens and the earth ('t hsmym w't h'rs)* (Gen. 1:1). Rabbi Ishmael asked Rabbi Aqiba [about this verse]. Said [Ishmael] to him: "Because you studied with Nahum of Gam Zo twenty-two years [the] *'k* and [the] *rq* [which] limit [the meaning of a verse and the] *'t* and *gm* [which] extend [the meaning of a verse], what is the meaning of the *'t* which is written here?"

B. Said [Aqiba] to him: "If it had said 'when God began to create the heavens and the earth [without the *'ts*], that would be the same as saying even heaven and earth are gods."

C. Said [Ishmael] to him: *"For it is no trifle to you* (Deut. 32:47). But if it is a trifle to you, [it is your fault], for you do not know how to interpret

[it]. Rather, *'t hsmym* [is said] to include [the] sun, [the] moon, [the] stars, and the planets. And *'t h'rs* [is said] to include [the trees, [the] grass, and the Garden of Eden."[18]

Genesis Rabbah 22:1:

A. *'t yhwh* (Gen. 4:1). Rabbi Ishmael asked Rabbi Aqiba [about this verse]. Said [Ishmael] to him: "Because you studied with Nahum of Gam Zo twenty-two years [the] *'k* [and the] *rq* [which] limit [the meaning of a verse and the] *'t* and *gm* [which] extend [the meaning of the verse], what [is the meaning of the] *'t* which is written here?"

B. Said [Aqiba] to him: "If it were said, 'I acquired a man *yhwh'* [without] the *'t*, the matter [would present a difficulty, for it would appear that *yhwh* were the man she acquired]; therefore, *'t yhwh* [was written to avoid any ambiguity]."

C. Said [Ishmael] to him: "*For it is no trifle to you* (Deut. 32:47). But if it is a trifle to you, [it is your fault, for] you do not know how to interpret [it]. Rather, *'t yhwh* [means] that in the past Adam was created from the earth and Eve [was created] from Adam; but, from this time forward [they will be created] *in our image and in our likeness* (Gen. 1:26). [This means] a man [can]not [be created] without a woman [and] a woman [can]not [be created] without a man, and both [can]not [be created] without the *Shekhinah.*"[19]

Genesis Rabbah 53:20:

A. *And God was 't*[20] *the lad* (Gen. 21:20). Rabbi Ishmael asked Rabbi Aqiba [about this verse]. Said [Ishmael] to him: "Because you studied with Nahum of Gam Zo twenty-two years [the] *'k* [and] [the] *rq* [which] limit [the meaning of a verse and the] *'t* and *gm* [which] extend [the meaning of the verse], what [is the meaning of the] *'t* which is written here?"

B. Said [Aqiba] to him: "If it were said 'And God was the lad' [without the *'t*], the matter [would present] a difficulty, [for it would appear that God was the lad to whom the verse referred]; therefore, *'t hn'r* [was written to avoid any ambiguity]."

C. Said [Ishmael] to him: "*For it is no trifle to you* (Deut. 32:47). But if it is a trifle to you [it is your fault, for] you do not know how to interpret [it]. Rather, *'t hn'r* [means that God was with] him, and his ass-drivers, and his camels, and his household."

In all three passages we discover that although Ishmael claims that Aqiba should employ the *'t* as an extending particle, it is Ishmael who uses the particle to extend the meaning of the verse. The editor(s) of these passages seem not to have been bothered by that fact that C does not follow from A. None of the texts suggest that Aqiba actually employed the techniques he supposedly learned from his teacher, while all three tell us that Ishmael did use this technique.

---

[18]Cf. bHag. 12a.

[19]From "in the past" to "Shekhinah" is attributed to Simlai in Genesis Rabbah 8:9.

[20]The *'t* here is a preposition, while in the other two texts its serves to mark the direct object of the verb.

Granted, the texts are highly stylized and clearly related with regard to form and content, but it is still striking that no one attempted to "correct" the text.[21]

VI

The following summary will aid us in examining Ishmael's exegetical activity and its relationship to the thirteen *middot* listed in the opening of Sifra. The most striking features are that he uses only a limited number of the techniques attributed to him in Sifra and that he employs many principles not included in Sifra's opening list.[22]

Items from Sifra's list: A *fortiori* (13); *gezarah shavah* (33); prototype based on one verse (2); prototype based on two verses (4); general statement-specific statement (5); specific statement-general statement (0); general statement-specific statement-general statement (4); general statement which requires a specific statement (0); specific statement which requires a general statement (0); anything which is included in the general statement and which is specified in order to teach something teaches not only about itself but also about everything in the general statement (0); anything which is included in the general statement and which is specified as a requirement which is in keeping with the general statement is specified in order to make the second requirement less stringent and not more stringent (0); anything which is included in the general statement and which is specified as a requirement concerning another requirement which is not in keeping with the general statement is specified either to make less or more stringent (0); anything which is included in the general statement and which is excepted from it by an entirely new provision you may not return it to the provisions of its original general statement unless Scripture expressly indicates that you may do so (0); a thing is to be explained from its context (4); a thing is to be explained by what follows it (0); two passages which contradict each other cannot be reconciled unless a third passage comes and decides between them (1).

Items not in Sifra's list: Analogy (14); pun (8); *heqqes* (3); repetitions (7); superfluous words, phrases, or verses (8); extension or limitation (12); plural or singular form of a word (4); solves a contradiction without bringing a third verse (1); all but three "ifs" in the Bible indicate a voluntary act (2); verse should be expounded by means of a msl (4); verse supplies a hint, zkr (1), interpretation of the particle 't (4); extending term follows an extending term only to limit (3); verse provides a rmz (1); two things which are specified in a general statement

---

[21]Segal most recent discussed the problem of these passages and notes those, such as Graetz, who did alter the text so that Aqiba used the techniques of his teacher; however, Segal's difficulty with these texts rests on the fact that he assumes that Ishmael *always* opposed the use of the principle of extension; A. F. Segal,*Two Powers in Heaven: Early Rabbinic Reports About Christianity and Gnosticism* (Leiden: 1977), 75-76.

[22]We see that Ishmael often employs principles normally associated with Aqiba. In fact, my study on the Ishmaelean corpus has demonstrated that Ishmael and Aqiba frequently employ the same exegetical methods; Porton, IV, 205-209.

multiply its teaching (1); anything which is in a general statement but is specified to teach something is removed from its general statement and it keeps its uniqueness (1); one cannot illustrate a case by something derived by analogy (2).[23]

VII

Our survey of the rabbinic texts has revealed a consistent picture of Ishmael's exegetical activity: *Ishmael did not employ many of the items attributed to him in Sifra's list, and he did exegete Scripture by techniques not assigned to him in Sifra.* If we cannot connect Ishmael with Sifra's list, to what can be tied? It is instructive to answer this question by referring to the traditions which discuss Hillel's exegetical methods:

Sifra Weiss 3a:

Hillel the Elder expounded seven [exegetical] rules before the Elders of Bethyra: 1) *a fortiori,* and 2) a *gezarah shavah,* and 3) two verses, and 4) a general statement and a specific statement, and 5) anything similar to it in another place, and 6) a thing is explained from its context. These are the seven [exegetical] rules which Hillel the Elder expounded before the Elders of Bethyra.

Avot deRabbi Nathan A 37:7:

Seven [exegetical] rules expounded Hillel the Elder before the Benei Bethyra, and these are they: 1) *a fortiori,* 2) *gezarah shavah,* 3) a prototype from one verse, and 4) a prototype from two verses, 5) by means of a general statement and a specific statement, 6) by means of a specific statement and a general statement, 7) anything similar to it in another place, 8) a thing is explained from its context. These are the seven [exegetical] rules which Hillel the Elder expounded before the Benei Bethyra.

Tosefta Sanhedrin 7:11:

Seven things expounded Hillel the Elder before the Elders of Petirah: 1) *a fortiori,* 2) *gezarah shavah,* and 3) prototype and one verse, and 4) two verses, and 5) a general statement and a specific statement, and 6) a specific statement and a general statement, and 7) anything similar to it in another place, and 8) a thing is explained from its context. These are the seven [exegetical] rules that expounded Hillel the Elder before the sons of Pitirah.

---

[23]The numbers in this section include those passages in which Ishmael uses the principle or it is attributed to him.

None of these lists contains *seven* exegetical principles; Sifra lists six items, and Avot deRabbi Nathan and Tosefta each contain eight rules.[24] Furthermore, only five items appear in all three lists: 1) *a fortiori,* 2) *gezarah shavah,* 3) the general statement-specific statement, 4) anything similar to it in another place, 5) a thing is to be explained from its context. Given this confusion in the transmission of Hillel's "seven" exegetical rules, we cannot ascertain which rules Hillel is suppose to have taught. Furthermore, a review of the exegetical traditions attributed to Hillel indicates that he did not use these principles. Neusner does not attribute to Hillel the use of the prototype from one or two verses, the general statement-specific statement, the specific statement-general statement, or a thing is explained from its context.[25] The use of the *heqqes* is attributed to Hillel;[26] however, this exegetical techniques does not appear in any of the lists of his exegetical methods. Hillel's exegetical activity is as poorly represented by his "list" as is Ishmael's by his "list."

When we compare Hillel's list(s) with Ishmael's, we discover some interesting facts. Four items appear in all three versions of Hillel's list and in Ishmael's list: 1) *a fortiori,* 2) *gezarah shavah,* 3) a general statement and a specific statement, 4) a thing is explained from its context. In addition, the following items are attributed to Hillel in Avot deRabbi Nathan and Tosefta and to Ishmael in Sifra: 1) a prototype from one verse, 2) a prototype from two verses, 3) a specific statement and a general statement. In brief, the list of exegetical rules attributed to Ishmael and the three versions of Hillel's techniques have *seven* items in common; the only item which they do not share is

---

[24]With regard to Sifra, Aaron ibn Hyym does not seem to realize that there are only six *middot*. He asks why Hillel employed only seven *middot* and then explains that Ishmael's "thirteen" rules are all included in Hillel's seven. Abraham b. David adds a prototype to Hillel's list in Sifra and interprets the reference to "two verses" as referring to two verses which contradict each other. The Wilna Gaon moves "two verses" after "a thing is explained from its context," but he still must have only six principles. Rabbenu Hillel adds both types of prototypes and takes the reference to "two verses" as referring to two contradictory verses. He reads *kll wprt and prt wkll* in Tosefta as one rule. With regard to the version in Tosefta see Lieberman, II, 159. In his translation of Avot, Goldin uses commas in a way which suggests eight items in the list; however, he does not comment on this discrepancy; J. Goldin, trans., *The Fathers According to Rabbi Nathan* (New York: 1974), 154. It should be noted that many of the sections of Avot 37 open with the word "seven" and that may have affected the opening of our section. In his commentary, Schechter merely refers to the others versions of the *sugya*. He realizes that the version of Avot is closest to the account in Tosefta; however, he does not comment on the fact that there are eight items listed; S. Schechter, *Avot deRabbi Nathan* (New York: reprint 1967), 110, n. 12. Cf. J. Neusner, *The Rabbinic Traditions about the Pharisees Before 70* (Leiden: 1971), II, 240-242, 274.

[25]Neusner, *Rabbinic Traditions,* I, 24.

[26]Neusner, *Rabbinic Traditions,* I, 241.

"anything similar to it in another place," which appears in all three versions of Hillel's techniques but not in Ishmael's list.[27] Thus, while the number "seven" does not describe the number of items in Hillel's list, it does correctly designate the number of rules which Hillel's and Ishmael's lists share.

A comparison of the two lists leads to one more interesting fact: With two exceptions, Ishmael uses only those items which his list and Hillel's list have in common. The only items which are "original" to Ishmael's list are his bringing a third verse to solve a contradiction between two other verses, which he uses once, and the general statement-specific statement-general statement, which he used three times. The items which Ishmael used most often, the *gezarah shavah* and the *a fortiori* argument, open the lists of both Hillel and Ishmael. If all we possessed were Hillel's list(s) and the exegetical pericopae in which Ishmael appears, we would conclude that Ishmael was a member of Hillel's "school," for the former most often employs techniques which appear in the latter's list. Even with Ishmael's list before us, we are struck by the fact that Ishmael most often employs techniques which were not "original" to him but which were also attributed to Hillel.

We have before us a complicated phenomenon. Given the two lists, we would assume that Ishmael and Hillel represent the same "exegetical school" and that the former built on the latter. Given the techniques attributed to the former, we would assume that Ishmael was closer to Hillel than is implied by a comparison of the former's and latter's list. Given Hillel's list and the Ishmaelean corpus, we must conclude that Ishmael has been pictured as an uninventive and unoriginal follower of the Hillelite "school" of biblical exegesis. When Ishmael breaks away from the Hillelite "school," he often employs techniques which are usually labeled as "Aqiban;" in fact, in many of the *sugyot* in which both Ishmael and Aqiba appear, there is little difference between them.[28] The importance of the awkward lists is that they show a clear relationship between Ishmael's exegetical activity and Hillel's list. When we compare the lists, we again see that Ishmael's, but not Hillel's, activity conforms to Hillel's list more than it does to Ishmael's list in Sifra.

Ishmael becomes even less original and inventive as an exegete when we delve into the origin of Hillel's list and exegetical activity. As Daube and Lieberman have demonstrated, Hillel's exegetical techniques and those employed most often by Ishmael are paralleled by the interpretive methods common in the

---

[27]Many have noted the similarity between Hillel's list and the list attributed to Ishmael. Aaron ibn Hyym and Rabbenu Hillel believed that all of Ishmael's thirteen principles were implied in Hillel's list. In addition see Derenbourg, 389; Frankel, 108; Bacher, 1; Petuchowski, 8; Mendelssohn, 649; Safrai 84.

[28]Porton, IV, 205-209.

Hellenistic rhetorical schools.[29] In addition, two other favorite Ishmaelean techniques, the pun, which he uses eight times, and the argument by analogy, which he uses fourteen times, were common Hellenistic rhetorical devices.[30] We are left with the impression that Ishmael exegeted the Bible much like Hillel was supposed to have done according to his list(s), although not as he did according to the Hillelite exegetical pericopae, that is, like any other Hellenistic sage. Ishmael's creativity and inventiveness as a biblical exegete cannot be maintained when he is placed in the wider context of the Hellenistic environment or in the more limited sphere of the rabbinic documents.

We have *two major descriptions* of Ishmael's exegetical activity: 1) the opening of Sifra and 2) Yohanan's statement in the Babylonian Talmud. However, when we compare these claims *about* the midrashic techniques which Ishmael *was suppose to have used* with those which *he actually employed* in the rabbinic corpus we discover that neither description is accurate. Rather than picturing Ishmael as an innovative biblical exegete who used a small number of interpretive techniques, we have uncovered an Ishmael who was much like any other rhetorician of his age. Ishmael employs techniques attributed to Hillel and those attributed to Aqiba. Furthermore, we have seen that the problems with Ishmael's list of exegetical *middot* are also found in the list(s) of Hillel's *middot*. Neither list actually reflects the activity of the sages as they have been transmitted to us. We must conclude, therefore, that the lists were attempts to systematize and categorize the exegetical activities of the two sages. However, these stereotypic accounts were not based on the corpora as they have been passed on to us. This is especially striking when we see that both the Tannaitic and Amoraic strata of our texts contain the same picture of Ishmael's exegetical activity. This means that the claims themselves are merely one part of those corpora and that they must be evaluated in the same way as any other piece of information. And our comparison of these statements *about* Ishmael's exegetical activity with those *sugyot* which purport to *report* his midrashic endeavors indicates that the former statements are inaccurate. The statements *about* Ishmael's exegetical practices reflect an attempt to place him at odds with Aqiba and to divide the early rabbinic schools of biblical interpretation into two balanced parts, one represented by Hillel-Ishmael and the other by Aqiba. When this took place we cannot say. Why Ishmael was chosen along with Hillel is unclear; however, the choice of Ishmael does balance with the importance attributed to Aqiba in this area of rabbinic activity. Who devised the picture is also unclear.

---

[29] D. Daube, "Rabbinic Methods of Interpretation and Hellenistic Rhetoric," *Hebrew Union College Annual*, XXII (1949), 234-264. S. Lieberman, *Hellenism in Jewish Palestine* (New York: 1950), 47-82.

[30] G. Kennedy, *The Art of Persuasion in Greece* (Princeton: 1963), 35, 45, 235, 246-247, 298. R. Pfeiffer, *History of Classical Scholarship* (Oxford: 1968), 203, 205, 208, 229, 266ff.

Perhaps the most important result of this study is that it teaches us not merely to rely on rabbinic statements to give us an accurate picture of their own data. In order to study a sage, his entire corpus must be investigated and evaluated. We cannot base our pictures of the rabbis merely on the statements they made about themselves or one another. We must measure those statements against all of the material available to us.[31]

---

[31]This adds support to the pioneering work of Jacob Neusner: J. Neusner,*The Development of a Legend: Studies in the Traditions Concerning Yohanan ben Zakkai* (Leiden: 1970). *Eliezer ben Hyrcanus: The Tradition and the Man* (Leiden: 1973). *The Rabbinic Traditions about the Pharisees before 70* (Leiden: 1971).

Chapter Two

The Yerushalmi and its Critics

Richard Eric Cohen

Brown University

"The Palestinian Talmud [the Yerushalmi]...for almost fourteen hundred years remained a 'sealed book.'"[1] Largely for historical reasons, the Babylonian Talmud, or the "Bavli," became the central text of Judaism and eclipsed the Yerushalmi. Apologists rationalized the neglect of the Yerushalmi by arguing that it deserved to be neglected because it was incoherent and incomplete. Today, scholars perpetuate this bias, criticizing the Yerushalmi as being unworthy of serious attention. When studied on its own terms, however, this document emerges as a highly sophisticated composition. It employs a remarkably uniform and coherent mode of argumentation to discuss a broad range of topics. The Yerushalmi appears to have been condemned without ever receiving a fair trial. The Yerushalmi's distinct and subtle mode of argumentation deserves more careful analysis.

The Yerushalmi as the Other Talmud

From the end of the Talmudic period, the Yerushalmi was overshadowed by the Bavli, which had become the normative and definitive text of Judaism. "It is virtually impossible to exaggerate the dominant position held by the Babylonian Talmud among Jews throughout the ages."[2] "What the Bible had meant for Talmudic civilization, the [Babylonian] Talmud now meant for medieval Jewish life," writes Gerson D. Cohen. "Medieval Judaism thus became synonymous with the law of the Babylonian Talmud."[3] Today, Conservative and Orthodox authorities continue to identify Judaism with the Bavli. According to Adin Steinsaltz:

---

[1]Louis Ginzberg, "An Introduction to the Palestinian Talmud," [1941] reprinted in *On Jewish Law and Lore* (New York: Meridian, 1962), p. 47.

[2]Eliezer Berkovits, "The Babylonian Talmud," *The Encyclopaedia Judaica* (Jerusalem: Macmillan, 1971), p. 767.

[3]Gerson D. Cohen, "The Talmudic Age," in Leo W. Schwarz, ed; *Great Ages and Ideas of the Jewish People* (New York: Random House, 1956), p. 210.

> If the Bible is the cornerstone of Judaism, then the [Babylonian] Talmud
> is the central pillar, soaring up from the foundations and supporting the
> entire spiritual and intellectual edifice. In many ways the [Babylonian]
> Talmud is the most important book in Jewish culture, the backbone of
> creativity and national life. No other work has had a comparable
> influence on the theory and practice of Jewish life, shaping spiritual
> content and serving as a guide to conduct. The Jewish people have
> always been keenly aware that their continued survival and development
> depend on the study of the [Babylonian] Talmud....[4]

From this perspective, the Bavli functions as the totem, the all-important and
all-encompassing symbol, of the community; it represents everything vital to
Judaism – the guide to everyday life, the source of spiritual life, the backbone of
national life. Indeed, Jewish destiny and survival is said to depend upon this
document.

As the Bavli became the central text of Judaism, the Yerushalmi was
relegated to the margins. Religious authorities personally identified with the
Bavli, portraying themselves as the continuators of the ancient tradition which
came to ultimate expression in this document. The Yerushalmi, in contrast, was
treated as merely the "other Talmud." This situation compares to the way men
have viewed themselves as the norm and women as "the second sex." Simone
De Beauvoir writes:

> Thus humanity is male and man defines woman not in herself but as
> relative to him; she is not regarded as an autonomous being... She is
> defined and differentiated with reference to man and not he with reference
> to her; she is incidental, the inessential as opposed to the essential. He
> is the Subject, he is the Absolute–she is the Other.[5]

Conservative and Orthodox authorities, the self-proclaimed heirs to the Bavli,
portrayed this document as the absolute authority on the essential issues of
Jewish law. Whereas the Bavli represented "the central pillar . . . supporting the
entire spiritual and intellectual edifice" of Judaism, the Yerushalmi was
considered dispensable. At best, the Yerushalmi functioned as an appendix,
providing an occassional supplement or exception to the rules established by the
Bavli. The Yerushalmi was rarely studied on its own terms as an autonomous
statement. It was evaluated only in terms of its relationship its Bavylonian
counterpart. The Yerushalmi was judged favorably to the degree that it was like
the Bavli, and unfavorably to the degree that it was different.

Scholars projected their own values into their portrayal of the differences
between the two Talmuds. On one hand, because they identified with the Bavli,
they saw in it the essential qualities which they most highly valued –

---

[4]Adin Steinsaltz, *The Essential Talmud*, Chaya Galai, trans. (New York: Bantam, 1976), p. 3.

[5]Simone De Beauvoir, *The Second Sex*, H.M. Parshley, trans. (New York: Alfred A. Knopf, 1953) xvi-xvii.

intelligence, logic, restraint, punctiliousness. On the other hand, they viewed the Yerushalmi as a mere curiosity, characterized by the lesser virtues of beauty, poetry, and imagination. For example, Steinsaltz trivialized the Yerushalmi by describing the most important Palestinian sage, Rabbi Yohanan, as a man of "great physical beauty," whereas he describes the sages responsible for the Bavli as "pious and noble" men with "incisive minds."[6] Solomon Grayzel considered the Yerushalmi to be a superfluous document which was inevitably neglected by medieval Judaism: "The Jews of that day stood in greater need of the strength and unity which result from the common law and tradition in which the Babylonians were stronger, than the poetic creations of beauty and imagination which the Palestinians emphasized."[7]

The language of scholarship reflects this bias towards the Bavli. In the same way that men often use language that allows them to forget that they represent only one species of the genus "human being," scholars of Rabbinic literature often use language that allows them to forget that the Bavli is only one species of the genus "Talmud." The Old English word *man*, meaning "person" or "human being" eventually began to also denote "adult male." "As long as most generalizations about people were made by men about men, the ambiguity nestling in this dual usage was either not noticed or not thought to matter."[8] Likewise, the generic term *the Talmud* came to refer both specifically to the Bavli and generally to Talmudic literature. This dual usage was possible because most statements about Rabbinic literature came from those who considered the Bavli to be normative. Generalizations about the Bavli were thought to apply to all Talmudic literature. In contrast, scholars invariably referred to the Yerushalmi as *the Palestinian Talmud*. The use of this modifier *Palestinian* indicates that the Yerushalmi represented only a sub-category signifying a specific Talmud and not the general category of Talmudic literature.[9] Whereas the Bavli signified the norm, the Yerushalmi represented nothing more than a special case.

The Bavli's Rise to Prominence

To understand the how the Bavli achieved dominence, we must look at the historical situation during the second half of the first millennium. After the completion of the Talmuds, the Babylonian and Palestinian Jewish academies

---

[6]Steinsaltz, pp. 40-55.

[7]Solomon Grayzel, *A History of the Jews, From the Babylonian Exile to the Present* (Philadelphia: Jewish Publication Society, 1968 [1947]), p. 270.

[8]Casery Miller and Kate Swift, *The Handbook of Nonsexist Writing* (New York: Lippincott and Crowell, 1980), 9-10.

[9]The standard notation system used to identify specific passages also reflects the perception of the Babylonian Talmud as the unqualified norm: *Rosh Hashana* 10b refers to a passage in the Babylonian Talmud, but references to the Palestinian Talmud require a prefix of *PT* or a *Y* (e.g., *Y Rosh Hashana* I. 10).

each focused on the locally composed document. The Jewish community prospered in Babylonia, but not in Palestine. When the ocean of Islam spread as far as Spain and Asia, the influence of Babylonian Jewish community spread with the tide to the farthest reaches of the Jewish world. As Babylonian Jewry became more prominent, so too did their Talmud. The Babylonian Jewish leadership had a vested interest in advocating their own Talmud, because they derived their religious authority from being the heirs, and the sole legitimate interpreters, of the Bavli. They portrayed the Bavli as the culmination of the Rabbinic period and the ultimate expression of Judaism. Not everyone, however, immediately accepted the Bavli: the Karaites rejected the authority of all Rabbinic literature, including the Talmuds, and the Palestinian community continued to be oriented toward the Yerushalmi. Following a fierce struggle, the Babylonian authorities eventually won out, and the Bavli became the central text of Judaism.

Medieval authorities perpetuated the bias against the Yerushalmi. Alfasi, an eleventh-century commentator, affixed a note to the end of the Bavli's Tractate of Erubin, relegating the Yerushalmi to the status of an occasional supplement. Henceforth, on questions of Jewish law, religious authorities referred to the Yerushalmi only when the Bavli did not contain a complete and unambiguous discussion. In concrete terms, this meant that there was a general lack of texts, commentaries, and codifications. The medieval texual commentators, such as Rashi, and the codifiers of law, such as Joseph Caro, rarely mentioned the Yerushalmi and may not have had access to any manuscipts. As a result, the Yerushalmi remained obscure and mystified. Only a few elite men were familiar with its contents. Because they distinguished themselves by this exclusive knowledge, they benefitted from perpetuating the obscurity of this document.

Today, religious authorities continue to focus almost entirely on the Bavli. Paradoxically, they ignore the Yerushalmi, even though they consider it to part of the revered canon of Rabbinic literature. The Bavli and the Yerushalmi are similar documents, yet one is exalted and the other is ignored. Theoretically, the Yerushalmi should be respected for the same reasons as the Bavli. Modern scholars, however, inherit an ancient bias against the Yerushalmi and are therefore relatively unfamiliar with its contents. They offer apologetic arguments to explain their neglect of this Talmud. Jonathan Z. Smith describes this process as the development of a theory of the "proximate other".

> While the "other" may be perceived as being either LIKE-US or NOT-LIKE-US, he is, in fact, most problematic when he is TOO-MUCH-LIKE-US, or when he claims to be-us. It is here that the real urgency of a "theory of the other" emerges.... [W]e are not so much concerned with the drama of "expulsion," but with the more mundane and persistent processes of "micro-adjustment." This is not a matter of the "far," but preeminently,

of the "near." The problem is not alterity, but similarity–at times, even identity.[10]

Apologists emphasize the difference between the two Talmuds. They rationalize the neglect of the Yerushalmi by arguing that it is an inferior text which deserves to be neglected. This polemic becomes a self-fulfilling prophecy: apologists developed theories to justify the historic neglect of the Yerushalmi. These theories lead to the further marginalization of this document. Although it is part of the same body of sacred literature, the Yerushalmi is not considered to be equal to the Bavli. In other words, there is a hierarchy in the canon of Rabbinic Judaism. In the same way as Christians often prefer the New Testament to the Old, Jews regularly focus on the Bavli to the exclusion of the Yerushalmi.

With the exception of a few scholars, such as Zacharias Frankel, Saul Lieberman, and Jacob Neusner,[11] the academic community also neglects and condemns the Yerushalmi. Recent scholarly monographs on Talmudic literature base their conclusions entirely on the analysis of the Bavli. If the Yerushalmi is mentioned at all, it is to provide a supplement or an exception to the rules established by the Bavli. The authors appeal to the usual polemic to justify their ignoring the Yerushalmi: this document is neglected because it is inferior and deserves to be neglected. Let us look at a few lengthy quotations in order to see how these authors explain the deficiency of the Yerushalmi. David Weiss Halivni writes in *Midrash, Mishnah and Gemara:*

> It has often been pointed out that the Babylonian Talmud differs from the Palestinian Talmud in that the argumentational material of the former is more complex, more dialectical, richer and more variegated in content, more removed from the *peshat* (the simple meaning) of the texts it discusses.... [T]he Palestinian Talmud is ... simple, narrow in focus, responding to the question at hand, and without a unique style, whereas the argumentational in the Gemara of the Babylonian Talmud is colorful, pulsating, outreaching, often presenting an interwoven and continuous discourse with a distinct, identifiable style of its own. For the purpose of tracing the various modes of Jewish learning, the Babylonian Talmud is more pivotal than the Palestinian Talmud; hence the heavy representation of examples in this book from the Gemara of the Babylonian Talmud.[12]

---

[10]Jonathan Z. Smith, "What a Difference A Difference Makes," in Jacob Neusner and Ernest S. Frerichs, eds., *"To See Ourselves as Others See Us:" Christians, Jews, "Others" in Late Antiquity* (Chico, California: Scholars Press, 1985), p. 47.

[11]Zacharias Frankel, *Mebo HaYerushalmi* (Breslau: 1870); Saul Lieberman, Al HaYerushalmi (Jerusalem: [1929] 1967), *Talmadah shel Keisarin* (Jerusalem: 1931) and *HaYerushalmi KiFeshuto* (Jerusalem: 1934); and Jacob Neusner, *The Talmud of the Land of Israel, A Preliminary Translation and Explanation*, vol. 35, *Introduction: Taxonomy* and *Judaism in Society: The Evidence of Yerushalmi* (Chicago: University of Chicago Press, 1983).

[12]David Weiss Halivni, *Midrash, Mishnah and Gemara: The Jewish Predilection for Justified Law* (Cambridge, MA: Harvard University Press, 1986), p. 82.

Likewise, Louis Jacobs ignores the Yerushalmi in *The Talmudic Argument* because

> A comparison of the Babylonian Talmud with the Palestinian demonstrates that the flavour of the former is all its own: the use of keen questioning and reply, of the thrust and parry of debate, of the liveliness of the arguments, especially of the stock framework into which lengthy discussions have been fitted.[13]

Robert Goldenberg reiterates the common assumptions in a recent textbook:

> There are two Talmuds. The earlier, the Jerusalem or Palestinian Talmud (it was really produced in the Galilee), dates from the first half of the fifth century. It takes the form of an extremely loose and elaborate commentary on selected tractates of the Mishnah. Proceeding paragraph by paragraph, it offers a jumble of textual elucidation, case stories and other stories, moral instructions both general and specific, theological speculation, legends about Bible characters and later people too, and so forth. It shows signs of insufficient editing: transitions, both within arguments and also between sections, are weak.... Dating from a century or two later, the Babylonian Talmud shows the result of more leisurely and more skillful preparation. The arguments in the legal sections are far more elegantly presented, with points made more trenchantly and with the help of a much larger arsenal of standard technical terms and rhetorical devices.[14]

Halivni, Jacobs and Goldenberg carefully substantiate their arguments concerning the Bavli, but they present offhanded attacks against the Yerushalmi without any documentation or analysis. They offer neither examples from the text of the Yerushalmi nor references to secondary sources. Halivni provides a single footnote which refers to the century-old source which he paraphrases.[15] It seems that these authors are simply passing on unexamined assumptions about the character of the Yerushalmi.

Steinsaltz succinctly summarizes the two lines of attack against the Yerushalmi. One criticism is that the Yerushalmi was quickly and haphazardly compiled:

> ...the Jerusalem Talmud was never properly edited. The material was compiled imprecisely and in haste, one of the reasons it was regarded for so long as a kind of appendix, a stepbrother to the Babylonian Talmud.

The other criticism is that the Yerushalmi is imperfect and incomplete, a rough draft of the Bavli.

---

[13]Louis Jacobs, *The Talmudic Argument: A Study in Talmudic Reasoning and Methodology* (Cambridge, England: Cambridge University Press, 1984), p. 22.

[14]Robert Goldenberg, "The Talmud" in Barry Holtz, ed., *Back to the Sources: Reading the Calssical Jewish Texts* (New York: Summit Books, 1984), p. 136.

[15]Frankel, 32b-35b.

Then again, the Babylonian Talmud received its final form in a later period and was therefore regarded as a more authoritative summary...[16]

Let us consider each of these assumptions to determine their validity. We shall begin with the second criticism, asking whether it is historically valid to study a document only in terms of later developments. Then we shall evalutate the first assumption by looking at a sample passage. By inductive analysis we shall determine whether the usual characterization is accurate: is the Yeushalmi a hasty and haphazard collection of material, a mere "jumble of textual elucidation"?

The Yerushalmi as a Rough Draft of the Bavli

Religious authorities have viewed the Talmuds primarily as repositories of Jewish law or Halakhah. In legal discussions, the latest ruling takes precedence. Therefore, because the Bavli was an expansion and emendation of the Yerushalmi, the Bavli was considered to be the more authoritative Talmud. This type of reasoning can be traced back to the eleventh century:

> The Jerusalem Talmud was completed a century and a half before the Babylonian, so that the editors of the Babylonian Talmud had it before them; thus any decision of theirs contrary to that of the Jerusalem Talmud meant that the latter was rejected. Alfasi followed the well-known halakhic principle which maintains that *halakhah ke-vatra'ei*, i.e., the final decision goes according to the last Talmudic authority.[17]

This argument may represent a valid legal principle, but it is not a valid theory of historical scholarship. The historian looks at each document in context of the situation in which it took shape. The fourth-century Palestinians lived in a different world than the sixth-century Babylonians. An historian may consider the various prior details which could have influenced the composition of a document, but she should not be prejudiced by later developments. The Yerushalmi must be understood on its own terms; the way the Babylonians copied, adapted or ignored the Yerushalmi is a separate issue. Moreover, Alfasi's argument is based on an invalid premise. The Bavli is not an expansion or emendation of the Yerushalmi. Through an inductive analysis of the two Talmuds, Jacob Neusner has demonstrated that they are autonomous compositions: each "presents its own message in its own way."[18] The Yerushalmi is not a rough draft of the Bavli. Therefore, historians can no longer

---

[16]Steinsaltz, p. 54-55.

[17]Berkovitz, 766.

[18]Jacob Neusner, *Judaism: The Classical Statement, the Evidence of the Bavli* (Chicago: University of Chicago, 1986), ch. 2. See also *idem*, "System or Tradition? The Bavli and Its Sources," in *New Perspectives on Ancient Judaism*, vol. III., "Judaic and Christian Interpretations of Texts" (Lanham, MD: 1987).

justify studying this important document "mainly through its reflection in the Babylonian Talmud."[19]

The Yerushalmi as a Hasty and Haphazard Compilation

The other common assumption, that the Yerushalmi is a hasty and haphazard collection of material, is more difficult to evaluate and will occupy our attention for the remainder of this article. Specifically, we wish to know whether the Yerushalmi is a "jumble of textual elucidation" as Goldenberg alleges or a carefully composed document which follows an identifiable plan. We can only determine the character of the Yerushalmi by inductive analysis. Let us look at a randomly selected passage – the portion of Yerushalmi which follows the citation of Mishnah Berachot 8:2.[20]

Topical Arrangement

When studied on its own terms, the Yerushalmi emerges as a carefully constructed document which carefully arranges material according to a set plan. This passage consists of seven discrete discussions, each of which treats a different topic. In other words, each of these paragraphs answers a different question. By listing these questions, we can analyze the topical arrangement of the passage as a whole. Let us compare the topical focus of the base Mishnaic pericope to the topics addressed by the passage as a whole. As we shall see, the arrangement of this passage follows a fixed plan – the mark of a well-composed document. The passage begins by closely analyzing the issues of the base Mishnaic pericope and then moves far afield according to the distinct topical interest of the Yerushalmi.

Base Mishnaic Pericope:

House of Shammai say: they wash the hands, and then mix the cup. House of Hillel say: they mix the cup, and then wash the hands.

(M. Berachot 8:2)

Commentary:

Paragraph	Relationship to Base Mishnaic Pericope	Topical Focus
I. A.	Direct	Are washings required – before mixing the cup of wine?
B.	Indirect	Are washings required – even if it is inconvenient?

---

[19]Steinsaltz, p. 55.

[20]For a more extensive analysis of this passage, see my "Topic, Rhetoric and Logic: Analysis of a Syllogistic Passage in the Yerushalmi," in Jacob Neusner, ed., *New Approaches to Ancient Judaism*, vol. III., (Lanham, MD: University Press of America, 1987).

C.	Indirect	Are washings required – before and after meals?
D.	Indirect	Are washings required – even if hands do not touch the food?
E.	Indirect	Are washings required – for all types of food?
F.	Indirect	Are washings required – more than once a day?
II. A.	Tangential	Does the same man say blessings before and after the meal?

The base Mishnaic pericope addresses the issue of whether ritual washings must be done before or after the mixing of a cup of wine to be blessed on the Sabbath eve. This Talmud's commentary is not limited to this topic. The document is structured as a commentary to the Mishnah. The Yerushalmi, however, has its own distinct topical program. It chooses to discuss certain issues among the broad range of possible questions which could be asked of the base Mishnaic pericope. Furthermore, the Yerushalmi addresses some topics which bear no direct relationship to this pericope. The Mishnaic pericope is concerned with the relatively narrow issue of when one should wash during the Friday night meal. In contrast, this passage of the Yerushalmi focuses on the broader issue of when washings are required before eating in general.

While the Yerushalmi has its own topical program, distinct from the Mishnah, it carefully arranges paragraphs according to their topical relation to the base Mishnaic pericope. The topics move from direct relationship, to indirect relationship, and finally to tangential relationship. The first paragraph (I.A.) is directly related to the topic of the whole Mishnaic pericope (the order of washing the hands and mixing the cup before the Sabbath meal). The next five paragraphs (I.B. – I.F.) consider various aspects of a related issue (washing the hands before any meal during the week). The topic of the last paragraph (II.A.) is only tangentially related to this pericope, directing our attention toward a different set of issues (the man who says grace). Clearly, the passage follows an identifiable topical plan; there is nothing haphazard about this arrangement.

Syllogistic Mode of Argumentation

More significantly, the Yerushalmi rigorously adheres to a uniform mode of argumentation in discussing the various topics. Every paragraph in our sample represents a carefully constructed argument. In each paragraph, the editors chose and arranged material according to syllogistic patterns in order to make a single point. Aristotle defined syllogistic logic as "a discourse in which, certain things being stated, something other than what is stated follows of necessity from their being so."[21] In plain English, this means that a syllogism is a logical construction which necessarily yields a conclusion. A typical syllogism is in three parts, with two propositions functioning as premises and a third functioning as the resulting conclusion.

1. **Premise**   All clowns are funny.

2. **Premise**   Sweepy is a clown.

3. **Conclusion**   (Therefore) Sweepy is funny.

According to syllogistic logic, the third proposition is the necessary conclusion of the syllogism.[22] I use the word syllogism to refer to a mode of argumentation, not a specific logical formula. For our purposes, the word "syllogism" – from the Greek *logizesthai* ("to reason") and *syn* ("together") – refers to any pattern of abstract causal reasoning in which propositions are structured and arranged in order to derive a certain conclusion.

Syllogisms consist of a series of propositional statements. Propositions are assertions of a single point which can be declared either true or false. They are the indivisible building blocks of syllogistic discourse. One type of proposition is the premise. A premise is a proposition which is assumed to be self-evidently true. By definition, a premise does not require any proof, justification or apology. A conclusion is also a proposition, but unlike premises, conclusions require proof, hence the need for the syllogistic argument. In our sample passage, three types of material function as premises.

- quotes of statements by authoritative sages
- reports of actions by authoritative sages
- citations from authoritative texts

This means that these literary units – statements, stories, and citations – function as propositions in syllogistic discourse. As we shall see, even relatively long statements, stories, and citations represent a single assertion.

In the passage at hand, we find three types of logical pattern: the unitary syllogism, the constructive syllogism, and the supportive syllogism.

---

[21]Antony Flew, ed., *A Dictionary of Philosophy* (London: Macmillan, 1979), p. 322.

[22]By definition, the two premises of a syllogism must have a common term – in our example, "clown." Logicians call this term "M" (for "middle term" or "medium"). Through a process analogous to subtraction, we can derive the relationship between the other two terms – "funny" and "Sweepy" – by removing the middle term.

1.	M	–	P	P = "funny"
2.	S	–	M	S = "Sweepy"
3.	S	–	P	

The unitary syllogism is the simplest logical pattern. In such a construction, a single proposition is, at one and the same time, a premise and a conclusion. Let me explain. For a proposition to be a premise, the text must (1) assume it to be true and (2) assume that the audience considers it to be self-evident. A conclusion, on the other hand, is the point which the text attempts to prove or justify. A proposition is a unitary syllogism if it is an authoritative source (premise) which is cited in order to make a point (conclusion). A unitary syllogism is a self-contained argument which is not part of a larger logical construction. That is, it does not require further elaboration or logical discussion in order to derive a conclusion. Our sample passage contains only one example of a unitary syllogism.

I. D.

1. *Samuel went up to visit Rav. He saw* [Rav] *eating with a napkin* [covering his hands]. *He said to him, "how so?* [I.e., are you doing this to avoid washing?]" *Rav replied, "*[No], I am fastidious [therefore I **wash as well as cover my hands with a napkin**.].*"

Here a story functions as a proposition. This proposition is cited to make a single point: hands should be washed, even if a napkin protects them from touching the food.

The second pattern, the constructive syllogism, derives new propositions (conclusions) from accepted propositions (premises). The premises are the unquestioned source of authority. In contrast, conclusions take on authority through their relationship to premises. The typical Aristotelian syllogism (all clowns are funny; Sweepy is a clown; therefore Sweepy is funny) falls into this category. Constructive syllogisms are constructed so that the conclusion is the necessary outcome. The conclusion therefore need not be explicitly stated, because it is implied by the structure of the argument. Indeed, the Yerushalmi is a remarkably economical document which chooses not to state conclusions which can be inferred from the structure of the argument.

The most common form of constructive syllogism is the dispute, the juxtaposition of opposing positions without any explicit resolution. A dispute contains two or three proposition, each attributed to a different sage. The propositions are expressed in one of three forms:

Opinion: a statement is attributed to a sage.

Narrated Opinion: a statement of a sage is presented as part of a story.

Story: a narration describing a sage's actions reflects his position on the disputed issue.

The conflicting positions appear without any commentary explicitly stating the relationship between the statements, such as "Rabbi X disagrees with Rabbi Y on issue A for the following reason...." The reader must therefore reflect on the relationship between the various positions in order to reconstruct the disputed issue. The disputants share common assumptions and only disagree on relatively minor issues. The implicit conclusion of a dispute syllogism is the point of agreement and the range of acceptable opinion. For example, **I.E.3-4.** is a dispute syllogism in which the first position is expressed in the form of an opinion and the second position is expressed in the form of a story.

I. E.

3. R. Yosah in the name of R. Hiyya Bar Ashi, and R. Johan and R. Hiyya Bar Ashi in the name of Rav, [said]: "one washes hands up to the **wrist for priests' rations and up to the knuckles for unconsecrated food."**

4. *Measha, grandson of R. Joshua b. Levi, said "If one was eating with my grandfather and did not wash his hands up to the wrist, grandfather would not eat with him."* [I.e., **wash up to the wrist for all food.**]

The implicit conclusion of this syllogism is that (1) it is agreed that priest's rations require washing up to the wrists, but that (2) there is a difference of opinion as to whether unconsecrated food also requires such extensive washing.

The third type of logical pattern is the supportive syllogism. Here the text begins with the conclusion and moves backward, explaining how this proposition is logically derived from a certain premise. In other words, a supportive syllogism announces the conclusion at the outset and then cites new premises to reinforce the authority of this conclusion. In the constructive syllogism, new propositions are implicitly or explicitly presented as the logical conclusion of an argument. In the supportive syllogism, on the other hand, the text does not establish a new proposition. The text merely reaffirms a proposition already known to the audience.

The one example of a supportive syllogism appearing in our sample analyzes the logical derivation of the base Mishniac pericope. The pericope functions is shown to be the logical conclusion of a syllogistic argument resting on authoritative premises.

I. A.

1. [Paraphrase of Tosefta Berachot 5:26:]
    a. *What is the reasoning of the House of Shammai?* [The cup cannot be mixed without washing the hands] lest hands make unclean the liquid [on the outside of the cup] and, in turn, the cup [and its contents].
    b. *What is the reasoning of the House of Hillel?* [The cup can be mixed without washing the hands because] the outside of a cup is always unclean [so washing would not help to protect the cup]. Another matter – hands should only be washed immediately before blessing [without interrupting to mix the cup].

2. *R. Biban in the name of R. Yohanan* [said]: "The opinion of the House of Shammai is in accord with R. Yosé and that of the House of Hillel with R. Meir* [i.e.,the House of Shammai and the House of Hillel in M.

Ber. 8:2, agree with the views of R. Yosé and R. Meir, respectively, found in M. Kel. 25:7-8.]

3. *"as we have learned there* [in Mishnah Kelim 25:7-8]:
    '[In all vessels, the outside, the inside, and the handle are distinguished (with respect to the transfer of uncleanness).] R. Meir says: "For unclean and clean hands." [I.e., unclean hands only make unclean the parts of a cup which they actually touch, not the entire cup.] R. Yosé says: "For unclean hands only." [I.e., unclean hands which touch any part of a cup make the entire cup unclean.]'"

The base Mishnaic pericope is shown to be the third stage of a three stage argument.

Stage One (second Mishnaic pericope – M. Kel. 25:7-8): Whether or not the parts of a cup are distinct with respect to the transfer of uncleanness.

Stage Two (Toseftan material – T. Ber. 5:26): Whether or not unclean hands touching the outside of a cup do make the inside of a cup and its contents unclean.

Stage Three (base Mishnaic pericope – M. Ber. 8:2): Whether or not hands must be washed before mixing a cup of wine to be blessed.

The first component (I.A.1.) takes us one step back in the logical unfolding of the argument, from stage three to stage two: the reason the Houses dispute in the base Mishnaic pericope over whether washing is required before mixing the cup is that they disagree on whether unclean hands which touch the outside of a cup make the contents unclean. The second component (I.B.1.), in turn, takes us to one more logically prior stage: the reason why the Shammaites are concerned with unclean hands touching the outside of the cup is that they (along with Yosé) presuppose that the parts of a cup are not distinct with respect to the transfer of uncleanness. If unclean hands touch the outside of the cup, they believe the inside of the cup and the contents become unclean. The Hillelites, on the other hand, are not concerned with unclean hands touching the outside of the cup, because they (along with Meir) presuppose that each part of the cup is distinct with respect to the transfer of uncleanness. If unclean hands touch the outside of the cup, they believe the inside of the cup and the contents do not become unclean. The Yerushalmi has thus outlined a two stage argument which reaffrims the authority of the base Mishnaic pericope.

The individual paragraphs of our sample passage have been carefully constructed according to three types of syllogism. Four of the seven paragraphs in our sample consist entirely of a single syllogistic argument without an extraneous word. The three other paragraphs contain a syllogism followed by an appended discussion. These appendices are also tightly constructed according to syllogistic patterns. They comment on the main argument of the paragraph, but they do not effect its meaning. The main argument would represent a coherent statement if it appeared independently, whereas the appendix would be incomprehensible without the main argument.

Logical Arrangement

We see that the individual paragraphs are not haphazard collections of material. Each paragraph represents a cogent discussion, carefully formulated to make a point. By listing the paragraphs in the order in which they appear, we can determine whether the passage as a whole follows an identifiable plan defined by the patterns of argumentation. As we shall see, not only are the individual paragraphs logically formulated, but the entire passage also represents a systematic exposition.

Paragraph	Topical Relation to the Base Mishnaic Pericope	Logical Pattern (Type of Syllogism)	Rhetorical Form	Appendix
I. A.	Direct	Supportive	Logical Derivation of the Base Mishnaic Pericope	–
B.	Indirect	Constructive	Dispute	Application of a Principle to a Specific Situation (I.B.2.)
C.	Indirect	Constructive	Logical Analysis of a Single Source	Negative Precedent (I.C.2.)
D.	Indirect	Unitary	Precedent	Precedent (I.D.2.)
E.	Indirect	Constructive	Series of Disputes	–
F.	Indirect	Constructive	Dispute	–
II. A.	Tangential	Constructive	Homogenization of Conflicting Sources	–

The paragraphs appear in a specific order. The passage begins with a supportive syllogism followed by a number of unitary and constructive syllogisms. The supportive syllogism appears first, immediately following the citation of the base Mishnaic pericope, because this pericope functions as the implicit conclusion of the construction. The syllogism identifies authoritative sources which reinforce the authority of this pericope. In the sample passage, we do not find any other logical patterns in which the base Mishnaic pericope functions as a proposition – either as a premise or a conclusion.[23] All subsequent paragraphs contain unitary and constructive syllogisms which have no logical connection to the base Mishnaic pericope. They neither derive conclusions from this pericope nor identify premises to support it. These syllogisms derive new conclusions from other authoritative sources besides the base Mishnaic pericope. They therefore appear at the end of the passage, removed from the citation of the base Mishnaic pericope. The unitary and constructive syllogisms are themselves arranged in a specific order, beginning with the more complex constructions, that is, the constructions which contain appended syllogisms.

The arrangement of paragraphs according to the type of syllogism corresponds to our earlier finding that paragraphs are arranged by topic. The supportive syllogism takes the base Mishnaic pericope as its conclusion.

---

[23]In the appended subunit I.B.2., a Mishnaic pericope from another tractate, functions as the premise of argumentation.

Therefore, by definition, a paragraph with a supportive syllogism will address a topic directly related to this pericope. In contrast, the unitary and constructive syllogisms take us far afield from the topical focus of the base Mishnaic pericope. Because these syllogisms bear no logical connection to this pericope, they can be used to address different issues. We have already determined that paragraphs which are only indirectly or tangentially related to the topic of the base Mishnaic pericope occur at the end of the passage.

Conclusion

We are now in a position to refute the usual criticisms of the Yerushalmi. Scholars almost unanimously consider this document as a jumble of textual elucidation, a haphazard collection of material. Our analysis of a sample passage, however, leads us to draw a very different conclusion: the Yerushalmi is a systematic exposition which rigorously adheres to a distinct mode of argumentation. The document consists of autonomous paragraphs which are constructed to make a single point. The editors argue their points by carefully selecting and arranging material according to syllogistic patterns. Furthermore, these individual paragraphs are placed in a specific order according to topical and logical patterns of arrangement.

The Yerushalmi's distinct and systematic mode of argumentation and arrangement has been completely overlooked. As we have seen, scholars inherited the ancient bias against this document. This bias has lead to distortion. Because the Yerushalmi has been studied only in reference to the norm established by the Bavli, any deviation from the norm established by the Bavli was viewed as an imperfection. For example, the Yerushalmi was found to be more dense than the Bavli. Because they assumed that the Bavli was superior, they explained the brevity of the Yerushalmi as a sign of poor editing. Nearly a century ago, Moses Mielziner presented the scholarly consensus: the Yerushalmi's "discussions are generally very brief and condensed, and do not exhibit that dialectic acumen for which the Babylonian Gemara is noted."[24] The Yerushalmi was concise, it was assumed, because the framers lacked time and skill. The document was supposedly composed under pressure during a time of persecution by Christian Rome: "That the work should suffer from shortcomings

---

[24]Moses Mielziner, *Introduction to the Talmud* (New York: Bloch Publishing Company, 1968 [1894]), p. 61.

was inevitable, for the age and the locale provided neither an abundance of leisure not peace of mind."[25]

We have seen, however, that Yerushalmi is "very brief and condensed" precisely because of the framer's "dialectic acumen." When the text is studied inductively, the brevity appears to be the result of tight argumentation:

> Where the discussion in the Babylonina Talmud tends to be prolix and discursive, that of the Jerusalem Talmud is succinct and concise. Where the Babylonian takes refuge in drawing sometimes farfetched comparisons and enters deeply into the essence of the matter being discussed, the Jerusalem relies upon logical argument.[26]

The Yerushalmi's syllogistic mode of argumentation allows it to express complex ideas in cogent, yet compact, form. The document only presents what is logically necessary to build an argument. A conclusion is not explicitly stated if it can be inferred from the structure of an argument. We recall that Goldenberg prefers the Bavli because it employs a "larger arsenal of standard technical terms and rhetorical devices." In contrast, the Yerushalmi carefully formulates its discussions according to syllogisms and expects that its audience understands these implicit patterns of argumentation. Therefore, it expresses arguments concisely without appealing to technical terms and rhetorical devices to guide the reader through its arguments. The reader must think through each syllogistic argument. In this way, the Yerushalmi is a subtle document which depends on the intelligence of its audience. The next generation of students of the document, framing their judgment on the basis of their own, sustained analysis of the Yerushalmi's traits in its own terms, may well appreciate the compliment that the authorship of the Yerushalmi pays its audience.

---

[25]Judah Goldin, "The Period of the Talmud, in *The Jews: Their History, Culture, and Religion*, ed., by Louis Finkelstein (New York: Harper and Brothers, 1952), Third Edition, p. 172. "In recent years, however, scholarly opinion has veered away from this oversimplification. Not only have large-scale Roman persecutions in the mid-fourth century been seriously questioned, but the Babylonian Talmud itself has been shown, under critical scrutiny, to have been far less "finished" than it had long appeared to be," writes Salo Baron in *A Social and Religious History of the Jews* (New York: Columbia University Press, 1952), Second Edition, Vol. II, Part II, p. 295-96.

[26]Louis Isaac Rabinowitz, "The Jerusalem Talmud," *The Encyclopaedia Judaica* (New York: Macmillan, 1972), p. 774-75.

Part Two

RELIGIOUS PROBLEMS

Chapter Three

Kavvanah for Prayer in the Mishnah and Talmud

Tzvee Zahavy

University of Minnesota

The common definition of the term *kavvanah* is "intention" or "concentration" during prayer or another ritual.[1] A precise definition of this word has been elusive because it refers to an intangible inner state of mind, an abstract concept of thought, and not a physical or tangible action. In this study we analyze several sources in the Mishnah and the Talmud which use the term *kavvanah* in reference to the recitation of the Prayer of Eighteen Blessings and the recitation of the *Shema'*

Obviously, the Talmud predates by centuries the development of the rich conceptual expressions of the modern disciplines of social science, especially of psychology and sociology. Accordingly, rabbinic texts use more indirect and primitive terminology and conceptualization to describe the inner states of a person's mind and the social aspects of prayer and ritual.

Even though rabbinic idiom was constrained by a limited terminology, rabbinic sources express sophisticated notions regarding inner states of consciousness. When we examine several rabbinic texts and translate into more contemporary terms some concepts of the rabbinic rules and interpretations regarding inner states of mind, we discover strikingly mature attitudes towards those aspects of consciousness, intention or concentration during prayer, called in the texts, "*kavvanah* for prayer."

In addition, an historical analysis of the concept of *kavvanah* in early rabbinic sources shows that the idea does not remain static within rabbinic thought but evolves in the various documents. Let us proceed to pursue these issues concurrently.

Although the Mishnah, Tosefta, Babli and Yerushalmi use the same term, one finds contrasts in the usage and understanding of the term within the distinct

---

[1]The term appears for instance several times in Mishnah referring not only to prayer but also to the performance of other rituals, such as the slaughter of sacrifices in the Temple and the offerings on the altar.

compilations, according to the preferences of each textual source, locale or historical context.

The earliest of our rabbinic texts, Mishnah, sets forth clear distinctions between the concepts of *kavvanah* associated with the recitation of the *Shema'* and with the recitation of the Prayer of Eighteen. These differences represent several separate substantive elements inherent in the rabbinic concept of *kavvanah.*

The first of the major relevant sources in Mishnah offers several rules relating to aspects of the disruption of *kavvanah* for the recitation of the *Shema'* and the Prayer of Eighteen. According to Mishnah, one who engages in these rituals must have *kavvanah.* But Mishnah speaks of two levels of *kavvanah* – a lower level, for one who recites the *Shema',* and a more intense level for one who engages in the recitation of the Prayer of Eighteen.

Mishnah Berakhot 2:1 says, "One who was reciting from the Torah [at Deuteronomy 6:4] and the time for the recitation [of the *Shema'*] arrived, if he directed his attention [to the goal of fulfilling the obligation of reciting the *Shema'*], he fulfilled his obligation."

Mishnah here uses the phrase "בון את לבו, directed his attention" – a clear reference to *kavvanah.* This suggests that one may simply concentrate and change one's state of mind at will to reach the desired level of thought and attention for the recitation of the *Shema'.*

In a text relating to the recitation of the Prayer of Eighteen, Mishnah presents a different picture of what is required for *kavvanah.* At M. Berakhot 5:1 we find, "One may stand to recite the Prayer [of Eighteen Blessings] only out of a solemn disposition. The early saints used to tarry for a while and then recite the Prayer, so that they might direct their hearts [i.e. their thoughts] to God."

The choice of the words "שיחכוונו את לבם, so that they might direct their hearts," implies that *kavvanah* is essential for the recitation of the Prayer. The added requirement of a solemn disposition[2] prior to such recitation presupposes that the framer of this Mishnah stipulated the need for a higher level of concentration and attention for the Prayer Service than for the recitation of the *Shema'* referred to in the text cited previously.

In the continuation of M. Ber. 2:1, Ushan Tannaim engage in a dispute regarding the ramifications of various interruptions in one's concentration while reciting the *Shema'.* According to R. Meir, if one encounters a fellow to whom he must show respect during the recitation of the *Shema'* he may extend a greeting to him if he pauses in his recitation between the paragraphs of the *Shema'* or return a greeting out of respect for him. But only if one encounters a figure of authority whom one fears while in the middle of reciting one of the paragraphs, may a person interrupt to extend or return a greeting. Meir

---

[2]The term in Mishnah is כובד ראש which suggests a form of deep concentration.

stipulates that a more rigorous form of intention and concentration must be maintained when one is in the midst of reciting of each paragraph of the liturgy.

Judah agrees in principle with Meir but disputes with him on the details of the law. When one pauses between paragraphs he may greet a fellow to whom he owes respect and may return the greeting of any individual. When one is engaged in the middle of the recitation of a paragraph of the *Shema'* he may extend a greeting to a figure of authority whom he fears, and he may respond to greeting extended to him by a person to whom he owes some measure of respect, but not to just anyone who comes along.[3]

The Tannaim argue here about the nature and significance of the social encounter for which one may intentionally disrupt his concentration for the recitation of the liturgy. The views in Mishnah exhibit some subtle differences in the understanding of the nature of concentration and interruption in the recitation of the *Shema'*. Both masters agree though that if an individual speaks to his fellow during the performance of the ritual, it does not invalidate the fulfillment of the commandment to recite the *Shema'*.

Mishnah's rule regarding the interruption of one's recitation of the Prayer of Eighteen is significantly different. Mishnah stipulates, "Even if a serpent were coiled to strike at his heel [while he was standing and reciting the Prayer of Eighteen], he may not interrupt (M. Ber. 5:1)." Clearly, as we proposed above, the rabbis envisioned the need for a more intense level of concentration for the recitation of the Prayer of Eighteen.

---

[3]The text is as follows [M. Berakhot 2:1-2]:

[D] "At the breaks [between the paragraphs of the *Shema'*] one may extend a greeting [to his fellow] out of respect, and respond [to a greeting extended to him].

[E] "And in the middle [of reciting a paragraph] one may extend a greeting out of fear and respond," the words of R. Meir.

[F] R. Judah says, "In the middle [of a paragraph] one may extend a greeting out of fear and respond out of respect.

[G] "At the breaks [between the paragraphs] one may extend a greeting out of respect and respond to the greeting of any man."

[A] These are the breaks [in the *Shema'*]:

[B] Between the first blessing and the second [of those which precede the scriptural passages of the *Shema'*].

[C] Between the second blessing and [the second paragraph which begins] "Hear O Israel" [Deut. 6:4-9].

[D] Between [the two sections which begin] "Hear O Israel" and "And it shall come to pass if you shall hearken [Deut. 11:13-21]."

[E] Between [the two sections beginning] "And it shall come to pass" and "And God said to Moses [Num. 15:37-41]."

[F] Between [the two sections] "And God said" and "True and upright" [the blessing which follows the scriptural passages].

[G] R. Judah said, "Between [the two sections] 'And God said' and 'True and upright' one may not interrupt."

Mishnah makes several other less explicit references to disruptions of a person's *kavvanah*. According to M. Berakhot 2:4, a workman may recite the *Shema'* while atop a tree. A householder may not. Moreover, fear of heights prevents a person from attaining the proper concentration for the recitation of the Prayer of Eighteen. Even the craftsman who is used to working high up must come down to recite the Prayer.[4]

Other emotions interfere with one's concentration during recitation. Mishnah elsewhere specifies, "A bridegroom is exempt from the recitation of the *Shema'* from the first night [after the wedding] until after the Sabbath, if he did not consummate the marriage (M. 2:5)." In this case, M. intimates, the anticipation or apprehension of the occasion diverts one's attention and prevents effective concentration.

The sorrow of mourning also disturbs *kavvanah* according to another Mishnaic source. From the time of the death of a relative until after the funeral, a mourner does not have the capacity to concentrate sufficiently for the recitation of the *Shema'* or the Prayer of Eighteen: "He whose deceased relative is lying before him [not yet buried], is exempt from the obligations to recite the *Shema'* and to wear tefillin (M. 3:1)." According to a conventional rabbinic explanation, the reason for the exemption is based on a general principle: one who is engaged in fulfilling a commandment (in this case, burial of the dead), is free from the obligation to fulfill another commandment (in this case, recitation of prayers). Nevertheless, we may add that the inner state of mind of a grieving individual prevents him from attaining the concentration necessary to properly recite the liturgy.[5]

---

[4]The text reads: "Craftsmen may recite [the *Shema'*] from atop a tree or atop a scaffold–something which they are not permitted to do for the [recitation of the] Prayer."

Tosefta adds: "[Workers may recite [the *Shema'*] from atop a tree,] and they may recite the Prayer from atop an olive tree or from atop a fig tree. But from all other kinds of trees one must come down to recite the Prayer below. And the householder must always come down and recite the Prayer below [Tos. 2:8]." [Though craftsmen are accustomed to the height, they are not as adept as fruit pickers who work in the trees and so may not recite the *Shema'* while up in a tree.]

[5]The Mishnah indicates that others who directly share in the grief of the funeral are included in the exemption from reciting: The [first set of] pallbearers, and the [next people] who replace them, and the [next people] who replace their replacements–whether they go [in the procession to the cemetery] before the bier, or they go behind the bier–

If they are needed to [carry] the bier, they are exempt [from reciting the *Shema'* and wearing tefillin].

And if they are not needed to [carry] the bier, they are obligated [in the *Shema'* and tefillin].

Both are exempt from [reciting] the Prayer [of Eighteen blessings].

(3:2)Once they [the mourners] have buried the deceased and returned [from the grave site]–

those who stand in line–the innermost [closest to the mourners] are exempt [from the recitation of the *Shema'*] and the outermost are obligated [to recite].

To recapitulate, in Mishnah's rules for the recitation of the Prayer and the *Shema'*, we may distinguish two levels of *kavvanah* (one for the *Shema'* and one for the Prayer of Eighteen) and three different forms of disruption of *kavvanah* (the emotional states of fear, desire, grief).

Tosefta, a later rabbinic compilation which serves as a complicated appendix to Mishnah, adds the notion that another form of intrusion disrupts one's concentration for prayer. In contrast to the "solemn disposition" required in M. Berakhot 5:1 as a requisite before reciting the Prayer of Eighteen, Tosefta says that lightheartedness disturbs one's ability to concentrate.[6] In Tosefta's words (Berakhot 3:21), "They may not stand to pray after conversation, or after laughter, or after lightheartedness [or after any idle matters], but only after [speaking] words of wisdom."

Tosefta offers here not a rigorous rule for recitation, but some sage guidance to a person as he prepares to pray each day. In order to properly concentrate in prayer, immediately before prayer, one must avoid moods and motivations which distract his attention.

This source extends the concept of *kavvanah* beyond the elementary stages set forth in M. M. stipulated that certain emotional states disrupted *kavvanah*. Tosefta adds that swings of mood also may interfere with an individual's state of *kavvanah*. Tosefta's shift in emphasis is slight but significant.

Sources in the two Talmuds, postdating and sharing knowledge of Mishnah and Tosefta, build on and extend this conceptualization. In the view of these later texts, other kinds of distracting thoughts and moods, not of a deep and pervasive nature, may unsettle a person enough to prevent him from attaining *kavvanah* for prayer.

In a pericope in the Yerushalmi, with a close parallel in Babli, the Talmud develops the proposal that one may start to pray only after engaging in "words of wisdom." The source gives us the following:

IV

- [A] R. Jeremiah said, "One should stand to pray only after [speaking of a] decision of the law."
- [B] R. Jeremiah said, "He who is involved with communal needs is like one who is involved [in the study of] words of Torah. [And he may pray immediately after he finishes serving a communal need]" [Y. Berakhot, Chapter 5, Mishnah 1].

The passage opens with an apparent explanation and addition to the Baraita in the Tosefta-passage cited which says that one may pray after "words of wisdom." The Talmud extends this to include the suggestion that one may pray

---

[6]The Hebrew terms highlight the contrast between these dispositions. For "solemn disposition" is the phrase is כובד ראש (literally: heavy headedness) and for lightheartedness it is קלות ראש (literally: lightheadedness).

after "a decision of the law" or involvement with communal needs." Yerushalmi then continues with specific examples of rules that illustrate the principle of praying after speaking of a rule of law:

[C] R. Huna said, "[Before praying one should speak of a law such as the following:] 'A woman who sees [a discharge of] a drop of blood the size of a mustard seed must sit and keep seven clean days [where she sees no discharge, then immerse herself before resuming regular marital relations].' [After reciting this law] then one may go and pray." [After reciting this stringent decision one will be able to turn one's attention away from further deliberation on the laws of the Torah.]

[D] Zeira bar R. Hinenah said, "[Before praying one should speak of a law such as the following:] 'One who lets blood from animals dedicated to the Temple [and uses the blood for ordinary purposes] has misappropriated Temple property.' This too is one of the [stringent] fixed laws [which one may recite to divert his thoughts from his studying before praying]."

[E] We learned: Bar Qappara said, "[Recite this stringent law before praying:] The [minimum number of] eleven days [which by law one must reckon] between one menstrual period and another, is based on a tradition received by Moses at Sinai.'" [A woman who saw a flow in any of the eleven days after the seven days of her menstrual period, must reckon that to be the flow of a *Zabah*, subject to a stricter law of abstinence. S.H.][7]

[F] We learned: R. Hoshaia [said], "[Recite this lenient law before praying:] 'A person may mix his grain with stalks [before bringing it into his storehouse] as an artifice to free it from the tithing requirement [since thereby it will resemble grain which has not been winnowed, which does not become liable to tithes when brought into storage].'" [According to Hoshaia, reciting a lenient law puts one in the proper frame of mind for prayer.][8]

The Babylonian Talmud has a slightly different version of this pericope:

[A] Our rabbis have taught:

[B] They may not stand to pray after judging [a case], or after [discussing] a matter of law, but only after [speaking of] a decided law.[9]

[C] What is an example of a decided law [which one may speak of before reciting his prayer]?

[D] Said Abaye, "[It is a law] like that of R. Zira."

---

[7]Babli's version omits this rule. Mareh Hapenim suggests that it may be because in Babli Niddah there is an explicit dispute over the rule between R. Yohanan and Resh Laqish. It therefore may not be an appropriate rule on which to reflect to divert one's attention from the distractions of study before turning to prayer.

[8]In Babli's version, he may mix the grain together with its own husks. In that case the rule refers to grain that has not been winnowed which is not liable yet to tithes. From Yerushalmi's version here we may infer that the ruse to avoid tithes works even for grain that has been winnowed and has become liable to tithes. Even in that case one may mix the grain with straw and bring it into the house to avoid the obligation of tithes.

[9]Rashi explains that if one deals with an undisputed law he will not be distracted to delve into it or ponder over it during his recitation of prayer.

[E] R. Zira said, "The women of Israel imposed a stringency upon themselves. For if they observe a [discharge of a] drop of blood [even as small] as a mustard seed, they sit and observe seven clean days [during which no new discharges are observed before resuming marital relations]."[10]

[F] Raba said, "[It is a law] like that of R. Hoshaia."

[G] For R. Hoshaia said, "A person may mix his grain with its chaff [before bringing it into his storehouse] so that his animal may eat it[11] and so that it will be free from the tithing requirement [since thereby it will resemble grain which has not been winnowed, and will not become liable to tithes when brought into storage].'" [According to Hoshaia, reciting a lenient law puts one in the proper frame of mind for prayer.][12]

[H] Or if you wish, an alternative [law which one may recite before rising to pray is one] like that of R. Huna.

[I] For said R. Huna, Said R. Zeira, "One who lets blood from animals dedicated to the Temple, one may derive no personal benefit [from the blood and one who uses the blood for ordinary purposes] has misappropriated Temple property."[13]

Putting aside the minor variations between the two versions,[14] the renditions in Babli and Yerushalmi represent a common approach to *kavvanah*. That is, one should turn to ponder certain legal rulings in order to reach a more intense level of concentration for the recitation of prayer.

We will be better able to analyze the theory inherent in this passage after we consider two additional pericopae in Yerushalmi which deal with other aspects of *kavvanah* for prayer.

The passage cited above from chapter 5, Mishnah 1 [IV] of Yerushalmi Berakhot continues as follows:

> [Before he went to pray,] Abdan asked Rabbi, "How many levels of holy things are there?"
> And he said to them, "Four."
> "How many levels of Heave-offering are there?"
> He said to him, "Three."
> Then [after speaking of these straightforward facts of the law, Abdan] went and prayed.

---

[10]They observed the more stringent law as required for a *zabah* who had seen discharges of blood on three consecutive days during the eleven day period between one menstrual cycle and another. See B. Niddah 66a, B. Meg. 28b.

[11]According to R. Ephraim in the commentary of Tosafot to B. Menahot 67b, s.v.כרי, this is the language the householder uses for the artifice, even though he intends to use the grain for himself.

[12]The obligation to tithe produce begins when one brings the grain into storage after it has been winnowed. See B. Pesahim 9a, B. Menahot 67b, B. Niddah 15b.

[13]See B. Me'ilah 12b.

[14]Notably, Babli omits Bar Qappara's view. His opinion in Y. [E] is similar to Huna's statement in Y. [C]. Both refer to strict laws regulating sexual relations. It appears that rather than to duplicate the point, Babli's editor simply omitted Bar Qappara's lemma.

A previous text in the tractate gives us a related tradition:

VIII

> Said R. Hiyya the great, "In all my days I never concentrated [properly on my Prayer.][15] One time I wanted to concentrate [properly]. So I meditated. And I said to myself, 'Who goes up first before the king? The *Arkafta* [a high dignitary in Persia][16] or the Exilarch?'" [He used this train of thought to help him concentrate on his Prayers. To induce the proper state of mind he thought about the Persian hierarchy.]
> Samuel said, "I count birds [to help me induce the proper state of mind]."
> R. Bun bar Hiyya said, "I count rows of bricks [in a wall to aid me in achieving the proper state of mind]." [Y. Berakhot, Chapter 2, Mishnah 4.]

Ostensibly, Yerushalmi speaks here of various means to enhance one's concentration, to modify a person's state of consciousness, perhaps to induce a special state of consciousness, close to what we might call a simple form of trance.

In light of this latter passage in Yerushalmi Berakhot 2:4, we may explain more amply the questions attributed to Abdan in the former text from Y. Berakhot 5:1. That brief exchange between Abdan and rabbi regarding the number of levels of holy things and of heave-offering, also served as an alternative means of focusing one's thoughts in preparation for prayer.

With the main texts now before us, the following additional explicit issues concerning the Talmudic conception of *kavvanah* for prayer present themselves:

1. What is the connection between *kavvanah* and speaking or thinking of undisputed legal sayings?

2. Of what value is it for a person to think of a legal decision prior to praying?

3. There are surely many other undisputed legal rulings in rabbinic literature. Why does the Talmud select the three or four specific rules cited in the passage?

4. What are the grounds for the dispute between Abaye, Raba, and the alternate opinion in Babli? [In Yerushalmi: between Huna, Hoshaia, Bar Qappara and Zeira.]

5. Finally, what distinctions can we draw between the views of the Baraita in the Talmud [which recommends attention be paid to undisputed laws prior to prayer] and the regulations of Mishnah [which refers to "a solemn disposition"]

---

[15] The traditional commentators naturally mitigate this statement. Pene Moshe explains that he was involved deeply in his study. Sefer Haharedim observes that it is unthinkable that such holy masters did not properly concentrate on their prayer. This must refer to instances of unavoidable disruptions of concentration.

[16] See M. Jastrow, *A Dictionary of the Targumim, Talmud Babli, Yerushalmi, and Midrashic Literature* (New York: 1967), p. 73.

and of Tosefta [which recommends praying after speaking of "words of wisdom"]. Is there a conceptual difference between these viewpoints? Do they in fact allude to the same idea using different means of expression? Can we trace some strands of historical development in the rabbinic ideas regarding *kavvanah?*

Let us return to the first issue. The connection between *kavvanah* and the act of speaking about an undisputed legal ruling makes sense within the context of rabbinic culture. The Talmud in general addressed itself to the average "disciple of the sages." The ideal scholar within a rabbinic circle of learning was expected to occupy himself throughout the day with the study of Torah. This meant that his mind was expected to be constantly busy with the questions and answers, the give and take of the Talmudic argument. No doubt, for this ideal rabbinic Jew it was a difficult task to desist from the intricate deliberations of such study and to turns one's perspective to thanksgiving and praise in prayer.

The remedy prescribed by the Talmud to divert one's thoughts from rabbinic debate and logical analysis was the "undisputed legal ruling." A scholar could turn his thoughts to a ruling which led him to contemplate to further debate, no questions and no answers, just a decided law. And through reflection on that law one could suppress further deliberations of study and clear his mind for *kavvanah* for prayer.

This then is the first basic concept in the main Talmudic passage which we have cited. To address the remainder of our issues we must advance more deeply into the theory behind the Talmudic dispute regarding which legal ruling one recites before he turns to prayer. Let us unpack the logic of each succinct rabbinic statement in the pericope.

The examples of undisputed laws given in the Talmudic passage are not chosen arbitrarily. Each is carefully selected to illustrate a specific point. Abaye in the name of R. Zeira suggests that a person ponder the stringent rule regarding a woman who discharges blood leaving a stain as small as the size of a mustard seed. To interrupt thoughts of legal give and take, Abaye posits, one must think about an especially strict rule. This breaks one's train of thought in learning and enables a person to turn his attention to prayer out of a humble spirit.

Raba differs. He perhaps believed that one should not come to prayer out of humility triggered by reflection over a stringency of rabbinic restrictions. Rather he recommended another avenue to enhance *kavvanah*. He advised the sage to consider a significant lenient rule such as an artifice to avoid tithes, a "tax loophole." Out of the delight associated with thinking of such a benefit, one can more easily divert his thoughts from learning and turn to prayer.[17]

The third alternative of the Talmudic source provides us with another perspective on preparation for prayer. Neither the excessive lowliness associated with contemplating a strict rule, nor the abundant joy connected with cogitating

---

[17]Another form of happiness is associated elsewhere with preparation for prayer. A baraita says, "One stands to pray...only out of the joy of [fulfilling] a commandment."

about a lenient precept, prepares a person's mind for prayer. Only meditating over an highly abstract principle of law such as the regulation that one is not permitted to let blood from an animal of the Temple, brings a person to the proper state of correct *kavvanah* for prayer.

Still, even if these interpretations of the views expressed in the Talmudic passage are correct, we have yet to explain why those three specific legal rules appear in the text. There are numerous stringent, lenient and abstract undisputed rules in the Talmud. By selecting these illustrations the rabbis expressed additional elements of their conceptions of *kavvanah* for prayer.

Abaye and Raba apparently saw the disciple's personality segmented by the tensions of everyday life. Ideally he lived in the world of Talmudic ideas and arguments in the study hall. In reality he also lived in the world at large, confronted by its many distractions.

From Abaye's perspective, concern over the everyday relationships between men and women constituted the primary distraction to concentration for prayer. To alleviate this one might turn his thoughts to a stringent ruling that inhibits contact between the sexes, such as we have in Babli's text.[18]

In Raba's view, mundane monetary worries were the chief sources of interference with a person's *kavvanah* for prayer. The average person, scholar or householder, rich or poor, had some measure of anxiety about money or taxes.[19] To mitigate this disquiet one could turn his thoughts to a great leniency in the law, the notion that a person may free himself of the obligation to give tithes, a burdensome fiduciary responsibility. After reflecting upon such a concept, one more easily might turn his attention to prayer.

According to the third alternative opinion in the Talmud, another more complex realm of daily interaction perturbed the individual and disrupted his *kavvanah*. This opinion proposed that the confrontation between a person and sources of authority might have created situations of frustration and helplessness and detracted from a person's ability to focus his thoughts for *kavvanah* for prayer.

In our text, the Temple stood as a symbol of a source of authority, the priests represented all bureaucracy, and the rule cited in the Talmud suggested the futility of trying to combat the system. One who let blood from a Temple offering, did so in order to benefit the animal, not for his own personal gain. Nevertheless, the Temple administrator saw only the minute requirements of the law. Accordingly, he declared such an action forbidden, and condemned a person who engages in it to be liable under the law.

---

[18]The same may be said of Bar Qappara's view in Y.

[19]Maimonides (in the *Guide for the Perplexed*, part 3, chapter 51) expresses this point directly: "Do not pray moving your lips with your face to the wall [as if you are engaged deeply in prayer] and all the while you are thinking of your business transactions...Do not think you have achieved anything [by doing these things]."

According to this third view, out of pessimistic thoughts of despondence, one might more easily turn his attention away from the distractions of the material world and its complex structures of authority and look with *kavvanah* towards the more spiritual realms of prayer.

Summary

In the Mishnah (early third century) we found the distinction between two kinds of *kavvanah*, one level designated for the recitation of the *Shema'*, and the other deeper form for the recitation of the Prayer of Eighteen. We also observed that Mishnah describes several situations which disrupt *kavvanah*, such as the states of mind associated with intense emotional experiences of fear, grief and affection. Mishnah also dealt with the conditions under which one might interrupt the recitation of the *Shema'*.

Tosefta expanded upon these basic ideas and added to them that everyday states of mind, such as discussion, mirth, and levity may affect one's concentration.

In two sources, Yerushalmi turned to the other side of the issue. It gave conventional suggestions for enhancing concentration, artificial means to aid in intensifying *kavvanah*.

Finally we found in another source in Yerushalmi and its parallel in Babli a completely rabbinic expression of ways to achieve correct *kavvanah:* thinking about or reciting undisputed legal rulings. We suggested several levels of explanation for the content of this pericope and a larger theory to account for the three-way dispute in the text.

Our analysis reveals that *kavvanah* cannot be reduced to a simple one-dimensional abstraction. Rather we have described several of the stages in the development of the concept of *kavvanah* for prayer from Mishnah through the Talmud, the formative ages in the history of Judaism. This idea continues to expand through history as rabbinic thought encounters mysticism and philosophy in the middle ages,[20] and as modern Jewish thought grapples with psychology and social science in contemporary times.[21]

---

[20]In rabbinic thought, especially as developed in the works of the medieval authorities, *kavvanah* was essentially understood to be an issue of turning one's thoughts towards a specified objective. This notion often took on strongly spiritual and even mystical connotations.

More recently the Israeli theologian Rav Kook expressed an acute formulation of the mystical notion of *kavvanah*. As he put it, people are always in a state of *kavvanah*. The problem a person faces is how to remove that substance which obscures the essence of concentration, how one may overcome that which infects the mind and diverts a person from true *kavvanah*.

This last point is cited by Rabbi Norman Lamm in his essay, "Nowadays we do not repeat [prayer] because of a lack of *kavvanah*." Rabbi Lamm suggests that the concept may also be found in medieval Jewish thought in the writings of Judah Halevi and others. See *Sepher Yevul Hayovloth* (New York: 1986), p. 241.

[21]Examples of recent works include Paul Bindler's two studies, "A Psychological Analysis of *Kavvanah* in Prayer," in *Proceedings of the Association of Orthodox Jewish Scientists*, ed. Fred Rosner, 3/4 (Jerusalem: 1976), pp. 133-143, and "Meditative Prayer and Rabbinic Perspectives on the Psychology of Consciousness: Environmental, Physiological and Attentional Variables," in *Journal of Psychology and Judaism*, 4/4 (Summer: 1980), pp. 228-248.

Also of interest are M.H. Spero, "Dream Psychology in Talmudic Thought," in *Proceedings of the Association of Orthodox Jewish Scientists*, ed. Fred Rosner, 3/4 (Jerusalem: 1976), pp. 123-132; R. Schatz, "Contemplative Prayer in Hasidism," in *Studies in Mysticism and Religion Presented to Gerschom Scholem* (Jerusalem: 1967), pp. 209-226; H.G. Enelow, *"Kawwana(!):* the Struggle for Inwardness in Judaism," in Phillipson, Newmark and Morgenstern, eds., *Studies in Jewish Literature in Honor of Kaufman Kohler* (New York: 1980, pp. 82-107; Riv-Ellen Prell-Foldes, "The Reinvention of Reflexivity in Jewish Prayer; the Self and the Community in Modernity," in *Semiotica*, 30, 1/2, pp. 73-96.

Chapter Four

The Maccabean Struggle to Define Judaism

Peter Haas

Vanderbilt University

When we read religious texts from Late Antiquity, we tend to see these as normative theological statements rather than as partisan documents produced in, and responding to, a particular social context. One of the contributions of Howard Kee has been to focus attention on the social background of religious movements of Hellenistic and Roman times. In this paper I shall carry forward this interest by adducing some of the social tensions behind the literature which describes the Maccabean bid for power in the middle of the second century BCE. I propose this area because it represents one of the earliest documented stages of the disintegration of Ancient Judaism into its various Hellenistic sects. By probing this series of events, we achieve insight into how a religious community, confronted with new and unprecedented change, struggles to absorb that change while still maintaining its traditional identity. The reading of the sources proposed here, then, differs from classical readings because it is not meant to reveal the thinking of a reputedly true or normative Jewish community. Rather, it is designed to bring to the surface some of the social and ideological tensions which provoked our authors to present the Maccabean enterprise in just this way. What I hope to show is that if we read these ancient texts as social documents, we open whole new worlds for understanding the intellectual background of the Maccabean movement.

A study of the books of Maccabees is particularly appropriate for this volume because these books, like the gospels on which Kee works, claim to be historical accounts of divinely significant events which occurred before the accounts were written and under the influence of which the author still lives. Like the gospels also, what we find in these texts is not an accurate report on "what actually happened," but a presentation of these events in the service of a particular theological or ideological perspective. Our interest in these books, then, is in the underlying perceived realities which compel people to interpretevents in one way and not some other. As our analysis will show, the Books of Maccabees do not represent a normative or self-evident position, but rather represent a limited and even controversial ideological stance. By examining this stance in relation to the other options against which the books react, I hope to draw out the social and political communities that begin to emerge at this crucial juncture of Judean religious history.

The Maccabean revolt, based largely on the accounts in the Books of Maccabees, has traditionally been portrayed as a struggle between those faithful to Judaism, on the one hand, and the Hellenists, on the other.[1] That is, we are asked to believe that two monolothic, mutually exclusive, cultural entities – Judaism and Hellenism – came into conflict, and that the Maccabees are the outstanding representatives of "Judaism."[2] Yet a closer reading of the primary sources, I and II Maccabees in particular, reveals a much more complex reality. Both works are fully aware that the Maccabees faced opposition from Judeans as well as from Greeks. There was, it is clear, no unanimity within the Judean community itself as to the appropriateness of what the Maccabees were doing. To be sure, the Books of Maccabees will reject their Jewish opponents as "faithless," "godless" or deluded pietists. The anti-Maccabeans, however, surely did not conceive of themselves in these ways. In their own eyes, they stood for the authentic and legitimate type of Judaism, a type now under attack by the radical Maccabeans. What we find in our sources, then, is that there werea variety of theories about what Judaism ought to be like in the Hellenistic age. Our goal is to understand these various communities and the expression of Judaism each represents. The end result, we hope, will be a fuller understanding of the nature of Judaism in this period.

---

[1]A classic articulation of this view in modern historical writings is given by Heinrich Graetz. See, for example, his *Popular History of the Jews* (New York: Hebrew Publishing Co., 1919) I, p. 366: "The consecration of the Temple marked the victory of Judaism over the refined Hellenistic idolatry, of the God of Israel over the idols." G. F. Moore popularized this view among Christian historians: "That the efforts of the king and his creatures to heathenize them [i.e., the Jews] ran counter not only to the attachment of the Jews to their religion but to their national sentiment is clear." [G.F. Moore, *Judaism* (New York: Schocken, 1971) I, p. 50]. Today two broad interpretations of these eventsexist. The one, represented by Victor Tcherikover [*Hellenistic Civilization and the Jews* (New York: Antheneum, 1970)] and Elias Bickerman [*God of the Maccabees* (Leiden: Brill, 1979)] argues that the actions in Jerusalem by the Seleucids were not so much acts of religious persecution in the modern sense as largely political in nature. They may even have enjoyed some support from Judeans themselves. The second view, represented mostly by Israeli scholars, still sees the struggle as one between Judaism and paganism. See for example, Y. Baer, "The Persecution of the Monotheistic Religion by Antiochus Epiphanes" in *Zion* 33:101-124. Also Menahem Stern, "The Hasmonean Revolt and its Place in the History of Jewish Society and Religion" in *Jewish Society Through the Ages*, ed. by H. Ben-Sasson and S. Etinger (New York: Schocken, 1972), pp. 92-106: "The events in Judeawere unusual in the history of ancient times in that they involved the total religious persecution of an entire nation... (p. 92)"

[2]Drawing a distinction between Judaism and Hellenism is misleading since it leaves the impression that the Judaism in question is itself not Hellenistic. In fact, we now know that all of the various manifestations of Judaism in our period are already Hellenistic religions. Hengel states matters exactly when he writes, "On the whole, it emerges that Hellenism also gained ground as an intellectual power in Jewish Palestine early and tenaciously. . . . From about the middle of the third century B.C. all Judaism must really be designated Hellenistic Judaism' in the strict sense...." [Martin Hengel *Judaism and Hellenism* (Philadelphia: Fortress, 1974), pp. 1-2. The emphases are Hengel's.]

The ideological description we adduce will of course be a function of the sources we choose to use. Our basic hypothesis must be that any source describing the events of the Maccabean revolt must by nature be an interpretationand that that interpretation belongs to the period of the document's composition and not to the time of the events being narrated. Before proceeding, then, we must briefly describe the primary sources available to us and evaluate what lightthey are capable of shedding on the social world of Maccabean times.

In dealing with the Maccabean revolt, we have essentially four sources. These are the Books of Daniel, First Maccabees, Second Maccabees and the historical writings of Josephus. Only the two books of Maccabees, as we shall now see, are suitable for our purposes. The Book of Daniel is in many ways an important document since it was published, apparently, during the time of the revolt mounted by Mattathias. As a source for history, however, it is of very limited use. Since it is unaware of the fact of Antiochus IV's death, which occurred in 164, the work must have appeared before this crucial event, thus placing its composition at the very beginning of the period in which we are interested. It is thus useless for understanding the revolt itself, or the reaction of people to the subsequent Maccabean victories and rise to power, since these occured subsequent to the book's composition. Furthermore, even as regardsthe events of which it does know the book presents formidable interpretative problems. It is written as an apocalypse, casting the Maccabean struggle in the mythic terms of a cosmic struggle. Thus the historical events it does describe are put in such a way that little useful social information can be garnered. Thus, despite its general applicability to the subject at hand, the book of Daniel turns out to be of little help in our investigation of the social forces at work during this period. Josephus also presents problems as a source for the history of the political and social struggles of the second century BCE. On the surface, the writings of Josephus seem a more promising source of data than does the Book of Daniel. The Antiquities of the Jews contains a detailed exposition of the Maccabean revolt and the reign of the early Hasmoneans. Unfortunately, this history was written only in the late first century CE, some 200-250 years after the events it describes. As Morton Smith and Jacob Neusner, among others, have shown, Josephus conceives of the parties and politics of the second and first centuries in terms of the social and political realities of his own time.[3] His writings are therefore useless for learning about Jewish self-perceptions in the Maccabean era.

The Books of Maccabees remain the most promising source of data for our purposes. In the first place, both documents have a fairly detailed discussion of the events in question. That is, they both give us a good deal of detailed

---

[3]See, for example, Morton Smith, "Palestinian Judaism in the First Century," in *Israel: Its Role in Civilization*, ed. Moshe Davis (New York: Harper & Row, 1956) and Jacob Neusner, *From Politics to Piety: The Emergence of Pharisaic Judaism* (New York: KTAV, 1979), especially Chapter Three.

information about the parties and politics of the time. In addition, these histories were most likely written within a generation or two after the Maccabees' final victory in the late 140's.[4] They thus emerge from a world whichis the immediate result of the Maccabean struggle. This proximity to events carries with it certain ramifications which we must keep in mind. First of all, both sources clearly will reflect the biases of the Hasmonean dynasty since both reach us as "normative" texts and not as sectarian writings. Second, both mirrormost strongly interests of survivors and heirs of the revolt rather than of its direct participants. At best, then, all we can claim is that these books provide information about positions which emerged and jelled during the revolt and which continued to be sources of concern and conflict during the succeeding generations. In short, these two texts offer insight only into the social ideologies of the heirs of the Maccabees in the decades immediately following the Hasmonean rise to power. If we fail to learn about the Maccabean brothers themselves, we nonetheless can adduce a good deal about some of the intellectual trends asssociated with the formative stage of the Hasmonean state, and so of Hellenistic Judaism in the middle to late second century.

One of our postulates in the investigation to follow is that the two books: First Maccabees and Second Maccabees – do not reflect the same perspective and ideology. This should be apparent from the simple fact that both books go over much of the same ground. Second Maccabees is, in effect, a detailed examination of a portion of the history covered in First Maccabees, namely the struggle led by Mattathias and the eldest brother, Judah. As the gospels themselves illustrate, the need to retell the same story once again, or to repeatpart of an already available story in more detail, masks a convction on the part of the latter author that the first telling misses, or misrepresents, the point. Second Maccabees is written, I claim, because it wants to correct, or disagree with, some aspect of First Maccabees. The different theological and stylistic characters of the two books have been recognized for a long time, but this difference has been presumed to be of no consequence for each book's portrayal of the essential historical events under discussion. In fact, as we shall presently see, each book evaluates the events of the revolt in a fundamentally different light, and draws different conclusions about what God wants, or does not want, as regards the community of Israel. Rather than two accounts of a single history, we have two historical sources concerned with the same events, but drawing different conclusions from them. Read as such, these two books reveal a much more complex, and interesting, picture of the state of Judaism in the last decades of the second century BCE than the traditional reading has allowed.

---

[4]Goldstein offers a detailed discussion of the dating of these documents. He concludes that both were written during the reign of Alexander Jannaeus, who reigned from 103 to 76. See *The Bible. I Maccabees*. Introduction and Commentaryby Jonathan Goldstein (New York: Doubleday, 1976), pp. 62-64.

Our analysis of these sources, as we said, must proceed in terms laid down for us by the character of these materials. According to both I and II Maccabees, the conflict is one over who will exercise authority over the Judean community. This focal concern of both authors indicates that the question of authority is a major category of definition and debate in the social worlds of our authors. Consequently, we will focus our attention on what these authors conceived to be the proper kind of authority for the people of Israel. We shall try to adduce, as far as is possible, what kinds of claims were being put forward as to what constitutes legitimate leadership and authority in Judea and the bases on which these claims were grounded. In fact, these questions move us to the very heart of Jewish self-perceptions of the second century, for the authority which one recognizes as legitimate for defining the religious life reflects in a profound way one's understanding of what that religion is. It follows that a struggle between different kinds of claimants to religious authority indicates fundamental disagreements as to what the religious tradition in question ought to be. It is this broader concern that will stand behind all of our subsequent deliberations.

Before turning to the texts themselves, it may be helpful to anticipate our results to an extent and indicate the kinds of authorities that our authors portray as in conflict. With these competing types in mind, the dynamics of the struggle constructed in each text become clearer. In this regard, as it turns out, both books share a general conception. For both books, there are three major types of authority that come into conflict. First is the power of the secular imperial authority, in this case the Seleucids. Since the founding of the Second Temple in the late sixth century, the imperial powers have been seen as instruments through which God works. These powers are given political control over Judea but allow the community to control its own internal affairs under the auspices of the holy Priests and according to the received ancestral traditions, "the laws of the fathers." The secular world powers, then, are the de facto political basis upon which the rule of Torah in Judea is based.

A second source of political power in the Judean community is the office of the High Priesthood. Although the High Priest must now be confirmed in office by the Seleucids, the office itself contains in it the potentiality of authority autonomous of secular rulers. According to Scripture, the Israelite priesthood was established by God himself, who conferred it everlastingly upon the descendants of Aaron. The priesthood is given exclusive right to regulate the Temple cult, to adjudicate matters of cultic purity, and to regulate the sacred economy of the community on the Holy Land. It comprises the characteristic institution of Israelite life, and constitutes the apex of Israelite society. From the point of view of the priesthood, of course, there is no intrinsic need for secular confirmation, even though this is now the status quo. In fact, the Maccabean claim to authority rests as we shall presently see on the assertion that one can be a true and legitimate High Priest even if the Seleucids do not recognize one as such.

The third source of authority which enters into the struggle is the Torah.[5] This revealed word of God requires that Israel be a holy people and spells out how this is to be achieved. Besides establishing standards for the cult, the lawimposes a certain lifestyle upon the community at large, observance of the Sabbath, for example, and abstinence from defiling foods. For at least some segments of the Jewish community in the second century, the Hasideans are a good example, proper adherence to these laws is of paramount importance. Those who understand the stipulations of Torah to be constitutive of the community will be willing to disobey even a High Priest if that priest is deemed to be improper according to the standards of the Torah law. It should be understood at this point that the precise nature of these stipulations is of course a matter of interpretation. What we shall find is not one group following Torah and another group not following Torah, but rather one group following one interpretation of Torah and a second group claiming that that interpretation is wrong. The point is that we shall soon encounter the phenomenon of high priests who are being challenged on the ground that they have misunderstood Torah. That is, the once self-evident link between priestly rulings and the meaning of Torah is being severely challenged in this period.

The tensions among these rival notions of authority, tensions which played themselves out in Jerusalem at this time, are understandable only in terms of the historical context of the struggle in which Judea was now finding itself. We need, then, briefly to review the events leading up to the revolt and the progress of the revolt itself. Such a review will allow us to see more clearly why the Jewish community became divided along precisely the lines that it did.

Let us begin with the three types of authority we just introduced. In theory, these various layers of authority could be made to operate in harmony and, it appears, did so for several centuries. The basic structure of the symbiosis was put in place by the Persians at the end of the sixth/beginning of the fifth century. The Persian emperor appointed an Aaronide High Priest over Judea who governed his territory according to the traditional priestly laws, as far as these

---

[5]By the second century BCE, this canon surely included at a minimum the Pentateuch and at least some, if not all, of the prophetic writings. See Norman Gottwald's discussion and chart in *The Hebrew Bible: A Socio-Literary Introduction* (Philadelphia.: Fortress, 1985), pp. 102-110.

were consistent with general imperial policy.[6] Thus we have a community in which the religious law of Israel is administered by a High Priest ruling with the concurrence of the secular king. Each of the three potential loci of power work together in an harmonious whole. This apparently stable symbiosis broke down only under Antiochus in the second century, although deep fissures began to form much earlier. To anticipate our results, it appears, again from the perspective of I and II Maccabees, that the dissolution proceeded in two directions. According to I Maccabees, the primary fissure was between the proponents of royal authority, the so-called Hellenizers, on one hand, and the upholders of divine law, the "righteous," on the other. This latter group claimed authenticity both because its leaders were of High Priest lineage, i.e., the Maccabees themselves, and because these priests alone properly understood and were faithful to Torah. In terms of the scheme we sketched above, the High Priesthood and the "law of the fathers" are allied against the imperial power. II Maccabees shows that eventually even this alliance broke down. According to the author of this work, a valid claim to authority can be made only by those who in their personal lives embody the traditional law. Occupancy of the High Priesthood is thus not in itself a sufficient ground for leadership. The thrust of II Maccabees seems to be that while Judah Maccabee was faithful, and thus a worthy High Priest, this was not so of his brothers and descendants. It follows that pious followers of the law must dissociate themselves from the latter Maccabees, even though they are priests and eventually do gain imperial recognition.

Let us now trace the development of these fissures. The stage for the Maccabean revolt was in some sense already set a generation earlier, under the reign of Antiochus III. In about the year 200 BCE, Judea was a province in the Ptolemaic empire centered in Egypt. A major change in this status occurred in 198, when the Seleucid emperor, Antiochus III, ruling from Mesopotamia, defeated the Ptolemaic Egyptian army and annexed the border province of Judea

---

[6]It is impossible to describe with precision the political organization of Judea under the Persians. In general, the Persian kings allowed the Jews to reorganize their national life and to live according to their ancestral laws insofar as these were consistent with Persian imperial law. A member of the priestly clan was appointed to administer the community. This "High Priest" was surely answerable to secular Persian authorities. There does not appear to have been a secular ruler as well. The general structure of this system remained unchanged under Alexander the Great and was passed down to his Seleucid and Ptolemaic successors. Hecataeus of Abdera, writing in the fourth century, describes the Jewish self-government as follows, "These same men [the priests] he [i.e., Moses] appointed to be judges in all major disputes and entrusted to them the guardianship of the laws and customs. For this reason the Jews never have a king, and authority over the people is regularly vested in whichever priest is regarded as superior to his colleagues in wisdom and virtue. They call this man the High Priest, and believe that he acts as a messenger to them of God's commandments." [M. Stern, *Greek and Latin Authors on Jews and Judaism* (Jerusalem: 1976), p. 28]. Also Ben Sira, in the late third/early second century describes the High Priest as the leader of the people, p. 50ff. Cf. Bickerman's description of the role of the High Priest in *Seleucid Palestine, God of the Maccabees* (Leiden: Brill, 1979), p. 35.

to his own empire. His immediate policy as regards this area was, of course, to integrate the new province into the social, political and economic life of his empire. It seems certain, however, that this shift in political status was not favored by all elements of Judean society. Although data are scarce, it appears that Egyptian rule over Palestine was on the whole benevolent. Hengel points out that Jewish literature of the time portrays secular rulers in a generally favorable light.[7] We also know that certain Judean families, the Tobiads, for example, gained considerable influence under the Ptolemies. There were, then, powerful interests in the community that preferred the status quo. On the other hand, the Egyptians seemed to have exercised tight control over Judea, especially in matters affecting the collection of taxes. The transfer of Judea to Seleucid control, then, would have certain beneficial effects for the common citizenry. They would be subject, apparently, to less close scrutiny in local affairs and would bear a lighter burden in taxes. In fact, transfer to Seleucid domination appears to have had broad support.[8] Insofar as there was popular, and apparently growing, support among the population for the Seleucids, at least vis-a-vis the Ptolemaic alternative, the Maccabean revolt against the Seleucids posed a real problem. Herein lies the seed of a fundamental division in Judean society.[9]

Antiochus III's military policy had a second profound effect. He left his successor, Seleucus IV, with considerable financial problems. These economic difficulties were exacerbated by a heavy tribute placed on the Seleucid throne by the Romans, who defeated the Seleucid armies in a series of battles (191-190). To meet his pressing need for gold and silver, Seleucus IV turned to the traditional storehouses of national wealth: local temples. He in fact died while attempting to plunder a temple in Elam. His son, Antiochus IV, inherited both the debt and the precedent of violating local religious institutions for the means to pay it.

Antiochus IV's need for money led him to actions which created in the province of Judea two foci of opposition to his rule. In 175 he began to meddle with the Judean High Priesthood, selling the office to the highest bidder.[10] The result was that soon almost Byzantine machinations surrounded the appointment of High Priests. As both books of Maccabees make clear, traditionalists interpreted this as a defilement of Israel's most holy office. It was becoming evident that the Seleucid rulers no longer could be trusted to uphold the honor of the High Priesthood. The old alliance between secular rulers and the rule of Torah was, at least for these people, beginning to unravel. This impending

---

[7]Hengel, p. 29.

[8]The role of the Tobiad family is discussed at length by Tcherikover, *Hellenistic Civilization*. See also M. Stern, "The Hasmonean Revolt..." in *Jewish Society Through the Ages*, pp. 94ff. For popular sentiment in favor of the Seleucids, see, for example, Hengel, pp. 23-29.

[9]Cf., for example, V. Tcherikower, *Hellenistic Civilization*, pp. 187-188.

[10]Bickerman, *God of the Maccabees*, p. 43ff.

crisis was further inflamed by a second assault against Judean religious sensibilities: in 169 Antiochus plundered the Temple in Jerusalem. This act of desecration meant that the symbiosis between the secular ruler and local religious law had fully broken down. In fact, the "law of the fathers" lost its official status shortly thereafter in the wake of what was apparently an aborted revolt against Seleucid hegemony.[11] It was virtually impossible now for one to be loyal both to the traditional priestly law of Judea and to the Seleucids. For people caught in this cruel dilemma, the secular ruler became an unacceptable authority for at least some segments of the population.

The process of internal disintegration has now been set in motion. Before turning to how our sources portray the different sides in the dispute, we need briefly to trace the course of events down to the reign of Alexander Jannaeus, the approximate time when our sources were written. The rebellion against Antiochus, led by the priest Mattathias and then by his son, Judah, scored its first success in 164 when the Temple was retaken from the Syrians and was rededicated. Shortly thereafter, Jerusalem itself fell into the hands of the rebels and the traditional priestly law – the Torah – was again established as the supreme authority in Judean life. To put matters in another way, we could say that the traditional authority of the Priesthood and the Torah now superseded the authority of the secular ruler. At this point it appears that the Seleucids attempted to make peace by reconfirming the position of the traditional priestly line and revoking their decrees against traditional Judean law. According to both books of Maccabees, these concessions satisfied many of the rebels. With the traditional priestly family again in power, ruling according toTorah, and with the backing of the now repentent secular authorities, the old modus vivendi was reestablished. Secular rule, the law of Torah and the office of High Priest again functioned together. The Maccabees, however, refused to be satisfied. Successive Hasmonean brothers continued the struggle with the Seleucids, until Jonathan won the High Priesthood for himself in 153. By 151 or so, Judea, while still a province of the Seleucid empire, was effectively ruled by the Hasmonean family. This general state of affairs lasted until about 143, when Jonathan, backing Demetrius in his claim for the Seleucid throne, was executed by Antiochus VI. Jonathan's younger brother, Simeon, remained loyal to Demetrius and when Demetrius emerged victorious, Simeon was appointed High Priest and Judea granted autonomy. In this way, some twenty years after their initial victory, in 140, the Hasmoneans achieved full control over the political life of Judea. The old alliance between secular, pagan overlordship on the one hand, and local priestly rule, on the other, was broken. The pagan authorities had in effect abandoned the field, vesting authority now in priest and Torah.

---

[11]The exact nature of the Assyrian actions in Jerusalem is not at all clear. Probably the most cogent attempt at reconstruction is that of Elias Bickerman in*God of the Maccabees*, pp. 53f. See also Jonathan Goldstein's lengthy discussion in "I Maccabees,"*The Anchor Bible* (New York: Doubleday, 1976), pp. 104-160, especially p. 112.

Simeon, as both ethnarch and high priest, ruled the newly resurrected independent state of Judea until his murder in 134.

Simeon was succeeded by John Hyrcanus I, the first Hasmonean ruler born after the original revolt of Mattathias. He saw his task not as carrying forward the idealistic struggle of his forebearers, but as maintaining and strengthening the Hellenistic military state that he inherited. He was a Hellenistic chieftan pure and simple. Under Hyrcanus, and his successors, Aristobolus and Alexander Jannaeus, Judea became a typical Hellenistic kingdom: its coins bear Greek pagan symbols, its rulers engaged in petty international politics; John Hyrcanus even looted David's tomb to raise funds for a mercenary army. As we move further and further away from the roots of the rebellion, Judean culture became more and more Hellenized, and its rulers acted more and more like the petty Hellenistic princesaround them. It is ironic that the dynasty which began as a rebellion against Hellenism became its patrons a generation later. Those who fought the Seleucids because of their introduction of foreign ways into Judea stood betrayed. The Hasmonean High Priesthood did not remain faithful to what traditionalists would consider the true spirit of the traditional law of Torah. Herein lies the cause for the second important breach in the Judean community: that between what the traditional way of life under the rule of Torah seemed to demand, on the one hand, and the actual character of the community and its High Priest, on the other. That is, the two remaining elements of authority, the office of High Priest and the rules of Torah, no longer seemed congruent. We must keep this tension in mind when we turn to the later of our two sources, II Maccabees.

Having laid out the historical framework, we now turn to our analysis of the sources. Again, we are interested in adducing who our sources perceive to be the primary contenders for religious authority among the Judeans. We will consider first I Maccabees and then II Maccabees.

The author of I Maccabees has no doubt that the Hasmoneans are the fully legitimate rulers of the people. Our author ascribes to them all of the outward signs of legitimacy. They are of priestly lineage (2:1; 14:29), faithful to the law (2:20-21), granted seemingly miraculous victories, and are eventually confirmed in office both by the gentile powers (10:20; 11:27, 57) and the Jewish populace at large (14:35-43, 49). Thus the author eventually invokes all of the elements of the old symbiosis to establish the legitimacy of his heroes. In fact, this book makes the Maccabees define the acme of holiness and righteousness in Israel. Against their standard all other actors in the historical drama are measured. If we place the Maccabees in the center of successive rings of holiness, we find that the group with the next most perfect status are other priests who fight against the Seleucids. These priests, however, do not enjoy the divine favor that Mattathias and his family members do as illustrated by the fact that they can not on their own gain victory in battle (5:61-67). Next, as we move out from the center, we have the supporters of the Maccabees, righteous men faithful to the law but not priests. These define a population which remains undefiled and pure (1:60-63) but which is nonetheless to be subject to Hasmonean authority. Further out are the Jews who side with the gentiles and oppose the Maccabees. These are described as "lawless," "irreligious," "godless" (6:22), "lawbreakers," "wrongdoers" (9:23-25) and "haters of their own nation" (11:23). Finally, furthest removed from the metaphysical center of holiness defined by theHasmoneans, are the Gentiles, who are "greedy" (3:28-29), "plunderers" (6:1-3) and "full of violence and lawlessness" (3:20). The Gentiles, in fact, pollute the land and finally must be expelled from the environs of Jerusalem (I Macc 14:36-37). This typology of peoples indicates that the author of I Maccabees conceives of his heroes as more than the heirs of fortuitous political events. In all ways they embody all those traits which are naturally to be expected of the leaders of the holy people, Israel.

The typology adduced above reveals the two basic criteria which, for our author, define legitimate holders of authority in Israel. These are 1) faithfulness to the law and 2) priestly lineage. This combination of priestly lineage and overall regard for the law on the part of the Maccabees is repeatedly stressed. This theme appears first, as we would expect, in connection with Mattathias. The first mention of his name includes the information that he is of priestly lineage (2:1) and his initial lament concerns the profanation of the Temple. On the other hand, his public statements deal consistently with the laws and the covenant (2:20-22, 27, 50, 58, 64). Interestingly, these two themes, priesthood and obedience to the law, are combined in Mattathias' public act of defiance in Modein. Upon seeing an Israelite prepare to offer sacrifices upon the pagan altar, I Maccabees tells us, "he burned with zeal and his heart wasstirred. He gave vent to this righteous anger; he ran and killed him upon the altar. At the same time, he killed the king's officer who was forcing them to sacrifice, and he tore down the altar. Thus he burned with zeal for the law, as Phineas did against Zimri, the son of Salu." (2:24-26). The closing reference to Phineas is significant. Phineas, scion of a priestly family, zealously defended the purity of the community when the Children of Israel were in the wilderness after having fled from Egypt. He was rewarded for his zealousness by having the priesthood conferred upon him and his descendants (Nu. 25:6-15).[12] The point of the allusion is that just as Phineas earned cultic leadership because of his devotion to the standards of Torah, so too did the Maccabees. Nor is Mattathias alone in these qualifications. Judah, Mattathias' successor, also is depicted as a conscientious priest who is faithful to the law. Before fighting Gorgias, for example, he and his followers prayed for victory: "[they] opened the book of the law to inquire into those matters about which the Gentiles were consulting the images of their idols. They also brought the garments of the priesthood and the first fruits and the tithes [which were to be eaten in Jerusalem], and they stirred up the Nazirites, who had completed their days [and owed offerings]; and they cried aloud to Heaven saying, 'What shall we do with these? Where shall we take them?'" (3:46-51) Certainly their devotion to the correct practice of priestly law could hardly be more forcefully portrayed. Upon recapturing the Temple, this description of devotion continues, for one of Judah's first acts was to appoint men to reconsecrate the altar. For this he chose "blameless priests devoted to the law" (4:42). At every opportunity, then, Judah is made to appear as a priest who upholds the law. The point is reiterated by Simon at 13:3, who says, "You yourselves know what great things I and my brothers and the house of my father have done for the laws and the sanctuary..." (cf. 13:47-48, 14:14-15, 29). I Maccabees then clearly appropriates for the Hasmoneans the powerful symbols of the law and the sanctuary. It is around these symbols that legitimate Jewish opposition to the secular Seleucid rulers is organized.

According to this portrayal of the Maccabees, they are the natural leaders of the Jewish ethnos. Yet we know, from evidence in I Maccabees itself, that some segments of the Jewish community did not join the Maccabean camp. In I Maccabees, these are dismissed as lawless, godless or, at best, deluded pietists (cf. 7:12f). As we examine the evidence more closely, however, we discover that in fact opposition to the Maccabees on the part of Jews is based on two rather ·

---

[12]This story has an important polemical function. The High Priesthood was traditionally the preserve of the Oniad line. These were descended from Jeshua, son of Jedaiah, a priest who is mentioned as having returned to Palestine for the Restoration (Ez. 2:36, Neh. 7:39). He himself was a descendant of the Zadok who was given the exclusive rights to the priesthood by Solomon (I Kings 1). The Hasmoneans, however, are not of this line but claim descent from another priest, namely Jehoyarib (I Maccabees 2:1). They thus can be considered usurpers by those who consider the High Priesthood to belong to the Oniad line alone. The comparison with Phineas serves, then, to establish a second claim to authority. This alternate priestly line of Jehoyarib is now chosen for special prominence just as Phineas once was.

The identity of this Jehoyarib is hard to pin down. At least three candidates exist. There is a Jehoyarib mentioned as a priest at the time of the Restoration (Neh. 12:6). This figure is mentioned as an equal along with Jedaiah, the ancestor of the Onaids, and Bilgah, from whom Menelaus (appointed as High Priest in 175) is descended (cf. Tcherikower's discussion of Menelaus' descent from Bilgah, pp. 403-404). The Maccabees' line is thus made equal to the other "functioning" priestly lines. Secondly, Neh. 11:10 mentions a priest, Jedaiah, who is the son of a Jehoyarib. It could be, then, that the Maccabees claim descent from the father of the Jedaiah from whom the Onaids stem. The third possibility is the Jehoyarib mentioned in I Chron. 24:7, who receives the first lot when David divided the priesthood into watches.

compelling themes. The first is that the Maccabees are opposing the duly constituted secular authorities who guarantee the existence of the Jewish commonwealth (6:21f, 7:33-38). As we have already said, loyalty to the secular ruler as an instrument of God is evident already in the late sixth century. The second is that they are not proper High Priests (7:12). Seen in light of these claims, the anti-Maccabean forces appear not as traitors but as serious thinkers who reject the Maccabees on perfectly legitimate bases. Let us now turn to an examination of the intellectual basis for opposing the Maccabees, on the basis of information presented by I Maccabees itself.

I Maccabees clearly indicates that some members of the Jewish ethnos felt that their primary loyalty was to the secular authority, the Seleucids.[13] 6:21f reports on a group of "ungodly" Jews who joined Greek escapees from the beseiged garrison in Jerusalem: "They went to the king and said, 'How long will you fail to do justice and to avenge our brethren? We were happy to serve your father, to live by what he said and to follow his commands.'" Another example of this attitude occurs in 7:33-38. In this passage a group of Jews attempts to indicate to Nicanor their continued loyalty to the Seleucids: "After these events, Nicanor went up to Mount Zion. Some of the priests came out of the sanctuary and some of the elders of the people, to greet him peaceably and to show him the burnt offering that was being offered for the king...." For these people, loyalty to the secular ruler was not inconsistent with being loyal to the Temple and its requirements. This would certainly be true after 164, when the Seleucids again became imperial patrons of the local Temple in Jerusalem.

The Maccabees were also rejected, we said, on the grounds that they were not of proper priestly lineage. 7:12f, for example, reports that "the Hasideans were the first among the sons of Israel to seek peace from them (i.e., Alcimus, the rival High Priest, and Bacchides, the Greek general) for they said, 'A priest of the line of Aaron [that is, Alcimus] has come....'" Apparently, Alcimus' claim to the priesthood was more convincing to these people than was Judah's. After all Alcimus was from the established priestly family, presumably the Zadokites, while the Maccabees were from a lesser known priestly clan. We have already in fact seen an attempt on the part of the author of this book to deny this claim by invoking the precedent of the usurpation of the priesthood – with God's blessing – by Zimri. Both themes, that the Maccabees are rebels against the established government and that they are of improper lineage, appear together in 7:5 ff:

---

[13]This position is in fact extremely plausible in light of the general situation painted by our sources. The Seleucids, of course, represented Hellenism, that is, modern (to them) civilization. Their efforts to effect the Hellenization of Judea certainly found favor among a large portion of the population, who saw entry into this larger world as beneficial. In those days lawless men came forth from Israel, and misled many, saying, 'Let us go and make a covenant with the Gentiles round about us, for since we separated from them many evils have come upon us...'" (I, Mac. 1:11). Indeed, Mattathias is encouraged to be the first in his village to concede to Hellenization "as all the Gentiles and the men of Judah and those that are left in Jerusalem have done" (I Mac. 2:18). Support for the Seleucids, and their general policy, seems to have been widespread. See, for example, Bickerman, p. 54.

"Then there came to him (the Seleucid ruler, Demetrius) all the lawless and godless of Israel; they were led by Alcimus, who wanted to be High Priest. And they brought to the king this accusation against the people: 'Judah and his brothers have destroyed all your friends....'" It is an interesting fissure in the Maccabee's propaganda that these people, loyal to the traditional priestly line must be called "godless."

Interestingly, opposition to the Maccabees seems to have gained momentum after Judah's death. At this point the immediate objective of the revolt had been accomplished: the Temple cult was reinstituted. With this accomplished, the popular swell of sympathy for the Maccabees, which grew out of Antiochus' desecration of the Temple, began to wane. The Temple was rededicated and a member of the old priestly family (Alcimus) was confirmed in office by the repentent Seleucids. Despite these victories, however, the Maccabean revolt continued, as we have already seen. Apparently, some who were willing to back Judah's attempt to recapture the Temple were not willing to see the Maccabees establish themselves as a permanent dynasty of High Priests in opposition to the Seleucids. Thus, to use the language of I Maccabees, "after the death of Judas, the lawless emerged in all parts of Israel and all doers of injustice appeared" (9:23). In fact, we are arguing, these are not lawless and godless people, but people who saw Judea's future to lie in a peaceful accommodation with the Seleucids (who had now recognized the legitimacy of the priestly law in Judea) and in the traditional priestly line. It is the Maccabees themselves, from this perspective, who are proposing a radically new status for the community.

This brings us to the interests of II Maccabees. The thesis of this work, as we shall see, is that the law stands at the center of all Jewish life, both interms of individual lifestyle and in terms of the proper management of the cult. Loyalty to the Seleucids is perfectly in order as long as these secular authorities grant the Jews the right to govern themselves in accordance with these ancestral laws. When the Seleucid policy results in defilement of the Temple and subversion of the law, revolt is justified and necessary. Insofar as the Maccabees intend to cleanse the Temple and reinstate the law, their revolt is legitimate, as far as Jewish law is concerned. This is not the case, however, if the Maccabees oppose the rule of Torah as instituted by the Seleucids and try to arrogate the priesthood for themselves. Now their claim to authority is to be challenged. On this reading of matters, we would expect the book of II Maccabees to portray Judah in a positive light, and his brothers in a negative light. This is precisely what we find. II Maccabees wants to justify loyalty to Judah's cause and explain his successes on the one hand and yet wants to oppose Judah's heirs, the later Hasmoneans, on the other.

The central thesis of II Maccabees is that there is a direct relationship between the purity of the high Priest and the prosperity of Israel. The history of Judea covered by this book moves through three stages. At first the High Priest, Onias III, was pure and the ethnos prospered. Then came the evil and defiled priests: Onias IV, Menelaus, Jason. Israel suffered. Finally, a new, pure leader arises, Judah Maccabee. Israel again prospered. The underlying message is that proper authority belongs to the pure and law abiding. The claims of all potential leaders for obedience are to be evaluated in terms of their righteousness, that is, their adherence to Torah-law (at least as understood by the writer). With this in mind, we turn to an analysis of how this theme is played out as regards the Maccabean bid for power over Judea.

Traditionally, the occupant of the office of High Priest needed to meet two requirements in order to be deemed the legitimate leader of the Jewish ethnos. He must first be a scion of a priestly family and, secondly, he must be confirmed in office by the ruling imperial power: the Persians, Ptolemies, or Seleucids. For the author of our document, this is not enough, however. The High Priest must above all be righteous, that is, faithful to the ancestral laws. Thus Onias III, who meets all three requirements, is a model of what a High Priest should be. "While the holy city was inhabited in unbroken peace and the laws were very well observed because of the piety of the High Priest, Onias, and his hatred of wickedness, it came about that the kings themselves honored the place and glorified the Temple with the finest presents, so that even Seleucus, the king of Asia, defrayed from his own revenues all the expenses connected with the service of the sacrifices (3:1-3)." Yet Onias' brother, Jason, who enjoyed the same lineage and who was duly appointed as High Priest by Antiochus to replace Onias, is not deemed to be a High Priest at all. Why? Because "there was such an extreme of Hellenization and increase in the adoption of foreign ways because of the surpassing wickedness of Jason, who was ungodly and no High Priest... (4:13)." Similarly, Alcimus, who was of the traditional priestly line and who was appointed High Priest by Demetrius, is considered by our author as unfit for the office. The reason is his "defilement" in having joined the Hellenizing forces at the time of Jason's High Priesthood (14:3). In contrast, Judah Maccabee is deemed a worthy leader even though he is neither a scion of the family from which High Priests traditionally came nor was he appointed by the Seleucids. His position of authority is credible, for our author, because Judah does not share in the defilement of Hellenization (5:27), that is, because of his righteousness.

The same standard of judgment, righteousness according to the law, is applied to secular powers as well. We already saw that Seleucus IV is depicted in a positive light, paying Temple expenses out of his own treasury (3:1-3). This, it should be noted, is in marked contrast to I Maccabees in which Gentiles are routinely depicted as evil. In fact, our author cites several examples of cases in which even Judah Maccabee entered into treaties with Gentiles, provided these recognized the validity of the ancestral laws. Thus an agreement was reached with Lysias in 164 (11:13ff.), and even with Nicanor (14:18ff). It follows that loyalty to any power is justified if it recognizes the validity of the Jewish law and, conversely, any ruler can be rejected if he fails to honor this law. There is no doubt that Judah Maccabee himself fulfills this requirement. There are some hints in II Maccabees, however, that the righteousness, and thus divine authority, of Judah do not extend to other members of his family. Twice his future successor, Simon, is depicted as beyond the plane of divine providence. The first occurs during the siege of the Idumean strongholds. "Maccabeus left Simon and Joseph, and also Zacchaeus and his men, a force sufficient to besiege them; and he himself set off for places where he was more urgently needed. But the men with Simon, who were money-hungry, were bribed...(10:19-20)." Such a scandal never occurred when Judah was in command. Later, Simon joined battle with Nicanor and was "checked" (14:17). This same Nicanor sued for peace as soon as Judah approached. In other words, the successors to Judah were clearly his inferiors as regards God's blessings. We have, unfortunately, no clear statement by our author as to what he felt about the later Hasmoneans. Yet his concentration on Judah, and his deprecations, however subtle, of Simon, are suggestive. Loyalty to Judah is clearly warranted. After all, he did reverse the Hellenization of Jerusalem and he did purify the Temple. But it does not follow from this that the entire future dynasty must be accorded loyalty.[14]

In many ways, the point of view of II Maccabees is congruent to the picture that I Maccabees paints of the Hasideans. The Hasideans, we recall, are a group who are zealous for the law (I; 1:60-63; 2:29). In particular they were meticulous about the Sabbath, and many died because of their refusal to fight on that day (I; 2:33-38). The importance of Sabbath observance is repeatedly stressed in II Maccabees (6:6; 8:25-28; 15:1-5). The Hasideans are also portrayed as joining forces with the early Maccabees (I: 2:42ff.), but then later abandoning the Maccabees and going over to Alcimus (I: 7:12). That is, once the sanctuary had been purified, the traditional law reinstated, and a priest from the traditional line confirmed in office, they are willing to live in peace with the secular authorities and the duly appointed High Priest. Presumably, some of the Hasideans who remained loyal to Judah joined in the mass defection when his brothers took over the movement (I: 9:23). These data are perfectly compatible with the theory of authority we have adduced from II Maccabees. This is not to say that the author of II Maccabees was a member of this group or is in some way their spokesman. It does indicate that the "lawless" and "godless" of I Maccabees may well have been acting out of an honest conception of what Judaism demanded of them, a conception shared also, at least in important ways, by the author of II Maccabees.

The victory of the Maccabees, and the continued reign of the dynasty they founded, has skewed our view of Judaism in the second century. We have come

---

[14]Cf. Goldstein, p. 33, who adds to these two instances two more failures on the part of Maccabean leaders. II Mac. 12:24 reports that a certain Dositheus was duped into releasing a captured Syrian general. Since Dositheus is a Greek equivalent for the Hebrew name Jonathan ("God gives"), it is possible, says Goldstein, that we have here a veiled reference to one of Judah's brothers. Also, in 12:36-40, slain soldiers who fought under Judah's divisional commander, Esdris, are found to be wearing pagan amulets. See also Goldstein's analysis of the anti-Hasmonean view of Jason of Cyrene, pp. 79-80.

to see them as in some way the defenders of "true" Judaism over against the corrosive and corrupting forces of Hellenism. What our analysis has shown, however, is that there was no single, "true" Judaism in the second century for the Maccabees to defend. Rather, the struggle concerns the very question of what the shape and substance of a true Judaism should be. The Maccabees, in this view, represent only one of a number of possible perspectives. Their efforts resulted not in the preservation of Judaism, but in the ascendancy of a particular definition.

Through our analysis of these sources, concentrating on the social ideologies implicit in their arguments, we have been able to spell out the content of one major focus of controversy in the late second century/early first century BCE – the question of proper authority within the faithful Judean community. Through this controversy we have seen emerge what came to be three mutually exclusive notions as regards the source of authoritative pronouncements for Judeans: secular, political government; the High Priesthood; and "the Torah." We have seen how the diverse communities within second century Judea defined themselves around these different notions of leadership, and how that conviction set them in conflict with other communities. What we have learned is that Judaism of the late second century was a more complex phenomenon than our sources, on the surface, seem to indicate. Further we have seen that what was at stake in the Maccabean revolt was not merely Judaism versus Hellenism, but rather, what particular definition of Judaism was to be the normative paradigm in the new, Hellenistic, age.

Truly to understand the ramifications of the Hasmonean victory in the mid-second century BCE, we need to know much more about their religious and political theories. We have here adduced only one important theme that emerged in the wake of their victory: that of authority. We would like to know what other beliefs or values the Maccabean party saw as bound together with its view of authority as adduced here. Unfortunately, the sources at hand will not allow us fully to reconstruct their religious theories. Yet we are not left without any insight. As I have tried to indicate, our sources do contain what at least the immediate heirs to the Maccabees considered to be the central points of controversy within the community of Judeans. By identifying the question of authority as the subject of heated and sustained debate we see what the sources themselves conceived to be the most basic components of Judean self-definition. It was, after all, these issues, and not others, which generated controversy. We can recover some sense, then, of what potentialities of self-understanding were contained in the Judaisms of the mid-second century. While a modest insight in and of itself, it does provide fresh insight into how a religious community, faced with rapid change, goes about meeting that change while still claiming to be faithful to the essential requirements of its tradition.

Part Three

PROBLEMS OF RELIGION AND SOCIETY

Chapter Five

Law and Society in Early Judaism: Legal Evolution in the Mishnaic Division of Agriculture

Alan J. Avery-Peck

Tulane University

One current trend in analyzing the evolution of legal systems grows out of the approach made famous by Weber in his study of the rise of capitalism. This approach suggests that developments in legal systems are best explained in terms of social, political and economic changes. This view argues that the communal infrastructure within which the lawyer works is the primary force in shaping the evolving legal system. The task of the legal historian, accordingly, is to ascertain the effect of politics, economics or religion in determining the shape that a legal system takes in each period.

This historical-functional approach is based on the assumption that lawyers and legislators, like all people, react to their environment, creating rules for conduct that make sense of the social and political world in which they live. In order to understand the legal systems they create, however, a further set of factors must be taken into account. For the antecedent legal tradition itself exerts a great influence, determining the parameters within which legal growth is possible. Lawyers and legislators, this is to say, tend to be conservative, innovating within the narrow confines of the inherited tradition, and forcing past modes of behavior to conform to present needs.[1] A second, cognitive-developmental approach to legal history accordingly focuses upon the legal tradition itself, seeing the internal dynamics of the existing legal system as the most important factor in producing legal change.

These two approaches to explaining the development of legal systems should go hand-in-hand. By explaining the parameters within which legal evolution is plausible, the developmental approach facilitates application of the historical-functional method, which locates the reasons for which, within those

---

[1] These first paragraphs draw upon the introductory observations of Shael Herman in a review of Alan Watson, *The Making of the Civil Law*, in *Israel Law Review*, Volume 18, Nos. 3-4 (1983), pp. 490-503. Herman makes this particular point on p. 491.

parameters, legal evolution takes one particuar course and not another. Despite the clear advantages of applying both the developmental and functional approaches, in practice, a great tension exists between the two, with scholars tending to focus upon one to the exclusion of the other. This points to an important methodological problem concerning the epistemological status of each of these theories of legal history. What, this is to say, can we expect to learn from each of these different approaches? How secure is the knowledge each provides? What happens when they are used alone or in juxtaposition?

To address these questions, this paper applies to a single legal system the two different approaches just described. I refer to the Mishnah, the first legal code of rabbinic Judaism, completed in the late second century C.E. By applying to that text first the developmental and then the functional approach, I hope to clarify the strengths and weaknesses of each method and to determine the range of understanding and degree of plausibility each provides.

Let me state my general conclusions at the outset. The developmental approach explains the internal logic of an evolving legal system, locating the source of specific legal themes and explicating the theoretical stance that accounts for legislation on particular topics. Accordingly, it leads to a picture of the cognitive world of the legislators, describing their legal philosophy and indicating how that philosophy is expressed through the legal corpus as a whole. Insofar as this approach focuses upon the concrete details of the legal system, it tends to be epistemologcally strong and must be the starting point for all analysis.

Yet the developmental approach leaves open the important question of why, within the many possible avenues of growth, the legal system evolved along one course and not some other. The second, functional approach therefore must be applied, so as to suggest the societal motivations likely to stand behind the evolving legal system. By focusing upon economic, political and religious context, this approach probes the human question of the significance for the particular group of the legal and philosophical system it creates.

As we shall see in detail, however, while this latter approach's results may be intellectually compelling, they tend to be epistemologically weak. Like much of historical argument, they stand or fall upon an argument of plausibility but are not subject to proof or refutation. For legislators rarely make explicit, and are not necessarily conscious of, the philosophical statement their legislation makes within the social infrastructure of their own day. Still, in light of the human significance of the historical-functional approach's line of questioning, its continued use surely is warranted.[2] My point is that this method's limitations must be taken seriously, so that the functional approach not be used to explain

---

[2] As the several examples found in section IV of this article suggest, abandoning the historical-functional approach would leave historians and anthropologists the rather mundane job of describing cultural phenomena but would largely eliminate the possibility of determining those phenomena's significance.

too much too soon. The cognitive-developmental approach must remain the initial and perhaps primary focus of scholarly interest. By working to explain the individual details as well as the larger structure of the legal system, it provides the data upon which the epistomologically weaker, historical-functional conclusions ultimately rest.

I. Functional and Developmental Approaches to Legal History

The character of scholarly conclusions about the formation of a legal system depends in a great degree upon the sort of information we have about that particular system and about the social context in which it was created. For instance, while we have little direct evidence for the social and economic goals of ancient Roman jurists, we do know how their law was applied in concrete cases. Accordingly, the historical-functional approach has been applied to Roman law with better success then in the case of early rabbinic law, which played only a minor role in an actual society.[3] Because this paper concentrates on the case of the Mishnah, which has unique characteristics as a legal system, I cannot claim to judge the ultimate value of applying these two methods in other legal systems. But an elucidation of the specific case of the Mishnah can put into perspective the overall character of each approach. In order to initiate this latter task, I begin 1) by explaining why the Mishnah consititutes a suitable legal system for such a review and 2) by outlining the basic considerations pertinent to the use of each of the approaches described here.

In recent years interpretation of the Mishnah has begun to focus upon that document viewed as a whole, on the theology it expresses and on the meaning it had for those who, in the second century C.E., formulated and redacted its laws. Recent scholarship thus has moved to the heart of the human issue, of how people in a particular time period conceived and made sense of their world and of how and why they preserved their perceptions in one literary form and not another.[4] Yet as in the study of all legal systems, the methodological problem – how to determine why those responsible for formulating and interpreting law thought and wrote as they did – has been brought dramatically to the surface. This methodological question is particularly pressing in the case of the Mishnah, which is compiled of materials collected over a period of centuries and which is

---

[3]For the case of Roman urban lease law, see, e.g., Bruce W. Frier, *Landlords and Tenants in Imperial Rome* (Princeton: 1980), discussed below, note 9.

[4]In investigating the social and psychological attitudes that stand behind the creation of this enigmatic document, this scholarship takes initiatives beyond those found in tradibnal study, which concentrated upon the meaning of and relationship among individual laws. It moves as well beyond early critical scholarship, which, along with focusing upon the meaning of the laws, established the text and worked to describe the history of its formulation. While starting from a pericope-by-pericope reading of the whole Mishnah, contemporary study narrowly defines the significance of exegetical questions. It deems them important only insofar as they illuminate the legal ideology that accounts for the form and content of the Mishnah as a complete, redacted document.

formulated expressly to conceal all evidence of social, political or theological context and motivation. How to move from the Mishnah's laws to their significance for the individuals who produced them accordingly presents the central problem for contemporary scholarship.

To date, the most familiar approach is known from the work of Jacob Neusner[5] and those of his students who have interpreted tractates of the Mishnah.[6] These commentators argue that the legal thinking of the Mishnah's rabbis was directly affected by the political environment of their own day. Accordingly they relate Mishnaic law to the presumed psychological needs and emotions of its creators. As in all historical reconstruction, this is done by drawing general conclusions about the point of the document in question and about the period in which it was created, and by then finding an explanation that seems plausibly to relate the two. As we shall see below, the result for the case at hand is a reading of the Mishnah as a program of social and theological reconstruction responding to the destruction of the Temple and the failed Bar Kokhba revolt.

Two methodological problems plague this historical interpretation. First, insofar as the Mishnah's authorities consciously hide all signs of outside influence, this approach depends here, even more than in other instances of its application,[7] upon the historian's judgment of "plausibility." Even though based upon a law-by-law analysis of the content and legal ideology of the Mishnah, such a historical reconstruction can neither be finally proven nor, for that matter, falsified.

Second, this approach depends upon a questionable underlying assumption, that developments in the Mishnah's legal thinking should be understood *first and foremost* as reactions to the evolving life situation of the Mishnaic lawyers. Scholars writing about other periods have increasingly noted that, in Shael Herman's words, "the true causes of legal evolution" can often be discovered more easily "in the legal tradition itself than in the broader (and more remote) social and economic context in which a legal system evolves."[8] The opposite view, perhaps most famous from Weber's study of the rise of capitalism,

---

[5]The results of his massive study of five of Mishnah's six divisions are found in his *Judaism: The Evidence of the Mishnah* (Chicago: 1981).

[6]See below, note 32.

[7]See by contrast the example below in section IV, concerning the theological function of the Deuteronomic history. In that case, as in the instance of Roman lease law (below, note 9), a range of historical evidence as well as the clearer content of the documents in question provide firmer warrants than are possible in the case of the Mishnah.

[8]Herman, *op. cit.*, p. 490.

continues rightly to have important proponents.[9] Yet, as Herman notes, the argument that "intrinsic legal forces are more powerful than [for instance] economic conditions in shaping law" was already "implicit in Weber's inability to explain why England achieved capitalistic supremacy without a 'calculable, logically formal legal system.'"[10] In short, the evidence from other legal systems does not uniformly support the premise that legal thinking reflects first and foremost the social, political or religious climate of its day.[11] While societal influence certainly is present in all legal systems, employing such influence as one's *primary* hermeneutic in explaining specific systems, such as that of early rabbinic Judaism, is prone to serious difficulty.

In light of the problematic nature of the historical-functional approach, students of the Mishnah have employed as well a developmental approach, explaining the Mishnaic legal system by referring to the inner logic of the antecedent legal tradition, beginning in Scripture. This approach envisions the Mishnah's laws as a legal tradition that evolves along lines explained 1) by the dynamics of human legal thinking in general and 2) according to the internal needs of the tradition itself. Accordingly, it leaves open the question of the relationship between the Mishnah's rabbis and the outside world.[12]

This approach shows the extent to which the Mishnaic framers' choice of ideologies flows logically from the legal tradition within which they worked. Yet since it does not question why these rabbis developed one particular legal ideology and not another it is essentially incomplete, a mode of description that

---

[9]This approach is exemplified, for instance, by Bruce W. Frier, *op. cit., passim* and in particular pp. 196-219. As Frier states, the ability convincingly to relate legal developments to social context depends upon the extent of our knowledge of the jurists' role in society, of their own social and political ideals and, of course, of the working of the courts in which their laws were employed. Frier argues that sufficient evidence is available for the case of Roman lease law, despite the fact that Roman juristic writing (like the Mishnah!) "for the most part simply declares the law, offering no intellectually sufficient explanation or justification" and that arguments "seem to conceal more than they disclose about the foundation of juristic decisions" (p. 197). The point in the following is that the character of the Mishnah makes historical explanation of its law considerably more tricky.

[10]Herman, *op. cit.,* citing J.M. Trubeck, "Max Weber on Law and the Rise of Capitalism," *University of Wisconsin Law Review* (1972), p. 720.

[11]Below I report in detail on legal evolution in the medieval period which points in this same direction.

[12]A good example of this approach is found in Howard Eilberg-Schwartz, *The Human Will in Judaism: The Mishnah's Philosophy of Intention* (Atlanta: 1986). Eilberg-Schwartz shows that the legal ideology prominent in the Mishnah reflects ideas found in Scripture itself. Below I cite his conclusions in detail.

stops short of explanation.[13] The larger point accordingly is that despite their weakness, historical reconstructions attentive to the outside world comprise a central aspect of the interpretive task. We simply must remember 1) the importance of beginning with the evidence internal to the document so as 2) not to use a historical-functional reconstruction to explain too much. While an integral aspect of the interpretation of any historical period, such interpretations must be used carefully, based on an initial exegesis attentive to the internal characteristics of the legal tradition being analysed.

Before turning to the historical analyses that comprise the body of this paper, we must understand the underlying themes and legal perspectives of the section of the Mishnah chosen for evaluation, the Division of Agriculture.

II. The Mishnaic Theory of Agriculture

The Division of Agriculture details the proper modes through which Israelites are to plant, harvest, process and eat the crops they grow for sustenance upon the land of Israel. For the Mishnah these matters concern, first, how Israelites are to pay agricultural tithes from the produce. These tithes support the poor and contribute to the maintenance of the priests and Levites who serve in the Temple in Jerusalem.[14]

Second, the division details the other Scriptural rules concerning the Israelites' proper use of their land. The crops, for instance, must be arranged in the field in ways that prevent different species from growing together. Other rules preclude the consumption of fruit from a tree's first three years of growth and prohibit the planting and harvesting of crops in the seventh year of the sabbatical cycle.[15] The division as a whole thus takes up the wide range of concerns that revolve around the production and consumption of food in the Israelite world.

For the Mishnah's rabbis, these agricultural laws comprise a theological system, detailing how Israelites are to maintain and use a land that ultimately is

---

[13]Rabbinic Judaism, this is to say, incorporated and made use of Scripture. But Scripture does not define the content and character of rabbinic Judaism. This important point is phrased by Jacob Neusner, *Comparative Midrash* (Atlanta: 1986), pp. ix-x. In note 2 he describes the theological force of the contrary claim that "'Judaism' really restates what is merely the plain sense of Scripture, so [that] it is the one authoritative continuator of Scripture." He notes that "this claim serves theological purposes as part of the apologetic against Christianity, but rests on no firmer analytical-descriptive and inductive foundations than the Christian view of the 'New Testament' as the authoritative continuator of the 'Old.'"

[14]In addition to describing each of the major tithes and providing rules for their separation (Tractates Peah, Maaser Sheni, Bikkurim and parts of Tractates Terumot and Hallah), the Mishnah's authorities discuss how the tithes are to be prepared for consumption (Tractate Terumot) and detail how Israelites are to make certain that they do not eat produce from which these tithes have not been separated at all (Tractate Demai). Tractate Maaserot and parts of Tractate Hallah describe when Israelites are required to tithe.

[15]The concerns listed here are taken up in Tractates Kilaim, Orlah and Shebiit, respectively.

the special possession of God. The Mishnah's rabbis, that is, do not understand the payment of tithes simply to be a method of maintaining the Temple-cult or of supporting the needy of their community. Nor do they understand the other regulations that control use of the land to fulfill only general agricultural, social or economic functions (e.g., the possible agricultural value of allowing all land to lie fallow once every seven years; the economic function of legislating that certain produce, or its value, be brought to Jerusalem). The Mishnah's authorities, rather, see in these regulations descriptions of how Israelites are to use their land in accordance with the specific nature of God's creation of the universe and in keeping with God's special relationship with the people and land of Israel.[16]

Since the Mishnah's themes and much of what the rabbis have to say about them are predictable on the basis of Scripture, what is significant for interpretation of the division must be narrowly defined. First is the very fact that the Mishnah's framers choose to take up in a systematic way these topics, which Scripture refers to in a smattering of verses[17] and discusses with no consistent theological agendum.[18] Second, the Mishnah's framers become intensely concerned about agricultural offerings destined for priest, Levite and

---

[16]In creating the world, God rested on the seventh day. The land of Israel, God's special possession, therefore must rest each seventh year (see Louis Newman, *The Sanctity of the Seventh Year: A Study of Mishnah Tractate Shebiit* (Chico: 1983), p. 15). In creating the world, God distinguished discrete species of plants. In planting their fields, too, Israelites must not mix together different kinds (see Irving Mandelbaum, *A History of the Mishnaic Law of Agriculture: Kilayim* (Chico: 1982), p. 4). Finally, since crops that grow upon the land of Israel partake of the bounty of God's property, they are bonded to God and may not be eaten until God's interest in them has been satisfied, through payment of agricultural offerings (see Richard Sarason, "Mishnah and Scripture: Preliminary Observations on the Law of Tithing in *Seder Zeraim*," in W.S. Green, ed., *Approaches to Ancient Judaism, Vol. II* (Chico: 1980), pp. 87-89 and p. 94, n. 17, and my *The Priestly Gift in Mishnah: A Study of Tractate Terumot* (Chico: 1981), p. 3).

[17]A total of 68 verses are scattered in nineteen passages, the majority of which contain only one or two lines. The overall number of verses is raised considerably by the long passage at Dt. 26:1-15, which discusses the liturgy for the presentation of the first fruits and for Scripture's "year of tithing."

[18]The unsystematic nature of Scripture's tithing laws has prevented scholars from reaching a consensus concerning their significance. The problem arises with the attempt to locate in Scripture a unitary system of agricultural offerings (see, e.g., Aharon Oppenheimer, "Terumot and Ma'aserot," in *Encyclopedia Judaica*, vol. 15, pp. 1025-1028). This approach leads to claims of a dual focus of the tithing system, upon piety, on the one hand, and taxation, on the other (see H. Guthrie, "Tithe," in *Interpreters Dictionary of the Bible*, vol. 3, pp. 654-655, and J. MacCulloch, "Tithes," in *Encyclopedia of Religion and Ethics*, Vol. XII, pp. 346-350). As Richard Sarason, *A History of The Mishnaic Law of Agriculture: A Study of Tractate Demai* (Leiden: 1979), pp. 3-10, points out, in contrast to the unitary perspective of the Mishnah, the Deuteronomic and Priestly sources contain two distinct theories of tithing. The former holds that the separation of tithes acknowledges God's ownership of the land of Israel and expresses gratitude for the land's fertility. The latter holds that the tithes go to the Levites and Aaronide priests as their pay for serving in the Temple. Mishnaic authorities take Scripture's diverse statements and in part conflicting definitions and derive from them a unitary and focused set of laws concerned with the sanctification of Israelite life.

Temple in a time in which the cult had been destroyed and the priest and Levite had ceased to have a concrete function in the consecration of Israelite life. Third, the Mishnah's rabbis have a particular interest in the processes of sanctification – that is, in how, by growing and processing food, Israelites cause holiness to come into being,[19] and in how, before eating, they must dispose of that holiness, whether in the hands of the priests or through other of their own actions. These issues are absent from Scripture which, for its part, is concerned that the priest and Levite receive their designated share, but which does not question how, in the hands of non-priests, produce becomes sanctified as that share.[20]

Having isolated the specific themes of the Division of Agriculture, let us focus as well upon the legal ideology expressed through those topics. For during the course of the growth of Mishnaic law, these themes receive varied treatment. A development occurs in the rabbis' approach to the law, such that the legislation deriving from each major period in the Mishnah's evolution reflects that period's own legal interests and sense of how one determines right and wrong.[21] Let me elaborate.

The earliest generations of rabbinic authorities, those living before 70 C.E. and in Yavnean times, are concerned primarily with matters of definition and with basic laws facilitating observance of rules that are only sketched in Scripture.[22] A single theory of law stands behind these materials. Yavneans consistently exclude attention to the motivations or perceptions of the Israelite whose deeds are under scrutiny. The reasons or perceptions that lead an individual to act, that is to say, have no bearing upon the permissibility of that behavior. The status of a deed, rather, depends solely upon the nature of the actions through which it is carried out. It does not matter to Yavneans why an Israelite collects stones in his field during the seventh year. The fact is that, in doing so, he makes possible the cultivation of the land, which is not allowed during the Sabbatical. Such actions therefore are forbidden. This is the case

---

[19]This specific interest presumably accounts for the failure of Mishnah's rabbis to speak systematically about first tithe, which is not consecrated. See my *Mishnah's Division of Agriculture: A History and Theology of Seder Zeraim* (Chico: 1985), p. 427, note 5.

[20]The Division of Agriculture has little to say about the actual transfer of agricultural offerings to the priests and Levites. It thus ignores Scripture's central interest in favor of its own primary concern, the role of the non-priest in the processes of sanctification.

[21]The following conclusions are based upon chapters two through eleven in my *Mishnah's Division of Agriculture*. There I systematically organize the rules of the tractates on agriculture so as to ascertain which ideas derive from each of the major periods of Mishnaic legislation.

[22]These rabbis, for instance, 1) give concrete measurements that define a field, 2) delineate what field labors may or may not be performed in the Sabbatical year, 3) outline the quantity of produce to be taken as each tithe and agricultural offering and 4) indicate specifically how the offering is to be set aside.

even if the individual simply desires to build a stone fence, a deed that itself is permitted.[23]

These ideas reveal the Yavneans' understanding of the existence of a preset order in the world, of an objective reality separate from any individual's perceptions of how things are or should be. Correct acts are those that conform completely to the ideal. Behavior, not intention, counts. The result of the action, not its underlying motivation, is determinative.

The later generation of authorities, those of the Ushan period, develop the Yavnean ideal in a consistent pattern. Ushans analyze actions in light of the intentions of the individual who performs them and on the basis of the perceptions of those who witness and interpret them. They thus understand the permissibility of field labor in the seventh year to depend upon the Israelite's intentions in carrying it out. An action is permitted so long as the individual does not intend to break the rules of the seventh year and so long as he works in a way that prevents others from assuming that he proposes to break the law.[24] Unlike Yavneans, Ushans thus recognize no order in the world other than that imposed by Israelites who, through their own intentions and perceptions, give meaning to their activities in planting, tilling and harvesting produce on the land of Israel.

The description just presented of the content and development of the Division of Agriculture provides the foundation for interpretation of the division. To summarize, the issues for interpretation concern 1) why, in the period after the destruction of the Temple and loss of Israelite sovereignty over the land of Israel, the Mishnah's framers began to focus upon topics so closely connected to the maintenance of the Temple cult[25] and with God's sovereignty over the land, and 2) the reason for the shift from the Yavnean understanding of the existence of a preset order in the world to the Ushan theory of a world in which order is imposed by Israelites themselves.

---

[23]Along these same lines, Yavneans define physical entities in light of their shape and form, without regard to the use to which Israelites intend to put them. They deem a field, for instance, to be demarcated by geographical boundaries, by hills, streams or trees that set off one area of land from adjacent lots. The farmer's own actions in choosing to treat one area as autonomous are considered immaterial.

[24]In the same way, the efficacy of the individual's separation of agricultural offerings depends upon the intention with which the separation is carried out, not upon the physical actions by which the deed is accomplished. In this view, finally, Israelites' own perceptions define which crops are orderly and distinct or disorderly and mixed together, so as to be permitted or forbidden to be planted together in a field.

[25]This fact of course is not unique to the Mishnaic Division of Agriculture, but pertains as well to three of the five other divisions, which also focus upon the Temple, its offerings and Temple-purity.

III.   The Evolution of Mishnaic Law:
A Cognitive-Developmental Approach

The developmental approach focuses upon facts internal to the Mishnah. It explains the Mishnah' legal themes and ideologies 1) as determined by factors internal to the legal tradition and 2) as reflections of the sorts of thinking found in human society in general. Beginning with the former aspect of the rabbinic agendum, we must recall the extent to which the Mishnah's authorities take up and develop Scripture's own topics. It is clear accordingly that they affirm the divine nature of Scripture and its centrality for the Judaic people and religion. While the orientation towards Temple and priest strikes us as unrealistic for the period in question, still, we must recognize that the rabbis' choice of topics largely follows the established framework of Judaic thinking, insisting upon the people of Israel's obligation to abide by the covenant.

This recognition is important for the case of the Division of Agriculture, the majority of the laws of which could be followed even in the aftermath of the destruction of the Temple. We may understand the rabbinic focus in the divisions which concern aspects of Temple-law that could no longer be practiced to be purely descriptive or, perhaps, utopian. In either case, we should not be too shocked at this group's taking up of legal categories that for millennia had defined the relationship of the people of Israel to their god.

The two different types of legal ideology found in the Mishnah likewise reflect ideals found in Scripture itself. The Yavnean realism represents the perspective portrayed, for instance, in the priestly creation story. Here God creates a complete, perfected world, leaving no room for human interference. God creates each thing "according to its kind," so as to leave humans an already ordered world, in which they will not need to apply their own powers of categorization. Seeing the completed world, God also takes responsibility for its sanctification, the final divine gift that creates the Sabbath.

Yet the relativistic approach espoused by the Ushan authorities also figures in Scripture. It appears in Leviticus' laws of holiness, which distinguish between Israelites' intentional and unwitting consumption of holy things. In explaining the Mishnah's attitude towards intention in general, Howard Eilberg-Schwartz has pointed out that the J tradition, found in the second creation story beginning at Gen. 2:4, is clear about the power of individual human beings themselves to define their world. This power is represented in Adam's naming the animals, thus completing God's acts of creation.[26] Both the Yavnean and Ushan legal approaches accordingly have antecedents in biblical law.

Both the content of and the ideologies expressed in Mishnaic law follow closely upon the legal tradition that the rabbis received and accepted as valid. As we shall now see, the character of the evolution of the Division of Agriculture's legal thinking, too, is not unique to the Mishnah but is familiar from other legal

---

[26]Howard Eilberg-Schwartz, *op. cit.*, Chapter Five.

systems. Scholars have, for instance, pointed out similar growth in medieval law.[27] In these developments, inattention to motive and circumstances gives way, in the growth of the legal system, to a set of laws that take carefully into account the human elements that stand behind specific actions. For the case of medieval law, this development is described by Charles M. Radding, "Evolution of Medieval Mentalities: A Cognitive-Structural Approach." Since Radding's description of the growth of medieval law clarifies what we have seen in the Mishnah's Division of Agriculture, I cite it in full:

> [In the period preceding the twelfth century] monks and patrons alike believed that piety demanded only the observance of a precise daily routine, and as late as the eleventh century they considered the performance of liturgical ritual to be the essence of monastic dedication.

The confusion – perhaps one should say interchangeability – of intention and behavior is also evident in secular law. In the *Leges Henrici Primi* of 1114-18, drawn primarily from Anglo-Saxon codes, the compiler discussed homicide – in scattered fashion through many different sections – without differentiating among intentional slayings, deaths caused by negligence, and those resulting from unavoidable fault. Generally, the penalty for homicide was owed "in circumstances in which a man cannot lawfully swear that a person was not through his agency further from life or nearer to death." The compiler included cases that seem strange to us: "If anyone sends for a person and the latter is killed while coming; if anyone, when summoned to a place by a person, suffers death there, if anyone, being brought to witness a public exhibition of a wild beast or a madman, incurs some injury at their hands; if anyone entrusts a horse or other thing to a person and thence some harm befalls him." The explanation of these rules, according to the compiler, was the maxim *qui inscienter peccat, scienter emendet:* who unknowingly commits a wrong knowingly shall make amends ...

Few questioned these legal or monastic practices for the six centuries before 1050. After that time, however, these rules and assumptions were increasingly challenged and discarded: the law described in the *Leges Henrici Primi* virtually disappeared in the half century following its compilation; the Cistercians abandoned oblation [that is, the previously widespread custom in which young children, unable to commit themselves to life as monks were in all events turned over to be raised in monasteries] around 1100 and it was moribund well before the Fourth Lateran Council finally prohibited it in 1215. In each case change was directed towards greater concern with the interior aspects of human nature. Because monasticism and law could only function with the support of medieval

---

[27]A complete list of sources is found in the bibliography of Charles M. Radding, "Evolution of Medieval Mentalities," in *The American Historical Review*, 83:3 (June, 1978), pp. 557-597.

elites, these shifts also indicate changes in the collective mentality of European society (pp. 578-579).

The development of attitudes towards culpability in medieval law exhibits the same pattern of growth found in the Division of Agriculture. In both legal systems an early view that ignores motivation gives way to a later understanding that takes the human element as central. The example of oblation shows how closely the shift Radding describes resembles the development in the laws before us. Since oblates had not, of their own accord, chosen to become monks, "high standards of asceticism or spirituality was hardly possible in their case" (p. 578). Later medieval law rejected the formalism inherent in such individuals' performance of their liturgical responsibilities, deeming priestly ministrations performed without proper intention to be invalid. This is similar to Ushan authorities' insistence that, to be valid, the designation of heave-offering must be carried out by an individual who has formulated the intention to consecrate that which he separates as the priest's share. Both the later Mishnaic law and the medieval legal thinking to which Radding refers thus come to consider as invalid any actions performed without proper intentions.

In light of the parallel from medieval law, interpretation of the Mishnah's legal development becomes a problem of explaining in general terms the reasons for growth of such similar character in obviously unrelated cultural, religious and political environments.[28] Radding states the interpretive problem clearly:

> These trends in mental attitudes have been examined by many historians
> – among them Fredrich William Maitland, Dom David Knowles, Marie-
> Dominique Chenu, R. W. Southern, and, most recently, Colin Morris –
> but none has succeeded in giving an adequate account and many have
> retreated to vague generalities. Sometimes the matter has simply been
> sidestepped by indefinite references to "social and economic change."
> Another approach has related the new ideas in law and religion to an
> intellectual renaissance of the eleventh and twelfth centuries, on the
> theory that the innovations were connected with the wider use of reason
> in human affairs. But more intellectual activity does not necessarily
> mean different thoughts. Equally plausible is the argument that
> dissatisfaction with old attitudes stimulated the growth of scholarly
> debate. The changes also have been attributed to the new institutions of
> the twelfth century ... (pp. 579-80).

The problem as Radding sees it is the impossibility of proving a connection between a shift in mental attitudes and changes in social, political and intellectual environment that could, after all, lead to a variety of different legal or philosophical responses. Radding therefore does not search for specific factors within the milieu of the eleventh and twelfth centuries that would explain the legal growth that he describes. Instead, he turns to the work of cognitive

---

[28]This fact poses the greatest challenge to the attempt to explain legal evolution through reference to external forces. See Herman, *op. cit.,* p. 492.

psychologists in order to show the extent to which both the earlier and later attitudes found in these legal systems represent stages in the growth of human thinking. Radding does not attempt to prove that a similar development occurs in all societies, by which a lack of interest in intention – that is, moral realism – gives way to a concern for the human elements that explain action. He shows, rather, that both types of thinking are usual for people in general, such that we should not be surprised to find them alone or in historical juxtaposition. Radding's inquiry again instructs us in explaining the rabbinic legal system.

Piaget pointed out that the lack of interest in intention exhibited in primitive law resembles the attitude toward rules – called "moral realism" – that are typical of children in all societies. According to Piaget, moral realism has at least three features: 1) the belief that any act that shows obedience to a rule is good and that any act that does not conform is bad; 2) the rule is not to be taken as something to be judged and interpreted but as something that is given, already made and external to the mind," so that the letter and not the spirit of the rule is obeyed; and 3) acts are evaluated in terms of their conformity with the rule and not according to the motive that prompted them (p. 582).

The notion that authority and doctrine are exterior to the individual's mind, such that they must be taken literally and uncritically, begins to change when children reach the age of about ten. Then, to use the example of their attitudes towards play, they see rules not as "sacred and untouchable," but as validated by agreement of all players.

"In short," as Piaget put it, "law now emanates from the sovereign people and no longer from the tradition laid down by the Elders." This less rigid attitude toward rules is founded on an increased ability to understand the other person and to cooperate on the basis of mutual development of subjective responsibility: "When the child is accustomed to act from the point of view of those around him, when he tries to please rather than obey," then "he will judge in terms of intentions. So that taking intentions into account presupposes cooperation and mutual respect" (p. 583).

The two stages Piaget points out in attitudes towards law and authority resemble the stages in the development of the law of the Division of Agriculture. The Yavnean perspective, which views Scripture's restrictions as preset and unaffected by circumstance, corresponds to the attitude of younger children, who judge matters in terms of the letter of the law and the concrete effects of action, not on the basis of the perceptions or intentions that lead to the specific behavior. The Ushan perspective resembles that of older children and adults, who look for the intent of the law and who determine the morality of an action in light of its conformity with that intent.

The preceding descriptions are not intended to argue that the evolution of culture and society parallels the growth of thought in individual human beings. I do not mean to say, that is, that phylogeny recapitulates ontogeny. Radding is careful to note that psychological theory can be applied to individual people alone, but not to societies as wholes (see p. 595). Indeed, the notion that the growth of cultures necessarily parallels that of human beings is disproven by the fact that in many instances of growing legal and cultural systems, the development that we have seen in Mishnaic law and which Radding points out in medieval society is lacking. He notes, for instance, that "the history of late Roman culture might show a reverse trend – from communitarian to authoritarian conceptions of morality" (p. 595). In the same way, as I noted above, the Hebrew Bible, which early and later rabbis read closely, itself contains important distinctions between intentional and unintentional acts, for instance, in providing special rules for manslaughter (Num. 35:9-20) or in noting that certain rules apply only to an individual who unintentionally eats a holy thing (Lev. 22:14).

The parallel between the medieval legal developments analyzed by Radding and what we have seen in the Mishnah therefore cannot be construed to claim a normative development, such that all societies are expected to grow in the same way that moral sensibilities arise in children. The lesson this parallel teaches, rather, must be narrowly defined. It teaches first and foremost that both the Yavnean and the Ushan approaches to the law are natural within individual human beings and therefore are expected within the conglomerates of individuals that comprise societies. Finding, first at Yavneh and then at Usha, a predominance of a certain mode of thought points to the close correspondence between the mentalities of individuals who live in a common social, cultural and political environment. The shared perspectives on law indicates the extent to which the rabbis at Yavneh and at Usha developed a communal intellect and common ethical perspective. This in itself may at least in part account for the development of the moral relativism of the later period, which, as Piaget noted, "presupposes cooperation and mutual respect" (cited in Radding, p. 583).

At the same time it is important to recognize the rarity – and therefore significance – of quick, large scale shifts in group mentality. "Usually, of course, one generation, through its interactions with the next educates it into the same ways of thinking, just as the intellectuals and leaders of the twelfth century – by the institutions they created and the questions they posed, and the students they taught – assured that their concerns would be those of subsequent generations" (Radding, p. 595). Since, in an extremely short period of time, the Mishnah's masters shifted entirely from one pattern of legal thinking to a quite different one, the quest for a reason seems particularly urgent.

IV. The Evolution of Mishnaic Law:
The Historical-Functional Approach

The identification of a historical document's central theme leads, as a matter of course, to a reconstruction which relates that theme to the political and social environment of its creators. This standard approach to the writing of history is illustrated, for instance, within the field of biblical scholarship, which commonly faces the problem of a document written in one period yet claiming to derive from and speak about a different time. Frank M. Cross's description of Noth's understanding of the Deuteronomist is illustrative:[29]

> The theme running through the framework of the Deuteronomistic history, according to Noth, is a proclamation of unrelieved and irreversible doom. ... The Deuteronomistic author, according to Noth, thus addressed his work to the exiles. His theology of history, revealed in the framework of his great work, justified God's wrath and explained the exile's plight.

This brief citation cannot do justice to Noth's argument; but it does illustrate the common method of historical reconstruction, which looks for a plausible relationship between theological or legal themes and the period in which they developed. Thus the specifics of Noth's description of the theology of the Deuteronomist have been modified, e.g., by Von Rad[30] and by Cross himself. The basic approach to understanding the Deuteronomic documents, however, remains unchallenged. Scholars seek the most plausible way to understand the relationship between a particular philosophy or theology and the period in which it develops.

In this way, recognition of the central themes of the Division of Agriculture and, indeed, of the Mishnah as a whole has lead to interpretations that relate these themes to the political context in which the Mishnah's rabbis worked. In particular, these interpretations point out a possible connection between the destruction of the Temple in 70 C.E., the failed Bar Kokhba revolt of 135, and the formation within the Mishnah of a system of law that, while insisting on the enforcement of Scripture's rules, does so by focusing upon the power of individual Israelites. My own comments concerning Tractate Terumot[31] illustrate this approach to the interpretation of the Mishnah:[32]

> To make the claim of God's continuing presence, the tractate ... focuses upon the actions and responsibilities of the Israelite who sets aside and protects the priestly due. By describing these actions and responsibilities, it makes the powerful point that even with the Temple gone, cultic sanctification remains. This means that God himself still rules over the people and land of Israel. He moves in response to the intentions and perceptions of Israelites who separate the offering which he mandated. This message is poignant. For as is clear, with the

---

[29]*Canaanite Myth and Hebrew Epic* (Cambridge: 1973), p. 275.

[30]See his *Studies in Deuteronomy*.

[31]*The Priestly Gift in Mishnah*, p. 7.

[32]For comparable interpretations of other tractates in the Division of Agriculture, see Martin Jaffee, *Mishnah's Theology of Tithing: A Study of Tractate Maaserot* (Chico: 1981), pp. 3-6, Mandelbaum, *op. cit.*, pp. 3-4, Roger Brooks, *Support for the Poor in the Mishnaic Law of Agriculture: Tractate Peah* (Chico: 1983), pp. 35-36 and Newman, *op. cit.*, pp. 17-20. For one of the original statements of this thesis, see Jacob Neusner, *Judaism*, p. 271.

Temple destroyed and the Land defiled, these intentions and perceptions
were all that remained to deny the events of history and affirm God's
Lordship.

The evidence for the development of the legal thinking found in the
Mishnah leads to a refining of the theory just summarized. In the period
immediately following the war in 70, Israelites expected the imminent rebuilding
of the Temple and the return of the sacrificial cult. Life was expected soon to
return to exactly as it had been before the destruction. This may explain the
apparent insistence of Yavneans that there exists a preset and hierarchical order in
the universe, as was represented by the presence, in their midst, of the Temple
and the God-ordained cult practiced in it. Only with the Bar Kokhba revolt, the
point at which any expectation for the Temple's being rebuilt could no longer be
maintained, did the circumstances ripen for new theological developments.
These place common Israelites at the center of Israelite theology by claiming
that, through their own perceptions and intentions, Israelites impose meaning
upon a world otherwise seen to be in a state of chaos. Israelites, that is, are
given the power themselves to recreate a world out of the ashes.

Viewed as a whole, the Mishnah's law reaffirms the validity of the covenant
described in Scripture. In many of its details, accordingly, it indicates how
Israelites are to carry out their obligations in that covenant, for instance, by
properly planting and harvesting crops. In making their statement, however, the
Mishnaic rabbis articulate a system of theology that uniquely symbolizes their
own historical, political and religious situation. This theology replaces the lost
cult and its priesthood with new centers of focus, the rabbis themselves, viewed
as the bearers of revelation, and the common Israelites, whose thoughts and deeds
are made primary to the creation of a perfected world.

The strength of this reconstruction is its focus entirely upon central aspects
of the Mishnah and on the period in which that document was formulated. 1)
The rabbis' evolving legal ideologies and their choice to develop areas of law
that, in their own day, largely could not be observed[33] represent the primary
keys to explaining their larger purpose and perspective. 2) The significance of
the destruction of the Temple and the Bar Kokhba revolt for Jews in the land of
Israel in the first centuries seems undeniable. 3) It is a commonplace that, in the
face of disaster, people consciously or unconsciously develop systems of law and
theology that strengthen their self-image and commitment to their traditions. In
its broadest parameters, the interpretation at hand thus does what good historical
reconstructions must. It takes the most prominent aspects of the known and
relates them logically. By doing this, it answers the basic question left open by
the developmental approach just reviewed, concerning why, in their own

---

[33]Even the agricultural law, large parts of which could be observed, is striking in this regard.
The Division of Agriculture legislates the support of Temple personnel who no longer have a
concrete role in Israelite cultic life.

particular period, the Mishnah's rabbis chose to deal with the topics they did, and why their legal ideology evolved in the particular way it did.

At the same time, as I already have stated, this approach depends upon what is, finally, an unprovable assumption, that an external event, the failure of the Bar Kokhba revolt, best explains the character and content of the Mishnah. This represents a serious methodological problem, formulated clearly by William Green:[34]

> The obsession of the Mishnah with halakot pertaining to the Temple at a time when it must have been clear that the cult was gone forever certifies that the document speaks of a world that no longer existed. The disjunction of the Mishnah's interests and the evidence of the historical record, therefore, contributes a fundamental component to the understanding and interpretation of the document as a whole. It establishes beyond a doubt that the substance of the Mishnah is not mimesis, but fiction, and this knowledge helps to direct our assessment of its preoccupations and ultimate purposes. But the broad political context does not explain the details of the text, nor does it show how these two events [that is, the destruction of the Temple and the Bar Kokhba revolt] affected the form of the document. The danger of reading a text primarily against this sort of background is that limited and particular data, fragments of the historical record, may be used to explain too much, to constitute the single reference point for understanding. The assumption, for instance, that the Mishnah is designed principally and primarily as a strategy of rectification in the aftermath of the two wars carries in its wake the inevitable tendency to seek out its elements of structure and stability and to ignore its traits of disorder, ambiguity, and inconsistency (pp. 194-195).

Interpretive strategies such as the one reviewed here suffer because it is largely impossible to prove a direct connection between particular legal or theological attitudes and changes in social, political and intellectual environment. In other words, people need not react to disaster in the way that the above reconstruction claims that the Mishnah's authorities did. Thus, while interpretations such as this are *suggestive*, they remain only *suggestions*.

Yet, this fact is hardly devastating to conclusions derived from the historical-functional approach. For the criticism that this method's conclusions are not finally provable or subject to refutation applies in almost all cases in which the scholar shifts from description to interpretation. We saw this above for the case of interpretation of the book of Deuteronomy. A second example derives from the work of Howard Eilberg-Schwartz, whose developmental approach to the Mishnah was described above. Examining Mishnaic menstrual taboos from an anthropological perspective, Eilberg-Schwartz suggests:[35]

---

[34]"Reading the Writing of Rabbinism," in *Journal of the American Academy of Religion* 51:2, June, 1983, pp. 191-206.

[35]"The Language of Jewish Ritual: An Anthropological Approach to the Menstrual Taboo in Judaism," *Approaches to Ancient Judaism* (Atlanta, forthcoming), manuscript p. 24.

> If the [human] body symbolizes the social body, then the orifices represent society's capacity for controlling its members. According to this interpretation, the Mishnah's rules about body fluids allude to distinctions within society itself.... One in a sense plays out on one's body the drama of social life."

As with historical-functional explanations, so this anthropological one takes as central ideas not made explicit in the Mishnah itself and not consciously held by the Mishnah's rabbis. Yet as Eilberg-Schwartz, following the lead of social anthropology, states, this does not comprise grounds for rejecting such interpretations. They stand or fall, rather, depending upon their ability to explain the details of the social or legal system. In locating these details, as I have said, the developmental approach is of primary importance. By focusing upon the cognitive world revealed by the particular legal system in its relationship to the tradition of which it is a part, that approach provides the evidence to support historical-functional reconstructions.

V.   Conclusion: Law and the Cognitive World of the Rabbis

The conclusion drawn here parallels that of Green, who stresses that Mishnaic law must teach first and foremost about the cognitive world of the rabbis, a world revealed in the specific concerns they address and in the legal theories that they develop. In this regard the cognitive-developmental approach's hypothesis regarding the internal legal evolution of the Division of Agriculture supports the conclusion Green draws from the formal traits of the Mishnah as a whole. He states:

> [T]he Mishnah may be envisioned as a kind of primal list, mastery of which determined competence and credibility in rabbinic society. But the absence in its lists of explicit hypotaxis suggests that expertise involved learning each single pericope, each separate unit, one after another. It also implies that in rabbinic discourse attention will be directed not to a picture of the whole but to details of the distinct components of the lists themselves. Because their autonomy is never nullified and because they are not formally bound to one another, the elements of Mishnaic lists are capable of virtually endless comparison and contrast, of nearly infinite combination and recombination, *in a system that maximizes the possibilities for ingenuity* (pp. 202-203, emphasis added).

Ingenuity, indeed, is what the Division of Agriculture, and with it the rest of the Mishnah, is about. For in this document, rabbinic masters envision a society in which each individual's intellect will work towards creating a perfected world, conceived by humans and yet believed to be in the holy image of God. While awaiting realization of this dream, these rabbis, powerless within their own nation, work at the elaborate puzzle that constitutes the Mishnah. Their highest value is seen both in their internal intellectual life and in their legislation. This value consists in using the mind to determine what God demands and so to participate directly in the processes of revelation and, ultimately, redemption.

Chapter Six

Dependency, Autonomy and Sexuality: Woman as Chattel and Person in the System of the Mishnah

Judith Romney Wegner
Williams College

This paper focuses on the relationship between women's sexuality and their status in mishnaic law. It asks specifically whether the framers of the Mishnah perceive women as chattels or persons, and concludes that the sages treat a woman as chattel only if her sexual function belongs to a specified man and only when the case involves a challenge to his ownership of that function. In all other circumstances, mishnaic law regards a woman as a person.

The recent groundswell of popular and scholarly interest in the problem of women's status in American society has focused on contemporary issues of secular law ("Should Congress pass an Equal Rights Amendment?") and religious law ("Should women serve as priests or rabbis?"). But those who ask such questions have largely ignored the historical background of current concerns. Conflicting claims about the legal status of women in patriarchal antiquity float about unanchored in a sea of obfuscation. On the one hand, feminists continue to claim that patriarchy has always treated women as chattel; on the other, entrenched orthodoxies insist that religious law treats women as persons equal in the sight of God and man. Here I propose to explore these claims with respect to one patriarchal system of antiquity – mishnaic law. As I shall show, the picture is neither as black as it is painted by Jewish feminists nor as white as it is washed by the champions of Jewish orthodoxy. Rather, the truth lies somewhere between those poles.

The traditional starting point for most discussions of women's status has been the writing of Simone de Beauvoir. In *The Second Sex*,[1] she repeatedly asserts that women in ancient patriarchal society were always and only regarded as chattel:

> [A] wife is [a man's] property like a slave, a beast of burden, or a chattel (p. 93).

---

[1] *Le Deuxième Sexe*, 1949, tr. H.M. Parshley (1953, Vintage ed. 1974.

> Attached to her husband's hearth she is no more than his chattel
> and the chattel of the clan into which she has been put (p. 94).

and makes blanket allegations of the following kind:

> [A]t the time of patriarchal power, man wrested from woman all
> her rights to possess and bequeath property (p. 92).
>
> The paterfamilias has the right to put the guilty spouse to death
> (p. 94).

Patriarchy, on this view, deprived women of significant rights of personhood. Such claims in the Gospel according to de Beauvoir have attained the status of dogma among feminist theoreticians, and nobody seems seriously to have challenged them. Feminists have apparently been so intent on injecting their own agendas into the exegesis (or eisegesis) of patriarchal texts that they have neglected to consider agendas implicit in the texts themselves.

This failure has been compounded, above all, by a dearth of systematic studies of ancient legal codes. Yet these are among the very texts most likely to shed light on women's status; for despite feminist denials that the reality of women's lives in antiquity can be gauged by analyzing androcentric texts composed by males, it seems probable that legal rules defining women's status either substantially reflected that reality or made a sizable contribution to it. Otherwise, the promulgation of lawcodes would be an exercise in futility. But even supposing that the Mishnah presents its framers' utopian vision of an ideal Israelite society, rather than depicting facts on the ground,[2] its discussion of any topic must at the very least reflect some stance towards that topic. Hence, no matter whether the Mishnah's rules on women depict historical reality or a utopian dream, they cannot have existed in a vacuum but must have involved attitudes and behavior towards real, live women that constituted a significant part of those women's reality.

Presumably this holds good for lawcodes in general. If so, my work on women in the mishnaic system could serve as a model for similar studies of women's status in other codes contemporaneous with the Mishnah – for instance, the Laws of Manu or the Institutes of Gaius (both placed by scholars in the second half of the second century C.E.). Such enterprises would at the very least provide concrete data for the testing of global generalizations about the chattel status of women in patriarchy – data that in many cases may turn out to

---

[2]The chief proponent of this viewpoint has been Jacob Neusner, who puts the matter, with a *caveat*, as follows: "The Mishnah fully expressed the world view and way of life of these men. That is not to suggest that the Mishnah exhausts the evidence about the group behind the Mishnah. But the Mishnah does exhaustively express a complete system – the fit of world view and way of life – fantasized by its framers. It is in theory a way of conducting the totality of life and constructing society, state and cosmos." *Judaism: the Evidence of the Mishnah* (Chicago University Press: 1981), p. 24.

refute rather than validate such theories. For though de Beauvoir explicitly includes in her strictures the culture of biblical Israel and the Jewish patriarchy that evolved from it,[3] investigation reveals that many of her claims simply do not fit the mishnaic system. To substantiate this assertion, I shall review here the principal findings of my study of the status of women in mishnaic law.

To state my conclusions at the outset: the legal status of women in the Mishnah depends largely on a variable that I call the "sexuality factor."[4]   This factor operates in both the private and public domains of mishnaic culture. In the domain of private legal transactions that forms the topic of the present paper, the term "sexuality factor" means *the presence or absence of a legal relationship in which some man owns the exclusive right to use or dispose of a woman's biological function.* If such a relationship exists, the system classifies the woman as legally dependent on the man in question; if not, the system grants her legal autonomy. It turns out that this mishnaic taxonomy correlates with striking differences in the treatment of dependent and autonomous women, above all in matters touching the ownership of the woman's sexuality. As I shall show, those differences hinge on the mishnaic perception of the dependent woman as chattel rather than person, *when – but only when –* the context is control of her sexual and reproductive function. The autonomous woman, by contrast, is never perceived or treated as chattel.

To understand what follows, we must define two crucial terms: *chattel* and *person*. These terms represent legal concepts. Webster's New World Dictionary, Second College Edition defines a legal person as "any individual .... having certain legal rights and responsibilities." A chattel (more accurately, a chattel personal) is defined simply as "a movable item of personal property." Examples include slaves and livestock. A legal chattel (even if it happens to be a human being) lacks by definition the legal incidents of personhood. As we shall see, whenever the Mishnah's framers perceive a woman as chattel, that perception leads to the suspension of entitlements and obligations normally assigned to her when contemplated as person.

Equally crucial to the present analysis is the proposition that personhood is not a fixed but a variable quantity. Thus, the terms *chattel* and *person* do not imply a simplistic dichotomy whereby an individual qualifies as a person if and only if he/she possesses incidents of personhood equal to those enjoyed by the most privileged members of the society. Rather, members of society possess different *levels of personhood* within the system. The individual's level of personhood depends on the particular assortment of legal powers, rights and duties assigned by the system. But society may impose significant differences among members, so that a class or individual blessed with more entitlements and

---

[3]See, in particular, *op. cit.,* pp. 90-91 and 93-96.

[4]See my doctoral dissertation,*Chattel or Person? The Status of Women in the System of the Mishnah* (to be published by Oxford University Press, 1987).

burdened with fewer obligations enjoys a higher level of personhood than one assigned more obligations and fewer entitlements. Within a given system, the yardstick for measuring personhood comprises the class of persons who constitute the norm for that system. The Mishnah's yardstick happens to be the free, adult Israelite male – as it were, the mishnaic W.A.S.P. This Israelite householder corresponds roughly to his better-known contemporary, the *paterfamilias* of Roman law; all "others" in mishnaic society – women, children, slaves and foreigners – occupy lower spots on the mishnaic totem pole.[5]

Yet, though the status of the Israelite woman never fully matches that of the Israelite man, she still enjoys a measure of personhood that de Beauvoir's strictures would utterly deny. Indeed, when it comes to the autonomous woman, the sexuality factor I have isolated operates to make her almost the equal of a man with respect to private transactions, *including transactions that involve her biological function*. Moreover, even a dependent woman's personhood remains surprisingly unimpaired, *except in situations that pose a threat or challenge to the ownership of her sexuality by the man in control.*

Owner of biological function	Dependent Woman	Autonomous Woman	Owner of biological function
father............minor daughter		adult............daughter	herself
husband............wife		divorcee...........herself	
levir............levirate widow		widow............herself	

The Mishnaic Taxonomy of Women

Mishnaic taxonomy (as the table shows) divides women into two main categories: dependent and autonomous. The sages recognize three subclasses of dependent women: the minor daughter, the wife, and the levirate widow. All these women are legally dependent on the man who, in each case, owns the sole right to use or profit from their biological function. In the case of the minor daughter (a girl under twelve and a half years of age), that man is her father; for

---

[5]Here I ignore indigenous caste distinctions among Israelite males, notably the division into Kohanim (priestly caste), Levites, and lay Israelites, which has no relevance to the present discussion.

the wife, it is her husband; and for the levirate widow, her levir (her late husband's brother).[6]

Corresponding to the three classes of dependent women, the Mishnah knows three kinds of autonomous women: the emancipated or adult daughter,[7] the divorcee, and the regular widow.[8] These three form mirror images of their dependent counterparts with respect to their legal rights and powers – a feature that stands out above all in cases involving the disposition of their sexual functions. We can pinpoint the precise relationship between dependency, autonomy and sexuality by showing how the Mishnah reverses the legal attributes of women perceived as polar opposites on the spectrum of legal status, according to whether or not they control their own sexual function.

In the case of the first pair – minor daughter and adult daughter – the minor girl's marriage is arranged by her father (M. Ket. 4:4), she having no option in the matter,[9] while the adult daughter makes her own contract with the suitor of her choice (M. Qid. 2:1). Likewise, penalties and damages for seduction or rape of a minor daughter accrue to her father (M. Ket. 4:1), while the violator of an emancipated daughter indemnifies the woman herself (M. Ket. 3:6). Both of these distinctions reflect the fact that the minor daughter's sexuality is the

---

[6]A levirate widow is one whose husband has died without heirs (meaning, in this context, without male issue). Mishnaic law, based on Deut. 25:5-10, requires her to marry her husband's brother unless the latter releases her by the rite of unshoeing(*halisah*). The primary object of the levirate law was to try to produce a surrogate son, hence lineal heir, for the deceased. De Beauvoir's statement (p. 96) that *all* Israelite widows were required to marry their levirs is simply incorrect.

[7]In mishnaic law, "adult daughter" means a girl who has reached the age of twelve and a half years and one day. This was calculated by adding six months to the age at which the girl is presumed to have grown two pubic hairs. That age, in turn, was conventionally construed as the twelve years and one day specified in M. Nid. 5:6 as the age at which a girl becomes liable to observe the commandments of the Torah. At twelve and a half years, the girl is automatically emancipated from her father's control; and unless he has married her off beforehand, she becomes completely autonomous.

[8]A regular widow is one who has borne a son to her husband, or whose husband already has at least one son by another wife.

[9]The right of a minor daughter betrothed in infancy to reject the selected husband when she reaches puberty belonged *only* to girls betrothed by their mothers or brothers (M. Yeb. 13:2). Apparently such a betrothal was allowed if the father had died before arranging the daughter's marriage. The girl's right of refusal here reflects the fact that her mother or brother does not control her as absolutely as did her father.

property of her father;[10] while that of the emancipated daughter belongs to herself.

As for the second pair – wife and divorcee – here too we see the mirror-image effect following ownership of the woman's sexuality. It accounts, for instance, for a husband's power to countermand his wife's vows if these tend directly or indirectly to impair conjugal relations (M. Ned. 11:1, 12; M. Naz. 4:5), while no man can revoke the vows of a divorcee (M. Ned. 11:9). Although her husband owns the exclusive right to her sexuality during the subsistence of the marriage, the wife alone controls this function from the moment of divorce, except that she must abstain from sexual relations for three months to avoid doubt as to paternity if it turns out she was pregnant at the time of divorce (M. Yeb. 4:10). From the moment he divorces his wife, the husband loses control of her future sexual choices. The Mishnah makes this point crystal clear by explicitly precluding the husband from modifying the writ of divorce with statements like, "Thou art now permitted to any man *except Reuben b. Jacob*" (M. Git. 9:1). As the sages take pains to point out, the essence of the writ is the formula, "Thou art now permitted to *any* man" (M. Git. 9:3).

Similarly with the third matched pair: while the levir inherits the sexual function of the levirate widow, who can marry no one else unless he releases her (M. Yeb. 4:7), the normal widow may remarry at will, because her sexuality is at her own disposal. Once more we observe the mirror image effect.[11]

Obviously the man with legal control of a woman's sexuality owns a valuable asset. To that extent – *but only in that limited context* – the woman is regarded as his chattel. This perception emerges even more clearly from the formalities whereby ownership of a woman's sexual function changes hands. In arranging the marriage of his minor daughter, the Israelite father effectively sells her virginity to the bridegroom for brideprice. True, by mishnaic times, the bridegroom no longer actually pays the money to the father, but holds the brideprice (along with the rest of her marriage portion, including dowry supplied by her father) in trust for the wife during the subsistence of the marriage (M.

---

[10]In this connection we note the striking omission of the daughter from the list of women with whom a man may not cohabit (Leviticus, chapter 18). Despite orthodox apologetics, this omission undoubtedly reflects the view that the daughter's sexuality belongs to her father (since that of all other women in the list belongs to other men). In biblical times, it is inherently probable that a man had as much right to use his daughter's sexual function as to dispose of it. Even in America today, incest forced by fathers on daughters is, regrettably, a common phenomenon; but we may ask ourselves whether it is any more reprehensible than, for instance, Lot's willingness, in accordance with semitic notions of hospitality, to surrender his virgin daughters to a mob of rapacious Sodomites (Gen. 19:8).

[11]This kind of binary opposition is typical of the Mishnah, which is suffused throughout with hellenistic logic of a type that one writer has felicitously dubbed "the Greek penchant for combining symmetry with alternatives." Sarah Pomeroy, *Goddesses, Whores, Wives and Slaves: Women in Classical Antiquity* (1975), p. 25. See also Wegner, "Tragelaphos Revisited: the Anomaly of Woman in the Mishnah" (in press).

Ket. 4:7).[12] Nonetheless, the bridegroom has paid for and acquired a valuable asset – the bride's virginity. Hence the rule that if she is not intact, he can claim damages from the father at once (M. Ket. 1:1). Conversely, the father (in mishnaic as in biblical law) collects damages from any man who rapes or seduces his minor daughter (M. Ket. 4:1), since her reduced value on the marriage market leaves him out of pocket.

As for husband and wife, the fact that an item of *property* (the bride's virginity) is what actually changes hands upon marriage explains the unilateral character of the marriage ceremony (M. Qid. 1:1). This ritual, as the Mishnah specifically indicates, mimics the transfer formalities of some other forms of property, such as Canaanite slaves and real property (M. Qid. 1:3,1:5).[13] What the husband acquires is not the whole woman (for she is no slave), but merely her sexual and reproductive function. The one-sidedness of the transaction is further underscored by a tannaitic assertion that while a man acquires a wife by the formal declaration, "Lo, thou art consecrated to me," no woman can acquire a husband by reversing the formula and declaring, "Lo, *I* am consecrated to *thee*" (T. Qid. 1:1). The most she can do is indicate her willingness to become "consecrated" by contracting with the bridegroom beforehand – just as the father does in the case of a minor daughter. Property clearly cannot acquire its owner, but only the other way about. Significantly, the Hebrew term *mequddeshet*, "consecrated" in this context means, simply, set apart for the husband's exclusive sexual use.

In exactly the same way, since the object acquired is the wife's sexual function, the mishnaic husband can dispose of his wife at any time by executing a unilateral writ of divorce (Deut. 24:1, M. Yeb. 14:1), that explicitly renounces his exclusive sexual rights (M. Git. 9:3). But since property can no more release itself than it could acquire its owner, a wife has no corresponding power to divorce a husband in mishnaic law.[14] At the same time, the limited nature of

---

[12]The historical origins of the *ketubbah* (marriage deed) are cloaked in obscurity. Tradition ascribes it to Simeon b. Shetah, a sage of the first century B.C.E. (B. Ket. 82b); its probable origins have been exhaustively discussed by M.J. Geller, "Some New Light on the Origins of the Rabbinic *Ketubah*," *HUCA* vol. 49, 1978, pp. 227-245.

[13]This is obvious from a comparison of the following items from the list that opens tractate *Qiddushin:*

"A wife may be acquired in three ways .... by money, by deed, or by intercourse" (M. Qid. 1:1).

"A Canaanite slave may be acquired .... by money, by deed, or by usucaption" (M. Qid. 1:3).

"Real property may be acquired by money, by deed, or by usucaption (M. Qid. 1:5).

These formulae are essentially identical, once we realize that in the case of a wife intercourse constitutes usucaption.

[14]The same is true in other systems, like Islamic law, grounded in similar jurisprudential principles. However, the prescribed rule can sometimes be modified by private contract. There is evidence that some Jewish cultures of antiquity (though not that of the Mishnah) permitted a wife to divorce her husband by inserting a clause to that effect in the marriage contract. See Reuven Yaron, *Introduction to the Law of the Aramaic Papyri* (Oxford, 1961).

the husband's ownership of his wife is reflected in the rule that precludes a husband from arbitrarily revoking his wife's religious vows, except those which could impair (directly or indirectly) the conjugal relationship – for instance, if she vows to forgo washing or adorning herself (M. Ned. 11:1).[15]

It is no accident that these rights of the husband are not matched by corresponding rights of the wife. The asymmetry reflects the fact that while *he* owns the sole right to use *her* sexual function, the converse simply is not the case. In the polygynous society of the Mishnah, even a monogamous husband may with impunity have sexual relations with other women, so long as those women are not married to other men.

The same basic assumptions concerning the other two groups of dependent women underpin the laws governing the levirate widow. Her chattel status as a potential reproductive vessel appears in the automatic inheritance of her sexual function by her husband's brothers, each in turn exercising the right to accept or reject her (M. Yeb. 4:5). Stripped of her personhood when viewed merely as an incubator, she has no option, unless all the levirs agree to release her. Her personhood is thus subordinated to her socio-sexual function.

In these few short pages we can do no more than sample the mishnaic rules governing women's status. But those already discussed suffice to demonstrate the fact that the mishnaic system reduces a woman to chattel *whenever this is necessary to establish or enforce the exclusive sexual rights of the man legally entitled to benefit from her biological function.*

In the patriarchal society of the Mishnah, the foregoing does not surprise us any more than it would have surprised de Beauvoir. What may, however, astound us – and presumably would have amazed de Beauvoir – is the extraordinary contrast between the status of the woman as sexual chattel and her far higher personal status in all other areas of mishnaic law. For these same women, in private transactions generally, are unequivocally treated as *persons*. Frequently, indeed, they enjoy legal rights equal to those of a man. To illustrate this proposition, let us consider the paradigmatic case of the wife in more detail.

A wife participates in a reciprocal nexus of personal entitlements and obligations between herself and her husband (and here we recall that the definition of legal personhood includes the possession of *obligations* as much as *entitlements)*. The wife must perform specified, but strictly limited, household chores in return for maintenance at a prescribed minimum standard (M. Ket. 5:5, 5:8-9). Moreover, her worknorm varies with the number of slaves she brought to the marriage (M. Ket. 5:5); and both worknorm and food allowance are suitably adjusted if she is nursing a baby (M. Ket. 5:9). Besides their general matrimonial entitlements and obligations, the spouses also have mutual

---

[15]This point, which emerges from close scrutiny of Mishnah *Nedarim*, chapter eleven, is confirmed by an express statement in T. Ned. 7:1, as discussed in my forthcoming book (see note 4 above).

conjugal rights and duties (M. Ket. 5:6-7) – in contradistinction to most other legal systems, including Anglo-American common law, which have traditionally construed sexual intercourse as primarily the *right* of the husband and the *duty* of the wife.[16]

Another significant right of the wife is enshrined in the rule that a married woman retains title to her property – which, again, was not the rule in Anglo-American law until the late nineteenth century – and even has power to sell it (though here she needs her husband's consent, since he is entitled to usufruct during the subsistence of the marriage and would be unjustly deprived of an economic benefit unless he agreed). The husband, in turn, cannot sell it without the wife's consent. The Mishnah prescribes safeguards to protect the wife here, namely, it is she who must sell the property and the husband endorse the sale, rather than the husband sell and the wife subsequently ratify his action (M. Git. 5:6).

Beyond the foregoing rights and duties, a wife possesses significant powers of legal action. She can appoint agents to transact her personal business (M. Git. 6:1); she can act as her husband's agent for sale of his merchandise (M. Ket. 9:4); and she even possesses a right of legal action against him, for she can petition the mishnaic court to compel him to divorce her for specified infringements of her rights (M. Ket. 7:1-5, 7:10). Furthermore, though the court cannot grant the wife *as sexual chattel* a divorce without the participation of a recalcitrant husband, the sages, perceiving her as a *person* morally entitled to be released, are willing to endorse draconian measures to force his cooperation. They even give their seal of approval to gentile authorities who beat or jail the husband until he agrees to the divorce ordered by the Jewish court (M. Git. 9:8).

By the same token, the court expects the wife, as a *person*, to perform her legal duties – which, as we said, constitute a mark of personhood no less than the assignment of rights. The sages provide a list of infractions for which a wife may be divorced with forfeiture of her marriage portion M. Ket. 7:6-7). For instance, she must not violate Jewish law or Jewish custom. Her duties in Jewish law include observance of the rules of cultic purity; she must protect her husband from intercourse during and following the menstrual period. As for Jewish custom, she must keep her hair covered and refrain from speaking to strange men; and she may be divorced with loss of her marriage portion simply for being a "loudmouth" – which the Mishnah defines as a woman whose voice can be heard by the neighbors when she speaks inside her house (M. Ket. 7:6)

What is the common denominator of all the wife's rights so far described? *None of them threatens or challenges the husband's exclusive ownership of the wife's sexuality.* Unlike cases that treat her as chattel, none involves a situation

---

[16]However, as discussed in my book, the unusual perspective of the sages rests on their almost certainly erroneous interpretation of the technical term *'onah* occurring at Ex. 21:10. It is far more likely that the term really meant "shelter," rather than "conjugal rights" as construed by mishnaic and subsequent authorities.

in which the wife has had, or may have had, or must be prevented from having, sexual relations with another man.[17] This observation leads to a further conclusion: the sages of the Mishnah treat the dependent woman as chattel *only* when some man's exclusive right to her biological function is called in question; in all other contexts, they contemplate her as a person. My analysis thus isolates the sexuality factor as the variable determining a woman's treatment in mishnaic law.

This thesis derives further support from the marginal cases with which the Mishnah's framers exhibit an obsessive concern. Thus, an interesting legal conundrum of woman-as-sexual-chattel versus woman-as-person arises when a woman's marital status falls into doubt. This can occur in two principal ways: a woman may have remarried on the strength of a writ of divorce which is later invalidated for technical error (M. Git. 8:5); or a woman's husband may return from the dead after she has remarried in reliance on witnesses' reports of his demise (M. Yeb. 10:1). These unfortunate women suffer dire penalties, because the law treats them as adulteresses; among other things they lose their matrimonial property rights in *both* marriages – that is, in the genuine first marriage as well as the spurious second one. Effectively, in any conflict between woman perceived as sexual chattel and woman perceived as person, the chattel aspect of the woman supervenes, wiping out her rights of personhood.

Why do the sages punish so harshly women who are guilty only of an innocent mistake? In part, it is because the Mishnah abhors ambiguity; for ambiguous objects defy classification, and the Mishnah is above all an exercise in taxonomy. The woman in the cases described looks like the wife of two men at once. The sages solve this intolerable situation by reducing her to the status of nobody's wife at all. But this solution, while it has the merit of unequivocality, involves an arbitrary suspension of the wife's rights of personhood. Forfeiture of both marriage portions (when the two men divorce her, as they must) is only one among many penalties prescribed (M. Git. 8:5, M. Yeb. 10:1). From being a *person,* possessor of clearly assigned rights, the woman suddenly becomes a tarnished *chattel,* discarded by both her "owners" alike. At the root of this treatment lies the fact that, no matter how innocently, a woman whose sexual function belongs to one man has allowed another to make use of it.

Another graphic portrayal of woman as chattel and person at once appears in the law of the suspected adulteress. According to tractate *Sotah,* based on the biblical "law of jealousy" (Num. 5:11-31), a husband may put his wife to the ordeal on the basis of mere suspicion. But if he chooses also to *divorce* her without actual proof, we have a legal dilemma. On the one hand, the wife as

---

[17]Even the court's willingness in some cases to force the husband to divorce the wife rests on the view that a husband who wilfully disregards his wife's rights has forfeited his moral claim on her; though, as legal owner of her sexual function, it is still the husband alone who can effectively execute the writ of release.

sexual chattel can be unilaterally discarded at any time, even without cause (M. Git. 9:10).[18]   On the other hand, a woman divorced without proof of fault remains a property-owner, entitled to collect the marriage portion that her husband holds in trust for her (M. Ket. 4:7); as *person*, she cannot be deprived of property without due process. How do the sages resolve this dilemma? They simply forbid the ordeal unless the husband has first warned his wife before witnesses to stay away from the suspected lover (M. Sot. 1:1). Then, if she continues to defy him by secluding herself with the man in question, he can use those witnesses to forfeit her marriage settlement when he divorces her for suspected, though not proven, misconduct (M. Sot. 4:5).[19]

A similar problem occurs in the law of divorce. As we saw earlier, a man may divorce his wife at any time, even for no reason (M. Git. 9:10), while she cannot in theory divorce him at all (M. Yeb. 14:1). Yet at the same time, the Mishnah lists many grounds that entitle a wife to petition for divorce (M. Ket. 7:1-5, 9-10). These include the husband's cruelty, such as forbidding his wife to eat particular foods, or to wear her favorite jewels, or to visit her parents at reasonable intervals. In all such cases, as *person* the wife is morally entitled to a divorce; but as *chattel* she cannot divorce her husband and must rely on the good offices of the court to try and compel him by all available means.[20]   Here again, the law perceives the woman as chattel and person at one and the same time.

In another divorce scenario, the law empowers a wife to send an agent to her husband to receive her writ of divorce (M. Git. 6:1). The power to appoint an agent is obviously a significant right of personhood. But since receipt of the writ will release the wife at once, the sages insist that the ultimate determination of that moment remain with the husband. If for some reason he does not wish to yield sexual control of his wife by handing the writ to her agent, the husband can countermand the agent's commission, transforming him from the wife's agent for receipt into the husband's agent for delivery. This delays the wife's release until the agent returns home and actually hands her the writ. Here too, the wife is placed in a context where her status as a *person* conflicts with her status as the husband's sexual *chattel*, and as always the sexuality factor defeats her rights of personhood.

---

[18]In this connection, we note that the affinities between the talmudic and Islamic laws of women's status are far greater than is generally realized. See Wegner, "The Status of Women in Jewish and Islamic Marriage and Divorce Law," *Harvard Women's Law Journal*, vol. 5, 1982, pp. 1-33.

[19]A subtle distinction is present here. Unlike the preceding case of the wife who mistakenly remarried, the sages cannot override the wife's rights of personhood here. Whereas in the earlier case it is *certain* that she has had sexual relations with another man, in the present case her husband *cannot prove this*. (If he could prove it, she would not be subject to the ordeal, but to a trial for adultery.)

[20]This problem continues to plague Jewish women to this day, and probably does more than anything else to bring Jewish law into disrepute among Jews and gentiles alike.

With the levirate widow, the same process operates in reverse. Inherited by her brother-in-law upon her husband's death without heirs, she is his *chattel*. But as soon as the levir declares his intention to release her, she becomes as it were her own *person* (subject only to carrying out the rite of release). The levir's mere declaration brings her personhood to the fore, letting her assume the active part in the release ceremony, as she removes his shoe, spits at him, and verbally expresses society's condemnation of the man who shirks his levirate duty (Deut. 25:9, M. Yeb. 12:6). Once more we see the anomaly of woman as chattel and person in a single context.

When we turn from dependent to autonomous women, we find the legal status of the latter considerably higher than that of the dependent woman, in that an autonomous woman controls *all* aspects of her private life. Thus, an emancipated daughter or divorcee who finds some object of value may keep it, in contrast to a minor daughter or wife, who must turn over her find to the father or husband as the case may be (M. B.M. 1:5). Likewise, the minor daughter's earnings accrue to her father (M. Ket. 4:4) and those of a wife to her husband (M. Ket. 6:1), while an adult daughter keeps whatever she makes (M. Nid. 5:7). The autonomous woman can buy and sell without impediment, because no man has any claim on her property – unlike the wife, whose husband's entitlement to usufruct during the marriage gives him a concomitant right to approve or disapprove her sale of her property, as noted above. And the vows of an autonomous woman – whether unmarried, divorced or widowed – cannot be revoked, since no man is in a position to countermand her (M. Ned. 10:2, 11:9).

The emancipated woman can also engage in private litigation. She may bring suit for personal damages (M. B.Q. 1:3), or for the return of her marriage portion upon the termination of her marriage by widowhood or divorce (M. Ket. 2:1), or to sell part of her marriage portion while it is still in the hands of her husband's heirs, to provide for her maintenance pending receipt of her settlement (M. Ket. 11:3).

Another important power of the autonomous woman is her legal competency to testify in lawsuits concerning her virginity or that of other women (M. Ket. 1:6-7, 2:5-6). Such a suit may be brought by a woman about to betroth herself, in order to establish her right to receive the brideprice of virgins, or by a widow or divorcee against her ex-husband or his heirs, if the latter should deny that she was a virgin at marriage to reduce the cost of paying her settlement now. These women's competency as witnesses constitutes an important exception to the rule that women may not testify (M. Shebu. 4:1). Like the other principal exception, which permits a woman to testify to the death of her husband if no other witnesses are available (M. Yeb. 15:1-3), it is no accident that these cases involve widows, divorcees, or emancipated daughters. For dependent women's incompetency stems from the desire of the men who own their sexual function to keep them from exposure to strangers in a public courthouse; by contrast, no man has a legal interest in the conduct of an autonomous woman, so the law permits her to testify in public.

Still more significant are the standards applied by the Mishnah's framers to evaluate a woman's testimony. The sages consider women's morality and intelligence equal to that of men; they gauge the credibility of a woman's testimony by precisely the same criteria that apply to men. In particular, they assess whether her statements stem from self-interest or altruism (M. Ket. 2:6), or whether her damaging admissions involve facts known to herself alone. Thus, a woman who asserts her freedom to marry by claiming, "I was once married, but now I am divorced" (M. Ket. 2:5) may be believed, since she need never have mentioned the previous marriage, of which no one knew. But a woman who makes that claim in response to other people's assertions that she is married must corroborate her words by producing her writ of divorce. A woman is also considered trustworthy to swear certain kinds of business-related oaths (M. Shebu. 5:1, M. Ket. 9:4).

But by far the most important power of an autonomous woman is her control of her own sex life. As noted above, she makes her own marriage arrangements, selecting the man of her choice from among her suitors. That power, quite simply, stems from the fact that her sexuality belongs to no man and thus is hers to bestow (M. Qid. 2:1). This fact also explains the rule forbidding a jealous husband to interrogate his wife concerning her sexual conduct before he betrothed her or after he divorced her, since affairs conducted while she was not under his control are none of his business and give him no grounds for putting her to the ordeal (M. Sot. 2:6).

The net effect of the mishnaic rules is this: in the minds of the Mishnah's framers, no event in an autonomous woman's life justifies her treatment as legal chattel. Unlike her dependent sister (and contrary to de Beauvoir's assertions), this woman remains a person at all times in the private sphere of mishnaic law.[21]

In closing, I reiterate that this paper has dealt only with the status of women in the *private domain*. Rules governing women's relationship to the *public*

---

[21] An apparent exception is the case (M. Qid. 4:9) of the emancipated woman who, having sent her agent to espouse her to one man, changes her mind and espouses herself to another. If there is no way to determine which transaction took place first, the sages solve the dilemma by requiring both men to divorce her or else to decide between themselves which one shall have her. At first glance, this seems at odds with the woman's autonomy, since she could now end up with the first man, whom she clearly had rejected in favor of the second. However, the sages seem to take the view that she becomes the victim of her own irresponsibility. Like the man who changes his mind after sending an agent to divorce his wife (M. Git. 4:1), she should have sent a second agent to intercept the first agent before he could execute his commission. Her failure to do so lands her in an *impasse* of her own making. Certainly this woman has less claim to clemency than the innocent women who remarried in error but were treated like chattel by the sages solely because of their abhorrence of ambiguity.

domain of mishnaic culture [22] tell quite a different story – one that supports de Beauvoir's contentions up to the hilt. As she rightly observes, patriarchal cultures did (and do) significantly diminish the personhood of women by systematically excluding them from the life of the mind and spirit "in the vast universe to which [the man] belonged" (p. 95); and here mishnaic law offers no exception. Yet even conceding the lower level of personhood of the Israelite woman as compared with the mishnaic W.A.S.P., it remains true that the law never demotes her to the status of chattel, except in the single context I have described. Failure to perceive this fine distinction was de Beauvoir's error and has become the error of many of her disciples. So I end as I began, with a plea for more detailed studies of ancient lawcodes and more rigorous analysis of the status of women depicted there. Only thus can scholars expect to test popular generalizations about the position of women in antiquity, thus gaining insights that could add more rigor to feminist theory and help to dispel the theological fog surrounding the place of women in Judaism and its daughter religions.

---

[22]There exists considerable confusion about what precisely is encompassed by the term "public domain." When discussing the mishnaic law of women, the confusion is compounded by the established mishnaic terminology of "private domain" *(reshut ha-yahid)* as meaning privately-owned real estate, while "public domain" *(reshut ha-rabbim)* generally means "land not belonging to a private individual." On that definition, a public forum such as a courthouse ranks as "public domain." However, in feminist literature, "public domain" generally and more usefully means the *public domain of culture* in the society under discussion. That is how I use the term here. Hence, a woman who engages in private litigation, whether as party or witness, is involved in a *private transaction,* and is not operating in the public *cultural* domain, even though the lawsuit is heard in the courthouse. The public domain of mishnaic culture refers to such institutions as the synagogue and study-house, from which women were systematically excluded – sometimes by outright prohibition, and sometimes by exemption which ultimately led to their exclusion in practice. A paper on this topic is currently in preparation.

Chapter Seven

Hierarchy and Interstitiality: The Bondman and The Freedman in the Mishnah's Caste System

Paul V. Flesher
Brown University

The system of the Mishnah, with its stress on the correct classification of all things and the discovery of the proper rules pertaining to each category, chokes on the interstitial category. Ordinarily, the Mishnah's framers erect high walls between different categories and refuse to confuse one category with another. But there is one important exception, an interstitial category which bears the power to mix otherwise unmiscibles. If we consider that the two most distinct and incompatible categories for the Mishnah's authorities are Israelite and gentile, we must find it astonishing that the framers give slavery the power to create a single category from the members of both categories. That is to say, the slave comprises a category that receives persons of every ethnic background – both Israelite and non-Israelite – and treats them as a single classification that obliterates all traces of their ethnic origins.

The capacity of the slave, which we shall call the "bondman," to accomplish this feat derives from the slave's total subjection to his master's control.[1] This control centers on the locus of the master's household, because, in the Mishnah's system, the bondman constitutes his master's property. This subjugation places the bondman at the bottom the master's household, below the householder himself, his wives, and his offspring. The householder's control further cuts off the bondman from his kinship ties. The bondman possesses no relationships to parents, wives, or children. In fact, no trace of the bondman's past remains at all. He, or his ancestors, could have been born Israelites or a gentiles; it would make no difference to his present status as a bondman. The only relationship a bondman possesses is that to his master, which now defines his place in Israelite society.

---

[1] I use the terms "bondman" and "freedman" to indicate both the male of the species and the species as a whole, i.e., both male and female. In doing this, I am following the gender indications of the original Hebrew terms.

Upon his manumission, the bondman leaves his subordinate location in his masters' household and enters the category of freedman. The class of freedmen constitutes a group of free Israelites, belonging to the same household categories as other free Israelites; an adult male, for instance, becomes a householder and can form his own household.[2] He constitutes no one's property and is totally free from the power of his former master. He can now form new kinship ties, by both marrying and producing offspring. He does not regain any ties, however, from the period prior to manumission. The freedman, having been a bondman, still lacks all ancestral ties. This means that, like the bondman, the ethnic origins of the freedman are null and thus bear no effect on his position as a freedman. His definition as an ex-bondman – as a person once subject to but now free from a householder's control – determines his standing in Israelite society.

The nature of the householder's power over the bondman and the effects of its removal from the freedman can be most clearly be studied in the context of the caste system. This is because the status of bondmen and freedmen in the caste system stems directly from their position vis-à-vis the householder's control. The bondman's standing results solely from his link to his master, while the freedman's position derives from his former subjection to and his present freedom from a householder's control.

The Caste System

The caste system hierarchizes all members of Israelite society by placing them into one of ten castes. The framers rank the castes according to their importance to worship in the Temple cult. They present the hierarchy in the following passage.

A. Ten castes came up [to Jerusalem] from Babylonia:[3]

B. (1) the priests,

    (2) the Levites,

    (3) the Israelites,

C. (4) the impaired priests [who have transgressed the rules of Lev. 21:7,13,14 and married women who are divorcees, or, in the case of a High Priest, a non-virgin],

---

[2] The same point applies to other types of freedmen, *mutatis mutandis*. Adult freedwomen enter one of the classes of free women, minor freedwomen become minor daughters, and minor freedmen enter the category of minor sons.

[3] This Mishnah pericope may reflect Neh. 7:5-65, which lists the different classes of people who returned to Israel from the Babylonian exile. However, the lists of people in the two passages only partially correspond. Both lists contain categories not found in the other and leave out categories that are found in the other. Furthermore, the passage in Nehemiah focuses on listing the sub-families of each class. It does not arrange either the groups or the sub-families into any sort of hierarchical order. Since the point of the M. Qiddushin passage is to present a hierarchical caste system, it cannot be anything more than a faint echo of Nehemiah.

D. (5) the proselytes [foreigners who have chosen to worship Yahweh] and,
    (6) the freedmen,

E. (7) the *mamzers* [who are the offspring of incestuous marriages, (Lev.
    20:17-21)],

F. (8) the *Netins* [foreigners who once were servants to the Israelites],

G. (9) the *shetuqs* [people who know who their mother is, but not their
    father (M. Qid. 4:2)] and
    (10) the foundlings [who know neither their mother nor their father (M.
    Qid. 4:2)].

M. Qid. 4:1[4]

The Mishnah's sages divide each of these ten castes into two levels. The primary level is for householders, the free, adult, male Israelites who comprise the heads of their households. The secondary level contains the categories of people who belong to those households: different classes of women, minor sons and daughters, and, as we shall see momentarily, bondmen.

The framers use the primary level of the caste system to measure a householder's capacity to participate in Temple worship. It divides Israelite society into the castes whose members are allowed to participate in worship and those whose members are denied the right to take part. To use sages' terms, they distinguish those who may approach Yahweh in the Temple from those who are forbidden to approach. The first six castes in the passage above comprise those who take part in Temple worship – priests, Levites, Israelites, impaired priests, proselytes, and freedmen – and the last four contain people denied the capacity to approach the Lord – *mamzers, netins, shetuqs* and foundlings.

This capacity to enter the Temple is part of the caste system's larger purpose of designating different cultic roles to the participants. Following Scripture, sages assign a specific set of duties in worship and a concomitant set of privileges to each caste that can enter the Temple. This is clear with regard to the three main castes of Israelite society. The priests are the Temple officials; they perform the sacrifices and are in charge of the Temple. Householders of the Levitical caste, by contrast, constitute assistants to the priests; they help the priests in various ways behind the scenes of worship and accompany the rites with music. Householders of the Israelite caste comprise the worshippers. The framers require them to attend the various Temple rites, to provide the sacrifices offered on the altar, and to give donations for the upkeep of the Temple. Clearly, each caste is linked to a specific role in Temple worship. This logic applies to the other castes who have a role in worship. The proselytes and freedmen, who we shall study later in this paper, in general take on the same duties as members of the caste of Israelites. While it is is not clear what cultic

---

[4]M. Hor. 3:9 presents an ranked list of social groups containing many of these castes. These groups are arranged in a different order from M. Qid. 4:1. There is no incompatibility between the two lists, however, for the criterion here in Qiddushin is role in worship, and the one in Horayot centers on the legal system.

role the impaired priests possess, that they have a role is apparent from the fact that sages place them in the group of castes who take part in the cult.[5] In this way then, the framers use the primary level of the caste system to assign different roles in worship to members of Israelite society.

The purpose of the caste system's secondary level is to ensure that all members of a household possess the same caste status. It accomplishes this task by assigning the caste status of the householder to the other people within the household. At this remove, they do not take on any assigned duties associated with the caste, but they do acquire its privileges. A priest's wife, for instance, cannot perform sacrifices in the Temple but she can eat priestly rations.

The criteria by which sages assign roles are complex, for the caste system reflects two different views of Israelite society. Each view determines membership in a caste, and indeed membership in Israelite society as a whole, according to different criteria. On the one hand, the caste system reflects the portrayal of the people Israel as an extended family. This depiction, we recall, derives from the Biblical myth that all Israelites have descended from the patriarch Jacob. As such, they are the inheritors of God's promises to Jacob and of God's Covenant with Moses. On the other hand, the caste system embodies the view that Israelite society constitutes a collection of households. Everyone who belongs to an Israelite household belongs to Israelite society. The issue of their membership in the extended family of Israel is peripheral. These two views of Israelite society are closely related; they constitute different ways of ranking the same categories of people in the same positions – except, as we shall see, for the category of bondman.

The myth of Israelite society as an extended family provides the foundation for the caste system. Since all members of a family are related to each other, this image of Israelite society centers on the notion of kinship ties; all those who have Israelite ancestry and marital bonds belong to the family Israel. The Mishnah's authorities, however, have hierarchized the members of this family. Some sub-families have a higher rank than others. In the Mishnah's system, the framers use the scale of the caste system to formalize this inequality. In this view of society, a person's ancestry and marital bonds combine to place them into one of the ten castes listed above. In general, a person's initial caste standing derives from his or her parents, but the transmission of parental status to offspring depends on the validity of the parental union. In a marriage between two members of the same caste – the most straightforward case – the offspring take their parents' caste. So too the child of two levites, for example, belongs to the caste of levites. But in marriages between members of different castes the validity of the marriage takes on a greater importance in determining the

---

[5]In the Mishnah, as well as in Scripture, the impaired priest's capacity to participate in cultic worship is unclear. Sages certainly exclude him from any duties specific to priests, but they do not deny him the right to take part in worship. This stems from the fact that he remains a member of the "congregation" of Israel and hence remains an active participant in society.

offspring's caste. In general, if a man and a woman are from compatible castes, the offspring takes the father's caste. Thus, if an Israelite man marries a levite woman, their children are Israelites. Similarly, if a priest marries an Israelite girl, their children are priests. But if the castes are incompatible, or if for other reasons the union is invalid, then sages determine the child's status according to different rules (see, for example, M. Qid. 3:12). Yet these rules too accord with the parents' standing. In all cases, then, a person's ancestry interacting with the validity of his parents' union determines his caste position.

According to the portrayal of Israelite society as a collection of households, membership in a household determines a person's caste status. The Mishnah's authorities envision that all members of a typical Israelite household – one in which the householder has formed an approved marriage – belong to the same caste. The wife takes her husband's caste and their offspring do likewise. In this way, the caste of the householder determines the caste of the other members of the household. Furthermore, the household places its members on one of the caste system's two levels. On the primary level, we recall, the householder receives an assigned role in the Temple cult, which consists of a set of required tasks and privileges.[6] The other members of the household – women and minor sons – belong to the secondary level of the caste system. They receive no assigned duties linked to the caste, but they do partake of its privileges. In this way, then, the household differentiates members of each caste.

The Caste System and The Bondman

Each of these two portrayals of Israelite society treats the bondman in its own way. On the one hand, the bondman belongs to an Israelite household. A householder joins his bondman to his household through the property link between them. Through it, the bondman becomes an Israelite and takes on a secondary status in his master's caste. On the other hand, the bondman has no part in the network of kinship ties that indicate membership in the extended family of Israel. The tie to his master cancels all kinship ties the bondman may possess – whether to members of Israelite society or to those of some other culture. In doing so, it denies the bondman a place in the extended family of Israel. The bondman's property relationship to his master, therefore, causes one image of Israelite society to exclude him from the caste system, while at the same time, it causes the other to include him. Let me illustrate how each view treats the bondman.

On the one hand, according to the view that Israelite society comprises a collection of households, the bondman's tie to his master grants him a secondary caste status. Since the bondman constitutes a subordinate member of his

---

[6] In theory, adult sons who have yet to leave the household also have assigned roles in the Temple cult. The Mishnah's authorities, however, do not discuss any passages portraying this particular situation.

master's household, he takes on his master's caste and its privileges. This becomes clear when we examine the case of priest's bondman who can eat priestly rations even when his master is temporarily unable to do so.

A. The uncircumcised [priest] and all priests who are in a state of impurity may not eat priestly rations;

B. [however,] their wives and their slaves may eat priestly rations.

M. Yeb. 8:1

Both uncircumcised priests and those in a state of uncleanness belong to the priestly caste and hence possess the right to eat priestly rations. They pass on their right, along with their caste status, to the members of their household – in this case, wives and bondmen. The priests themselves may not eat priestly rations because they do not meet further conditions placed upon individuals whose caste status otherwise qualifies them to do so. Once they meet these further conditions – they circumcise themselves or they attain a state of cultic purity – the priests themselves may eat. In this way, bondmen take on a secondary membership in their master's caste because they belong to his household. Their caste status depends on their master's caste status, not on the master's capacity to exercise his privileges at any particular moment.

On the other hand, the link that attaches the bondman to his master and enables the master to provide the bondman a caste status also cuts the bondman off from all kinship ties. Thus he does not, and indeed cannot, belong to the extended family of the people Israel. This becomes clear when we discover that the Mishnah's framers do not consider slave parents to be related to their offspring or even to each other. If sages do not allow bondmen to form a nuclear family, then even more certainly they do not consider slaves to belong to the extended family of Israel. A passage concerning the institution of levirate marriage demonstrates this assertion. Levirate marriage provides for the continuance of a dead man's family. It is invoked when a married Israelite dies before any of his wives bear him offspring. The Mishnah's authorities, following Scripture (Deut. 25), consider this an undesirable situation and resolve it by requiring the dead man's brother to marry one of the widows and produce a heir his name. At issue below is whether this law applies to the offspring of bondwomen and gentile women.

A. [A dead man] who has any kind of brother, [this brother] imposes the duty of levirite marriage on his [deceased] brother's wife [if she has borne no children],

B. and he counts as [the dead man's] brother in every respect, unless he is the son of a bondwoman or a gentile woman.

C. [A man] who has any kind of son, [this son] exempts his father's wife from the duty of levirate marriage [if his father should die] ...

D. And he counts as a son in every respect, unless he is the son of a bondwoman or a gentile woman.

M. Yeb. 2:5

Sages do not consider the father to be related to his sons (C-D), or the sons as related to each other (A-B). Hence, such sons do not free the widow of a childless man from levirate marriage nor are such sons subject to levirate marriage themselves. This is because no member of a family of slaves can form a kinship tie to any other. This fact stems from the incapacity of their enslaved parents to form valid kinship ties. The fact that the father is not his son's kin shows, on the one hand, that they are not directly related. On the other hand, it also reveals that neither the father nor the son forms a kinship tie to the woman, otherwise they would be related to each other through her. Since bondmen are thus incapable of forming kinship ties to those who should constitute members of their nuclear family, they cannot possess the relationships that would make them part of the extended family of Israel.

The interstitial of the bondman's status becomes clear when we compare it with that of other categories, we can chart how the two perspectives of the caste system rank the categories of Israelite society. In this way, we can graphically pinpoint the bondman's position.

Social Category	The Extended Family of Israel: Kinship Ties	Households: Level in Caste System
Householder	Full member	Primary
Minor son	Full member	Secondary
Women	Full member	Secondary
Bondman	Non-member	Secondary
Foreigner	Non-member	Non-member

Fig. 1

As we can see clearly from the chart, the bondman straddles the boundary of Israelite society. He stands at the only point where the view of the caste system as a network of kinship ties is not coextensive with the portrayal of the caste system as made up of members of households. While the slave stands totally outside the extended family of Israel, his place in his master's household gives him a secondary status in his master's caste.

The Caste System and The Freedman

The main distinction between the bondman and the freedman is that the bondman's status is controlled by his master but that the freedman has no master to exercise such control. This change derives from the master's act of manumission. In the Mishnah's scheme, once a householder frees his slave, the status of the (now) freedman depends on own characteristics and not those of his ex-master. The immediate result is that the freedman loses the secondary status in his master's caste that allowed him to participate in that caste's privileges. Sages reveal this point in a passage comparing manumission to other means by which a bondman's tie to his master becomes severed, such as the sale of the slave or the death of the master. In these cases, the framers discuss how a priest's bondman – who, as a secondary member of the priestly caste, has the right to priestly rations – loses his caste privileges when the tie to his master becomes severed.

> A. [In the case of a priest's] bondman who was eating priestly rations and [messengers] came and said to him
>   (1) "Your master has died," or,
>   (2) "He has sold you to an Israelite [i.e., a non-priest]," or,
>   (3) "He has given you as a gift [to a non-priest]," or,
>   (4) "He has freed you." [In each case, the bondman's tie to his priestly master, and thus to the priestly caste, is severed, hence rendering him no longer qualified to eat holy food.] ...
> B. Rabbi Eliezer [holds that once the bondman's ownership has changed – whether or not the bondman knows it – he is liable for misuse of priestly rations and therefore] requires [the bondman to pay] the principal and the added fifth. [Eliezer holds that the bondman was ineligible to eat priestly rations at the time in question and so must pay.]
> C. And Rabbi Joshua exempts [the bondman from the fine of the added fifth but requires him to repay the principal]. [In other words, the bondman was not allowed to eat the priestly rations and therefore must restore the principal, but since he did not do so intentionally, Joshua rules that he does not have to pay the fine.]
>
> M. Ter. 8:1[7]

A lists different ways, including manumission, that bondmen become severed from their masters' control. At A1, a bondman's master dies, thereby removing himself as the source of control. At A2 and A3, the master cuts off his own power by transferring the bondman to the control of a second householder. Finally, at A4, the bondman has been freed by his master. In all four cases, the bondman's release from his master's power abruptly cancels the bondman's secondary caste position and therefore removes his right to eat priestly rations.

---

[7]This discussion is actually a dispute between Eliezer and Joshua concerning whether the bondman is culpable for misappropriating priestly rations. Joshua holds that the bondman is not culpable at the point of time in question. However, Joshua's position does not contradict our point here, because he agrees with Eliezer that the bondman's master still controls his status. He simply adds a further criterion, namely, that a slave's self-perception governs when the master's act takes effect to change his status. In this way, it becomes clear that to Joshua it is the bondman's intention that is important, not his act alone. Thus, only when the bondman learns of his actual situation does his status change. This point is further discussed in William S. Green, "Redactional Techniques in the Legal Traditions of Joshua B. Hananiah," in J. Neusner, ed., *Christianity, Judaism and Other Greco-Roman Cults* (Leiden: Brill, 1975) vol. 4, pp. 1-17, J. Neusner, *Eliezer ben Hyrcanus: The Tradition and the Man*, 2 vols. (Leiden: Brill, 1978-79) pp. 61-2, and Alan J. [Avery-] Peck, *The Priestly Gift in Mishnah: A Study of Tractate Terumot* (Atlanta: Scholars Press for Brown Judaic Studies, 1981) pp. 229-30.

This becomes clear in the dispute at B-C. Eliezer's position (B) is straightforward; he holds that the bondman is no longer attached to the priestly caste. Since at the moment the bondman was eating, he had no right to consume priestly rations, he must restore the amount eaten and pay a fine. Joshua (C) agrees with Eliezer in principle, but he adds a second consideration, namely, that of knowledge. Joshua holds that the bondman's ignorance of his true status affects his liability for the fine of the added fifth. In doing so, he follows a literal view of Lev. 22:14, which states "If a man [i.e., a non-priest] accidently eats holy produce" he must pay the fine. The bondman knew he was eating holy produce and so did not eat "accidently." It was his own status that he did not know. Thus his act does not fit the description in this verse. But since he did eat food to which he had no right, he must replace it. Thus, both Joshua and Eliezer agree that manumission severs the bondman from his master and the master's caste. Clearly, then, manumission releases freedmen from the control of their former masters. Since the freedman can no longer be defined by his relationship to an Israelite householder, the Mishnah's framers define him according to his own characteristics.

The main question for our study is therefore, what status does the freedman have in the caste system and what effect does the householder's control have on it? The most fundamental fact concerning the status of freedmen within this system is that they constitute a caste in and of themselves. Let us reexamine the caste list to see what place in the hierarchy of castes freedmen possess.

A. Ten castes came up [to Israel] from Babylonia:
B. (1) the priests,
   (2) the Levites,
   (3) the Israelites,
C. (4) the impaired priests [who have transgressed the rules of Lev. 21:7,13,14 and married women who are divorcees, or, in the case of a High Priest, a non-virgin],
D. (5) the proselytes [foreigners who have chosen to worship Yahweh] and ,
   (6) the freedmen,
E. (7) the *mamzers* [who are the offspring of incestuous marriages, (Lev. 20:17-21)],
F. (8) the *Netins* [foreigners who once were servants to the Israelites],
G. (9) the *shetuqs* [people who know who their mother is, but not their father (M. Qid. 4:2)] and
   (10) the foundlings [who know neither their mother nor their father (M. Qid. 4:2)].

M. Qid. 4:1

The hierarchy of the caste system is centered on the castes that possess pure, native, Israelite ancestry, and those that, for some reason, do not. The first three castes, of course, comprise those whose members possess native ancestry. The members of the fourth caste, that of defective priests, also possesses native ancestry, as we have mentioned, but they married women who possessed improper marital statuses. Momentarily passing over the proselyte and the freedman, the next caste, that of *mamzers*, consists of the offspring of parents whose union was incestuous. Next, the *netins* are the descendents of a people, not originally Israelite, who at one time agreed to act as Temple servants. The last two castes consist of people whose ancestry is not fully known. The status of the freedman in the caste system, along with the proselyte, therefore lies between those castes whose members possess pure, Israelite ancestry, and those castes whose members' ancestry is invalid, non-Israelite, or simply unknown.

The freedman's middle position stems from the primary criterion for determining rank in the caste system's hierarchy, namely, a person's ancestry. The freedman, as an ex-slave, has a distinctive characteristic in that regard, he lacks ancestry. Bondmen we recall, have all their kinship ties cancelled by their relationship to their master. The Mishnah's framers hold that, at manumission, the relationships are not restored but remain cancelled. Freedmen can of course form new kinship ties – through marriage or having children – but there is no way to restore the lost ancestry. The same point holds true for proselytes. When they enter Israelite society, all marital and ancestral ties that they once possessed are cancelled. Thus both freedmen and proselytes lack ancestry.

The case of a newly-freed bondwoman provides a clear demonstration of this point; the ex-slave remains cut off from all relationships which she might have formed during her slavery, even from ties with her offspring. By discussing whether the sons of a newly-freed slave are related to each other, the Mishnah's framers here ask whether her offspring are related to her. The central question is whether they must fulfill a commandment enjoined upon brothers, specifically, whether one son must marry the other's wife – that is, perform levirite marriage – should the other die childless. In this passage, sages raise this question as an appendage to an examination of a proselyte and her sons. Their conversion is the result of their own choice and is accomplished by undergoing a public ceremony involving sacrifice at the Temple (M. Ker 2:1). As a result of their actions, the Mishnah recognizes proselytes as bona fide Israelites who may participate in the Temple cult and may marry other Israelites. Here, the framers treat freedmen like proselytes.

A. [Concerning a] female proselyte whose sons converted with her –
B. they are not [required to undergo] the rite of removing the shoe (*'yn hwlzin*) and they are not [required to marry] the wife of their dead brother [because they are not considered to be brothers],
C. even if the first was not conceived in holiness [i.e, before conversion] but was born in holiness [i.e., after conversion] and the second was conceived and born in holiness. [That is, the first is not related to his mother because at conception she was a gentile, not a proselyte. Thus, even though the second child is related to his mother – because he was conceived after she converted – he still is not related to the other son.]
D. And the same [applies] to a bondwoman whose sons were freed with her. [The points made concerning the proselyte and her sons at B and C apply *mutatis mutandis* to the freedwoman and her offspring.]

M. Yeb. 11:2

This passage makes it clear that the freedwoman's sons, like the proselyte's sons, are not related to her. To explain this, I shall refer to A-C as if they were discussing the freedwoman, since that is how D expects us to interpret them. The two sons, at B, are not bound by any kinship tie and therefore are not required to marry the other's wife if he should die childless. That this results from the mother's enslavement is clear from C. There sages distinguish the two sons by the fact that one was conceived while his mother was still a bondwoman and the other when she is a freedwoman. She therefore has no kinship ties to the first son, but is related to the second. Since she has no kinship link to the first son, neither does the second son. Thus, the freedwoman lacks kinship ties to the offspring conceived while she was a slave, just as she lacked them while she was a bondwoman. Her freedom does not restore any relationships that she might have established while a bondwoman.

A second passage further supports the point that newly-freed slaves, by definition, have no relatives. Here sages focus on the payment of compensation after a person is injured. The victim is a pregnant woman, who was accidently injured while standing near a fight. The Mishnah's framers discuss how to determine the amount of damages and to whom it is paid. Simeon holds that women recently freed from slavery lack kinship ties and hence receive no payment.

A. And a man who intends to [strike] his fellow, but [misses and instead] strikes a [pregnant] woman and [thus causes] the offspring to come forth–
B. he must pay the value of the offspring.
C. How do they [calculate] the amount of payment?
D. They determine how much she was worth before the birth and how much she is worth after the birth.
E. Said Rabban Simeon ben Gamaliel, "If so, then after the birth, she rejoices. [Simeon's point is that this way of determining the fine will not work because the woman is worth more after the birth than before and thus there would be no fine.]
F. "Rather they determine the value of the offspring, and give [the money] to her husband.
G. "And if she has no husband, he gives it to [the dead man's] heirs.
H. "[And if she was] a bondwoman who had been freed or a proselyte, [the tortfeasor] is exempt [from paying any fine at all]."

M. B.Q. 5:4

The crux of the matter is that the compensation, however it is determined, must be paid to the injured woman's husband or to his heirs (F-G). The strict application of this principle to a newly freed slave woman results in no compensation being paid. Sages thus indicate that the freedwoman, like a female proselyte, has no male kin. That is to say, she formed no kinship ties to any males – whether offspring or consorts – while she was enslaved. Furthermore, it is clear that the framers do not hold that she has formed any links to free males. According to H, the woman was first impregnated and then freed. Thus she has not yet produced any free offspring since manumission and is unlikely to have acquired a free husband. This passage confirms that the process through which freedmen become full members of Israelite society leaves them without any kinship ties from the period prior to manumission. This lack interferes with their capacity to exercise power through relationships, but it does not prevent them from forming new relationships. Thus it is clear that the freedman, like the proselyte, lacks all kinship ties and most importantly all ancestry, from the period prior to his becoming a free Israelite.

The freedman's lack of ancestry results in his position in the middle range of the caste system. This is because it grants him, along with the proselyte, a broader selection of marital partners than any other caste. Indeed, according to the passage below, they can marry members of nine different castes. Only members of the priesthood stand beyond their grasp. These nine castes are divided into two groups which cannot marry each other – the castes of pure Israelite ancestry (except the priests) and those of defective ancestry. Sages place the caste of freedmen, along with that of proselytes, between the two groups.

A. (1) Priests, (2) Levites and (3) Israelites are permitted to marry each other (*lbw' zh bzh*).

B. (2) Levites, (3) Israelites, (4) impaired priests, (5) proselytes and (6) freedmen are permitted to marry each other.

C. (5) Proselytes, (6) freedmen, (7) *mamzers*, (8) *netins*, (9)*shetuqs*, and (10) foundlings – all of them are permitted to marry each other.

M. Qid. 4:1b

As we can see, freedmen can intermarry with the groups of castes listed at B and C, but not with the group at A. To understand why, we start with A, the list that excludes freedmen. This list comprises the original castes of the Israelite community. These are native Israelites who possess pure descent from those who made the covenant with Yahweh at Sinai. Since freedmen have no ancestry at all, the framers do not include them. By contrast, C lists those castes conforming to the opposite definition. That is, it comprises those castes of Israelite society who lack pure descent from the original Israelites. *Mamzers* possess impure Israelite ancestry, the ancestry of *shetuqs* and foundlings is unknown, while freedmen, proselytes and *netins* lack native-Israelite ancestry altogether. Despite being placed together, there are really two sub-groupings in this list. The main group consists of those castes whose ancestry sages consider invalid: *mamzers, netins, shetuqs* and foundlings. No one belonging to these castes may marry a native Israelite of pure descent. The second group consists of freedmen and proselytes. The framers do not forbid them, as we shall see, from marrying native Israelites and so they do not belong to the first group. However, they may marry members of the first group because they themselves are not native. Thus the freedman's ability to marry members of these castes stems from his lack of Israelite ancestry.

The list at B comprises the opposite of those castes whose ancestry is invalid, namely, those castes whose ancestry is not invalid. That is to say, it contains both native and non-native castes whose ancestry is not considered impure. Freedmen, like proselytes, can marry Israelites and levites. This is because their ancestry is valid, or more accurately, not invalid. Since they lack any ancestry prior to becoming a freedman, they have no invalid ancestry and hence can be treated as valid marital partners for native castes.

The same lack of ancestry that makes freedmen valid partners for Israelites makes them invalid partners for members of the priesthood (B). The framers, following Scripture, hold that priests can marry only native Israelites. There are two reasons for this. First, priests possess a higher level of holiness than other native Israelites. They are sanctified and set apart from the rest of the people Israel. As Yahweh says in Lev. 21:8, "for he [i.e., the priest] is holy to his God. Thou shalt sanctify him therefore; ... he shall be holy to thee." Thus, the framers forbid freedmen to marry priests because they do not want non-Israelite ancestry mingling directly with that of the priesthood. Second, Scripture expressly commands High Priests to select their brides only from native Israelites. The High Priest "shall take a virgin of his own people [= native Israelites] to wife" (Lev. 21:14). Since any priest may potentially become the High Priest, the framers apparently apply this Scriptural ruling to the whole priesthood. The priests' special position makes freedwomen unsuitable marriage partners for them because freedwomen lack Israelite ancestry.

Conclusion

From its interstitial position, the category of bondman derives the power to accomplish a task otherwise treated as impossible by the Mishnah's framers; it removes the differences between Israelites and gentiles and makes them the same. Specifically, the bondman comprises a category that accepts people of every ethnic background and places them into a single category that obscures all traces of their ethnic origins. A householder's control over his bondman produces the same effect on everyone, whether they derive from the family of Israel or stem from foreign origins. That control abrogates the former kinship ties of the slave and substitutes a property tie to link him to Israelite society and its caste system. This tie places the bondman within Israelite society – that is, Israelite society defined as a collection of households – but outside the kinship network of the family Israel. On the one hand, the householder's power cancels the ancestral and marital ties of an enslaved Israelite, thereby removing him from the extended family of Israel. The householder's control does not place him outside Israelite society, however, but only outside the family Israel; his status as property now links him to the Israelite community and determines his caste status. On the other hand, a slave originating outside Israelite society has radically different social ties, but his enslavement puts him in the same place occupied by enslaved Israelites. Prior to enslavement, the gentile's kinship ties bind him to a foreign society and he has no links whatsoever to Israelite society. But once enslaved, the householder's control places him in the same interstitial position; the householder's power cuts his kinship ties, places him within Israelite society defined as a collection of households, but does not bring him into the family of Israel. In this way, sages have positioned the category of bondman vis-à-vis the caste system in the one place where it can have the power to accept both Israelites and gentiles and homogenize them into identical people.

As a result of this process, the freedman lacks all kinship ties and, most importantly, all ancestry from the period prior to his becoming a free Israelite. He is not the only free category of Israelites without ancestry, however, the proselyte has also been cut off from his ancestral and other kinship ties. Despite this similarity, there are two important differences between freedmen and proselytes that cause the the Mishnah's framers to rank the proselytes higher in the caste system than freedmen. Proselytes enter Israelite society through a public process – involving a Temple sacrifice – and by their own free choice. Freedmen, by contrast, enter Israelite society through the private actions of their masters which are not subject to control by any public institution. Furthermore, the bondman never chooses to become an Israelite, he is forced to do so by his master's actions. Freedmen and proselytes are thus equivalent in that they both lack ancestry, but the framers rank proselytes higher in the caste system because of the difference in the way they lose their ancestry.

We can now explain why the caste of freedmen, along with that of proselytes, occupies the middle location in the caste system. The problem stems, we recall, from the makeup of the caste system, in which all castes of Israelite society, except for freedmen, proselytes and *netins*, either belong or claim to belong to the extended family of the people Israel. The question facing us has been to determine why the freedman occupies a middle slot and not one somewhere below people descended from native Israelites. The answer is that no ancestry is better than bad ancestry. For even though the lower castes descend from Israelites, their ancestry is somehow defective. The framers therefore place the freedman, that is, a person with non-defective ancestry, above those with invalid ancestry. The freedman's caste status, therefore, derives from his past (or his ancestors' past) as a bondman subject to the full extent of his master's control, a control which cut off all the freedman's former ancestral and kinship ties.

Chapter Eight

Todos and Rabbinic Authority in Rome

Baruch M. Bokser

The Jewish Theological Seminary of America

In assessing the role that Palestinian rabbis played in the Roman Empire in the early centuries C.E., scholars often cite a tradition found in the Tosefta and the two Talmudim regarding a *Todos* or Theudas of Rome.[1] Taking the account at face value, they generally deduce from it that rabbis wielded actual authority in that city.[2] But the recent work of archaeologists and historians who emphasize the independence of the Mediterranean Jewish communities and their diverse forms of organization and religiosity[3] causes us to question such a claim. The present paper addresses this problem. As I will demonstrate that a careful

---

[1]The name is a possible abbreviation of Theodosius, found in Greek writings and papyri; Victor A. Tcherikover, et al. *Corpus Papyrorum Judaicarum*, 3 vols. (Cambridge: 1957-64), 3:176-78; Emil Schuerer, *A History of the Jewish People in the Time of Jesus Christ*, 2d rev. Engl. ed., 2 divisions in 5 vols. (New York: 1891. Reprint. Jerusalem, n. d.) 1.2:168 n. 36; and Walter Bauer, William F. Arndt, and F. Wilbur Gingrich, *A Greek-English Lexicon of the New Testament* (Chicago: 1957), p. 360.

[2]See, e.g., Heinrich Graetz, *Divre Yime Yisrael*, ed. and trans. S. P. Rabinowitz (Warsaw: 1907), 1:467; Hermann Vogelstein and Paul Rieger, *Geschichte der Juden in Rome*, 2 vols. (Berlin: 1895-96), 2:70; Cecil Roth, *The History of the Jews of Italy* (Philadelphia: 1946), pp. 16-17; Louis Finkelstein, *The Pharisees*, 3d ed., 2 vols. (Philadelphia: 1962), 2:621; Solomon Zeitlin, "Review of Goodenough, *Jewish Symbols*," *JQR* 45 (1954):71-72; Gedalyahu Alon, *Toldot haYehudim beEres Yisrael biTequfat haMishnah vehaTalmud*, 4th prin., vol. 1 (Tel Aviv: 1967), pp. 145-46, 352 [Eng. ed. *The Jews in their Land in the Talmudic Age*, 2 vols. (Jerusalem: 1980-84), 1:231-32; 2:566]; Moshe Beer, "Theudas of Rome and Emperor Worship in the Reign of Domitian" [Hebrew], *Zion* 26 (1961):238, 239; EJ, s.v. "Theodosius of Rome" (15:1102), by Daniel Sperber; Shmuel Safrai, *The Jewish People in the First Century*, ed. idem and Menahem Stern (Philadelphia: 1974), p. 210; Menahem Stern, ed. *The World History of the Jews. The Diaspora in the Hellenistic-Roman World* [Hebrew] (Tel Aviv & Jerusalem: 1983), pp. 20, 151; cf. Saul Lieberman, "Response to the Introduction by Professor Alexander Marx" (1948), reprinted in *The Jewish Expression*, ed. Judah Goldin (New York: 1970), p. 129. E. J. Goodenough *Jewish Symbols in the Greco-Roman Period*, 13 vols. (Princeton: 1953-68), 1:14-15, a noted exception in claiming that the account indicates the lack of authority, still accepts the historicity of what is purported and relies on the corrupted b. Berakhot version.

[3]See A. T. Kraabel, "Social Systems of Six Diaspora Synagogues," in *Ancient Synagogues*, ed. Joseph Gutmann (Chico: Scholars, 1981), pp. 79-91, and references; Shaye J. D. Cohen, "Epigraphical Rabbis," *JQR* 72 (1981):1-17; and Baruch M. Bokser, "Recent Developments in the Study of Judaism. 70-200 C.E.," *The Second Century* 3 (1983):2-3, 7-10.

analysis and comparison of the several versions of the Todos tradition reveal that the earliest one, from the Tosefta, does not even testify regarding second-century rabbinic authority and that the later versions at most may illuminate the self-image of third- and fourth-century rabbis.

***

The earliest version of the Todos tradition appears in Tosefta Yom Tov (Besah) 2:15:

> Said R. Yose, Todos of Rome directed (הנהיג את) the Romans to take lambs (טלאים) on the nights of Passover and they prepare them roasted whole.
> They said to him, He in turn [thus] nearly causes them to eat holy things outside [the holy precincts], because they [the Roman Jews] call them [the lambs] *pesahim* פסחים).

(T. Yom Tov 2:15, pp. 291, lines 60-62)

To understand the reference of the passage to lambs roasted whole, let us turn to M. Besah 2:7, which the Tosefta supplements. This Mishnah (balancing M. Besah 2:6's triplet of stringent rulings by Rabban Gamaliel) lists three cases in which Rabban Gamaliel took the lenient position and sages the stringent one; the third case, treating a kid roasted whole, is the one that interests us:

> [A] Moreover [in addition to Gamaliel's three stringencies set out in M. 2:6] he said three things to be lenient:
> (1) They sweep between the couches [to gather food particles]; and
> (2) they put spices on the fire on the holiday; and
> (3) they prepare a kid roasted whole[4] (מקלס) on the nights of Passover.
> [B] And sages forbid [these actions] (אוסרין).

(M. Besah 2:7 = M. Eduyyot 3:11)

The third item deals with preparing a lamb in the manner that Ex. 12:9 prescribes for the passover sacrifice: "Do not eat any of it [i.e., the passover lamb] raw, or cooked in any way with water, but roasted – head, legs, and entrails – over the fire." As Gedalyahu Alon observed,[5] this apparently made up a post-70 attempt at preserving the details and atmosphere of the passover sacrificial meal even without the offering. But, as I have shown elsewhere, this particular act of preparing a lamb did not form part of the response to the loss of the sacrificial cult that became dominant in rabbinic circles. Rather, rabbis

---

[4]See Saul Lieberman, *Tosefta Ki-Fshutah [= TK]*, 8 vols. to date (New York: 1955), 5:957-58, and the references in Baruch M. Bokser, *The Origins of the Seder* (Berkeley: 1984), pp. 140-141 nn. 3-4.

[5]Alon, *Toldot*, pp. 164-66.

evolved an approach that not only offered a new meaning of redemption applicable to a Jewry lacking full autonomy, but also restructured the rite so that it would become independent of the sacrifice. Transcending the scriptural paradigm that made the unleavened bread and bitter herbs secondary foods to the paschal lamb, they elevated the former two, the *matzah* and *marror*, to an equal status with the offering. The early rabbis thus led Jews to believe that they could enjoy the main elements of the celebration and that they would not miss the sacrifice, for, it was asserted, the offering had comprised merely an additional element available to those in the holy precincts. Although the predominant approach did not entail substitutions for the lost sacrifice, some rabbis, judging from tannaitic sources such as Besah 2:7, believed that certain Jews initially did employ these imitative acts.[6] T. Y.T. 2:15 indicates that Todos and Roman Jewry were associated with such substitutions.

We can now return to the Tosefta's account of Todos. After providing a definition of *gedi mequlas* (גדי מקולס), T. 2:15 employs a pattern used in the Tosefta's preceding section to supplement Gamaliel's first two lenient positions. In all three instances we have: (a) a restatement of one mishnaic position; (b) a narrative account running counter to the opinion cited in (a); and (c) a response to the narrative account in (b) undermining its precedent and therefore supporting the initial position in (a). While T. 2:13-14 takes Gamaliel's two lenient positions as the point of departure, T. 2:15 leads off with an anonymous opinion that accords with sages of Mishnah *and not Gamaliel*. In this sequence, the pattern continues with the report of the practice of Todos and Roman Jews, which in effect does not accord with the preceding opinion; and then, third, a response to discount the precedent of Todos and to validate the original statement, thus supporting (a) against (b). The Tosefta reads:

[A] What is a *gedi mequlas?* ...
[B] They prepare a kid roasted whole *(gedi mequlas)* on [even the nights of] the first day of the Festival [Sukkot] and on [even the nights of] the last day of Passover, [they prepare] a calf roasted whole *(egel mequlas* עגל מקולס*)* [even on the nights of] the first day of Passover but not a kid roasted whole *(gedi mequlas)*. [Because the calf never served as a passover offering, using the calf would not represent an imitative act of the sacrifice. Similarly, because the passover offering was eaten Passover night, eating it roasted whole *(mequlas)* at other times, when there is no synchronization with the passover offering, would be unobjectionable.]
[C] Said R. Yose, Todos of Rome directed (הנהיג את) the Romans to take lambs (טלאים) on the nights of Passover and they prepare them roasted whole.
[D] They said to him, He in turn [thus] nearly causes them to eat holy things outside [the holy precincts],

---

[6]See Bokser, *Origins*, pp. 102-3.

[E] because they [the Roman Jews] call them [the lambs] *pesahim* (פסחים).

(T. Yom Tov 2:15, pp. 290-91, lines 56-62)

Yose, an early second-century master, in C offers evidence for a position that differs with B's prohibition of a kid roasted whole on Passover evening. Since Gamaliel in the Mishnah teaches that one may prepare a *gedi mequlas,* C in effect adduces in the practice of Roman Jews a precedent for Gamaliel. In using Todos as the example, it depicts him as a leader who had an impact on the ritual life of Roman Jews. Since he lacks the title Rabbi and is placed in Rome, we should, however, assume that he was not a member of the rabbinic group.[7] D-E, by referring to the established rule that prohibits eating holy things outside the holy precincts, rejects that precedent.[8]

Let me highlight the point that D, using the phrase, "[they] said to him," which does not identify the subject, has "sages," the conventionally assumed referent of this phrase, address the previous speaker, here *Yose,* who is told that his precedent is inappropriate. In the two supplements to the preceding two mishnaic cases, this phrase likewise introduces the response to the citation of the precedents. Hence we should not follow the lead of many writers in imposing on the Tosefta a later understanding, rendering the clause on the basis of the gemarot's construction, *as if the unstated sages were speaking to Todos.*[9] Rather we should follow the standard mishnaic and toseftan usage, as exemplified in T. Megillah 2:4:

[A] If one read it [the Megillah] at night, one did not fulfill one's obligation.

[B] Said R. Yose, (מעשה:) there was a case in which R. Yohanan ben Nuri read it in Sepphoris at night.

[C] They said to him, The time of an emergency is not proof.[10]

---

[7]Roman epigraphical and other sources mention diverse functionaries but not a rabbi; Harry J. Leon, *The Jews of Ancient Rome* (Philadelphia: 1960), pp. 167-94; Cohen, especially p. 15, n. 27.

[8]See, e.g. M. Zevahim 2:2, 5, ch. 5, especially 5:8 (and Albeck, *Shisha Sidre Mishnah,* 6 vols. [Jerusalem: 1954-59], 5:356); T. Zevahim 2:1 (p. 481, ls. 14-24); and M. Hullin 6:2. On the phrase QRWB L-, see T. Yevamot 6:9, and Sifra*Shemini* 1.2 (p. 47a).

[9]See note 2 above. Notable exceptions are C. J. Kasowski, *Thesaurus Thosephthae,* 6 vols. (Jerusalem: 1932-61), 1:404, and S. S. Margaliot, *haSofeh* 7 (1923):213-14 n.4, though it is unclear how they would assess this version historically. Although Gideon Leibson, "Determining Factors in Herem and Nidui During the Tannaitic and Amoraic Periods" [Hebrew], in *Shenaton ha-Mishpat ha-Ivri* 2 (1975):307-308, recognizes that the two Talmudim add to the Tosefta, he still assumes that rabbis threatened Todos.

[10]Page 349, lines 7-8. See T. Y.T. 2:13-14, lines 52 and 56, which respond to the dicta undermining Gamaliel's two lenient positions; and the instances opening with the term (מעשה), in the Mishnah: Eruvin 8:7; Sukkah 2:7, 3:8; Nedarim 6:6; Sanhedrin 7:2. And in the Tosefta: T. Terumot 1:1, especially 2:13, 3:18; Shevi'it 4:4; Shabbat 13:9; Eruvin 5:24; Sukkah 1:1, especially 1:7, 2:9-10; especially Yevamot 14:6; Sanhedrin 2:8; Ohalot 2:6; Nedarim 4:17, 8:5.

T. Y.T. 2:15D, therefore, comprises a retort to Yose, stating that the precedent of Roman Jewry is inappropriate because it entailed the negative side effect of a near desecration. E explains how that unwanted side-effect emerged, to wit, it arose because the Romans refer to the non-sacrificial substitute with the name of the offering, *pesahim*.[11]

Consequently, as far as the Tosefta was concerned, Todos personally was not addressed but his action became the subject of rabbinic discussion. By presenting Yose's account of Todos after an anonymous opposing position, the Tosefta suggests that a disagreement in the Mishnah reflects divergent practices. The Tosefta, like the Mishnah, however, downplays the imitative substitutions for the lamb. T. Y.T. 2:15D-E (the response to the citation of the Todos precedent) does so by claiming that Gamaliel's option is religiously counter-productive or dangerous, and M. Besah 2:7 does so by labelling Gamaliel's disputant as "sages." But both sources elsewhere refer to people following that practice and a text such as M. Pesahim 7:2 reports that Gamaliel himself had a kid roasted whole prepared at most only slightly at variance from the standard *mequlas* method. Hence, despite the questioning of Todos's practice, Yose, who associated Todos's action with the imitative approach, may indeed have believed that it comprised a viable custom.[12]

The versions of the Todos tradition in the Palestinian and Babylonian Talmudim, though not identical, diverge from the Tosefta in an important way. We first examine the PT version, found in Pesahim 7:1 (34a), Besah 2:7 (61c), and Moed Qatan 3:1 (81d).[13] The fact that the PT's Todos tradition may represent a distinct version and not just a corrupted citation of one part of an earlier, larger passage may be signalled by the y. text itself. After presenting as a single unit a very close analogue to T.2:15A-B's definition of *gedi mequlas* and the opinion prohibiting a person from preparing an exact imitation of the *gedi mequlas* on the first night of Passover, y. Pesahim and Besah then continue with the analogue to T. 2:15C, that is, Yose's report, but place before it the term

---

[11] See Lieberman, *TK*, 5:959, which notes that this formulation fits Simeon's version of the beraita, mentioned on b. Pes. 53b; and David Halivni, *Meqorot uMesorot*, 4 vols. to date (1:Tel Aviv, 1968; 2 4 Jerusalem, 1975), to Pes. 53a, pp. 426-29.

[12] See R. Samuel b. Joseph Strashun (RSS), annotations to b. Pes. 74 and Besah 23a; Samuel Safrai, "He'erot Historiyot leMishnah Pesahim Pereq Asiri," in *Bible and Jewish History. Studies in Dedication to the Memory of Jacob Levir*, ed. Benjamin Uffenheimer (Tel Aviv, 1971), pp. 299-302, especially n. 19; Halivni to Besah 21b, pp. 308-9 n. 2; especially Bokser, *Origins*, pp. 101-106. On the continued power of Temple symbolism in the diaspora, cf. Kraabel, p. 86, and the story cited by Lieberman, "Response," p. 130.

[13] Found in L MS and, for the Pesahim version, Samuel Loewinger, "New Fragments from the Yerushalmi Pesahim ch. 5-7," in *Alexander Marx Jubille Volume*, ed. Saul Lieberman [New York: 1950], Hebrew Section: 264-65 (on which see Saul Lieberman, "The New Fragments from the Yerushalmi," in ibid., p. 285); idem, *Hayerushalmi Kiphshuto [=YK]* (Jerusalem: 1934), p. 479, and TK, 5:957-59. On the sugya's original location, see Israel Francus, ed., *Talmud Yerushalmi Massekhet Besah, im perush Eleazar Azikri* (New York: 1967), p. 36; and below.

TNY, which indicates that the following material circulated as a separate source. That this material could circulate by itself is likewise attested by the y. M.Q.'s sugya, which totally lacks an analogue to A-B and thus opens with Yose's report. Let us now turn to this text:

> [A'-B' = a definition of *gedi mequlas* and the prohibition on eating thereof on the first night of passover = y. Pesahim and Besah.]
>
> [C'] It is taught (תני), *Said R. Yose, Todos of Rome directed the Romans that they should eat kids roasted whole* (gediim mequlasim) *on the nights of Passover.*
>
> [D'] Sages sent and said to him, Were you not Todos, would we not put you under a ban?
>
> [E'] [Providing an interpretation of Todos' name which explains why Todos was respected:] What does Todos mean?
> Said R. Hananiah,[14] He would send maintenance (פרנסתהין)[15] for rabbis.
>
> [F'.1] [A continuation of D' which has been expanded by F.2:][16] Do you not end up bringing the public (הרבים) *to eat holy things outside [the holy precincts]?*
>
> [F'.2] And whoever brings the public to eat holy things outside [the holy precincts] should be put under a ban.

While C', Yose's report, follows the Tosefta version, D', the response to it, differs considerably. Instead of *unnamed* individuals speaking to Yose to invalidate the cited precedent, "sages" send a message to Todos, as if they are in contact with him, could be expected to impose their will on him, and are able to put him under a ban. By explaining the etymology of Todos's name with a play on words that suggests Todos, rather than being a divine gift, is a giver of divine gifts, E' attributes to Todos a trait with which amoraim tried to inculcate the public so as to raise support for their students, a theme quite fitting in the third century but not in the late first or early second century.[17] F adds an explanation for the ban ("Do you not ...") paralleling E of Tosefta's explanation that Todos' act had proved problematic because people had called the animals *pesahim*. That the language of F'.1 may be shaped by the Yerushalmi and that F'.2, the clarification for the explanation, "and whoever...," may comprise the gemara's expansion of the tradition, is reflected in the use of these formulations in the y. M.Q.'s parallel. There, Yose's report, which as we already noted opens the pericope, appears as the third in a series of accounts of people meriting a ban and

---

[14]The Loewinger fragment reads "Haninah," either a first generation amora or else a scribal variant for "Hananiah," a fifth-generation amora; see the references in Baruch M. Bokser, *Post Mishnaic Judaism in Transition* (Chico: Scholars, 1980), p. 177 n. 435.

[15]See Targum to Job 38:39, Paul Lagarde ed., p. 115.

[16]Z. W. Rabinovitz, *Sha'are Torath Eretz Israel* (Jerusalem: 1940), p. 228.

[17]See Reuven Kimmelman, "R. Yohanan and the Rabbinic Class" [Hebrew], *Shenaton ha-Mishpat ha-Ivri* 9-10 (1983): 329 n. 4; and esp. Israel Ben Shalom, "A Favorite Saying of the Rabbis in Jabneh" [Hebrew], in *Milet* [Everyman's University Studies in Jewish History and Culture] 2 (1985):151-69, esp. 161-62.

each ends with a line like F', "do you not ..." ([ה]נמצאת[ה] לא), along with a clarification for the explanation, "and whoever ..." (שכל...).[18] In appreciating how the phrasing points to the tradition's redaction into the larger sugya, we further understand PT's use of the term *harabim* (הרבים), in F', instead of the more limited "Romans" – as above in Yose's report in C' – or the pronoun, "them," as in the Tosefta's reference.

Comparing the PT with the Tosefta reveals a shift in the image of Todos, who now appears to have been reprimanded by rabbis. Before discussing the import of this divergent perspective on Todos, let us look at the BT version, found in Besah 23a, Pesahim 53a-b, and Berakhot 19a. We quote from Besah:

> [1] It was taught (תניא), R. Yose says [MSS + parallels: *"Said R. Yose"*], *Todos of Rome directed the Romans to eat a kid roasted whole on the nights of Passover.*
> [2] They sent to him, Were you not Todos, we would decree a ban on you,
> [3] because you *cause* (the children of)[19] *Israel to eat holy things outside [the holy precincts].*[20]

Again we find Yose's report of Todos and the response thereto circulating as a separate tradition, distinct from an analogue to Tosefta's definition of *mequlas* and the application of the prohibition of *mequlas* to only a kid and to only Passover night (T. Y.T. 2:15A-B). The explanation of Todos' character, not interpolated into the b. beraita, as it had been in the PT, appears as part of a separate pericope on b. Pesahim 53b after an analysis of the beraita and it, like the PT, suggests that Todos assisted rabbis. Except for lexicographical variations, the b. and y. versions differ in only one major point. BT, lacking a clarification for the explanation of the problematic aspect of Todos's behavior, simply presents (in clause 3) the principle that makes Todos's behavior objectionable. On the other hand, like the PT, it formulates the response as a

---

[18]Cf. Leibson, p. 308 n. 80.

[19]BNY = in Besah's printed edition but missing in MSS; Raphaelo Rabbinovicz, *Diqduqe Sofrim [= DS]*, 12 vols. (Reprint. New York: 1960), Besah, p. 55 n. 10; Vatican MS 134, *(Manuscripts of the Babylonian Talmud in the Collection of the Vatican Library:* Series A. 2:172). To Pesahim: Sassoon MS 594 (published by Valmadonna Trust Library [London: 1984]); Vatican MSS 109, 125; Munich 6; JTS MSS R 1623, R 1608.

[20]A gloss adds: "[Actual] holy things outside [the holy precincts] you might think? Rather say, 'That which is similar to holy things.'" While found in Besah (including Vatican MS 134, [vol. 2:172]), the clause is less textually secure in the parallels. In Berakhot, it is missing in some MSS and clearly a gloss (with variations in wording) added in other readings; DS 91:5, to which add the *Babylonian Talmud Codex Florence*. Florence National Library II I 7-9, 3 vols. (Jerusalem: 1972), 1: 49, where the gloss is visible on the margin. On Pesahim, see: *DS* 153:8, to which add Columbia MS X893-T14 and JTS 1623, which lack the clause but, in line 3, have the formulation "because you *nearly* cause ... "; the other MSS in the previous note, in which the gloss is found only in MSS JTS 1608 and Sassoon 594; and Halivni, Pesahim, p. 427 n. 3.

direct address to Todos and uses for the object not "them" or "the Romans" [i.e.,
Roman Jews] but a more general term, here "Israel."

* * *

Let us now compare the several versions.

Tosefta	PT	BT
A. What is ...	A'. ..... [Pes + Bes]	
B. They prepare ... [the night of] the first day of Passover but not a kid roasted whole.	B'. ..... [Pes + Bes]	
C. Said R. Yose, Todos of Rome directed the Romans to take lambs on the nights of Passover and they prepare them roasted whole.	C'. TNY Said R. Yose, Todos of Rome directed the Romans that they should eat kids roasted whole on the nights of Passover.	1. TNY' Said R. Yose, Todos of Rome directed the Romans to eat a kid roasted whole on the nights of Passover.
D. They said to him, He in turn nearly causes them to eat holy things outside,	D'. Sages sent & said to him, Were you not Todos, would we not put you under a ban? E'. [Interpreting Todos's name]	2. They sent to him, Were you not Todos, we would decree a ban on you,
E. because they call them pesahim.	F'.1.Do you not end up bringing the public to eat holy things outside?	3. because you cause Israel to eat holy things outside.
	F'.2. And whoever brings the public to eat holy things outside should be put under a ban.	

As seen in the attached chart, the PT and BT agree with each other in:
structure; the initial report of Todos's action; the attribution of the retort; and
the nature of the retort. But while the Talmudim share with the Tosefta (a) the
similar overall structure and (b) the basic rationale for the retort (causing the
eating of holy things outside, בחוץ, F.1 in PT, and 3 in BT), they differ with the
Tosefta in: (a) the wording of the attribution ("they sent" (שלחו) or "sent and
said" instead of "they said"); (b) the person addressed; and (c) the content of the
first part of the response (D' in PT, and 2 in BT).[21] In simple terms, what has

---

[21]The variation between "causing them nearly (קרוב) to eat holy things" of Tosefta and "causing
them to eat holy things" of PT and BT (except for two MSS cited above, which, if not corrupt,
may incorporate into the tradition a gloss that other texts present after the tradition) may
reflect the variation which the gemara projected between Simeon's and Yose's versions
regarding what had occurred. See b. Pes. 53a-b, and Halivni, pp. 426-29. All our preserved
versions notably, however, are attributed to Yose!

changed is that sages address Todos, and what has been *added* is that sages said that Todos deserves to be put under the ban.   Modern scholarly accounts obviously have followed the amoraic sources which center on Todos being called to task, despite the fact that this feature is lacking in the Tosefta.

While theoretically one might hold that both the Tosefta and the Talmudic accounts represent two early versions,[22] I believe the Talmudim's version is a revision of the Tosefta account and we should not impose the former on our understanding of Todos' role. Four factors support this claim. The first, a literary consideration, is suggested by the textual history of the b. Berakhot 19a sugya. As noted by Raphaelo Rabbinovicz and subsequent critical readers,[23] the current printed editions contain a correction in the attribution as to who sent word to Todos. Instead of "sages," it has "Simeon ben Shetah," a chronological impossibility if we believe Todos lived in the first or second century C.E. But early printed editions and MSS correctly have "sages," the reading in the Pesahim and Besah parallels.[24] The corruption undoubtedly arose under the impact of the preceding account of Honi which forms part of a sugya dealing with cases in which masters deserve to be put under the ban. The BT cites M. Taanit 3:8's account of Simeon ben Shetah castigating Honi with the very words associated with the sages' response to Todos: "were you not Honi, I would decree a ban against you" (אלמלא חוני אתה עליך נדוי). This similarity may have caused the Todos tradition to become contaminated by the preceding pericope. I therefore submit that the mention of *niddui* itself in the Todos tradition may have been generated by the Honi material. Significantly, the design of this b. Berakhot sugya is analogous to that of the y. M.Q. version. Y. M.Q. deals with similar instances of masters who deserved excommunication. In fact it cites M. Taanit's Honi tradition with a revision explaining why Honi deserved to be put under the ban, i.e., because Honi had caused potential harm that would have caused the profanation of God's name.[25] This concluding portion, as mentioned above, comprises a structure employed in the Honi, Todos, and a third tradition to explain the error and to set out the rationale justifying the ban. As we concluded above, by supplying an identical structure for the explanation and the

---

[22]See the aforementioned Bavli claim that Yose and Simeon taught two versions of this text. A question on b. Pes. 53b may attest that the Tosefta version in fact also circulated in Babylonia. Cf. Halivni, pp. 426-27 n. 2.

[23]Rabbinovicz, *DS*, 91:4; Margaliot, p. 213; Alon, *Toldot*, 1:146; Wilhelm Bacher, *Aggadot haTannaim* (Tel Aviv: 1928), 2.2:210 n. 1; Mordechai Vogelmann, *"Todos ish Romi," Scritti in Memoria di Sally Mayer* (Jerusalem: 1956), p. 197; esp. Beer, p. 239; Leibson, p. 308 n. 80; Halivni, pp. 426-27 n. 2; cf. Jacob Neusner, *The Rabbinic Traditions about the Pharisees before 70*, 3 vols. (Leiden: 1971), 1:104.

[24]The printed edition also has "Yosef" instead of "Yose," the reading found in the MSS and all texts of Pesahim and Besah, an error which probably was produced by an incorrect resolution of the abbreviation R"Y; cf. Leibson.

[25]See W. S. Green, "Palestinian Holy Men: Charismatic Leadership and Rabbinic Tradition," *ANRW* 19.1 (1979), 2:637.

clarification for the explanation, the three traditions have been redacted together. Consequently, and this is the key, both the BT and PT circles that transmitted the Todos tradition, associated that tradition with cases in which individuals were believed to have violated Pharisaic or rabbinic authority. In both we also have R. Yehoshua ben Levi's comment that there are twenty-four instances of a ban. From the literary point of view, it is therefore possible that the gemarot's version of the tradition, especially the mention of the ban, may have been modeled after M. Taanit's account of Honi.

But we also have three historical factors that make it understandable how amoraim might claim that Todos deserved and was subject to the punishment of excommunication. The first factor is the waning popularity of the ideas Todos had supposedly advocated. While both gemarot, like the Tosefta, speak of causing others to "eat" or "nearly eat holy things outside the holy precincts," amoraic sources take a more stringent view that condemns *even appearing* to eat holy things outside the holy areas, including eating things merely resembling the holy.[26] Although some amoraim did accept *symbolic* substitutions for the passover offering, they avoided substitutions that were exact duplicates as well as anything that would suggest that a substitute was being used. Thus some amoraic circles restricted roasting any meat on Passover eve, thereby transforming M. Pesahim 4:4's toleration of this practice in those communities that had been accustomed to eat roasted meat other than lambs.[27] Accordingly, in amoraic eyes Todos's action seemed all the more outlandish.

The second historical factor is what appears to be an increasing intolerance of divergent customs, which may stem from the rabbis' perception that it was now possible more openly to express their true convictions regarding such variations.[28] We discern this development not only by recognizing, as noted above, that the gemara to M. Pesahim 4:4, which mentions the custom of certain locales to eat roasted meat on Passover night, considerably restricts the mishnaic rule, but also by comparing all of M. Pesahim chapter 4 with its companion gemarot. The Mishnah comments on what it considers valid customs and closes with reference to six practices that the Jerichoites followed, three of which the "sages" did not protest (לא מיחו בידם), and three of which they did protest.[29] This may suggest the general posture imagined by those responsible for the Mishnah. Rabbis could express their displeasure and at times protest; meanwhile, they ruled on what was and what was not acceptable. But

---

[26]Safrai, p. 300, made this important observation. Cf. Halivni, p. 427 nn. 7-8.

[27]See b. Pes. 53a and 116b; and y. Pes. 4:4, 31a, and *YK* ad loc.

[28]Prof. David Goodblatt, in a personal letter, additionally suggests that amoraic attitudes to divergent customs may have reflected ideological convictions while earlier Patriarchal circles responsible for the Mishnah may have followed a more latitudinarian approach to keep the peace.

[29]N.b., T. Pes. 4:19 speaks of not only protesting but also expressing displeasure. We do not consider the postmishnaic addition to the text commonly printed as M. Pes. 4:8.

the gemarot contain numerous pericopae in which sages project themselves as arbiters of what comprises a proper custom and in which they scrutinize the behavior of rabbis and nonrabbis; the gemara emphasizes how failure to listen to the rabbinic ruling or the proper local custom would be inauspicious *(siman ra),* causing disastrous results, or would lead to excommunication. While BT to 4:1 treats this somewhat more extensively than y. 4:1, the PT reflects this perspective as well, not only recording the curse that a certain rabbi Ammi imposed on certain people for following a certain custom but also in relating the subject of diverse customs to the larger issue of *bal titgodedu,* causing divisions in Israel.[30]

The third historical consideration centers on the divergent uses of the *niddui* in tannaitic and amoraic sources. As scholars have observed, tannaitic sources, using the term *niddui* (נדוי) (and *herem* (חרם)) to denote a temporary excommunication, in general refer to the imposition of a ban only in limited cases where it apparently is designed to enforce tannaitic authority and order within the Pharisaic or rabbinic group, in particular relating to a minority opinion vis-a-vis the majority rule. Amoraic authorities represented in the BT and PT, though possibly differing over details of application of the the ban and over nuances of terminology such as *niddui* and especially the Aramaic *shamta,* further develop the notion of excommunication and extend its use to those outside rabbinic circles, in particular to force people to abide by a rabbinic decision.[31] Whether or not people actually followed rabbinic bans, amoraic sources would have us believe that rabbis were successful in forcing people to abide by a rabbinic decision. As noted in different ways by Peter Brown and Shalom Albeck, however, the effectiveness of a ban ultimately depended on the cooperation of the community members in withdrawing themselves from the banned person. Hence, a first- or early second-century Todos does not seem to be a likely candidate for such a ban. But in amoraic times it was obviously

---

[30]Cf. Y. D. Gilat, *"Lo titgodedu," BIA* 18-19 (1981):79-98.

[31]See *EJ,* s.v. "Herem" (8:343-55), by Moshe Greenberg and Haim H. Cohn; and Lawrence H. Schiffman, *Sectarian Law in the Dead Sea Scrolls* (Chico: Scholars, 1983), pp. 168-73, especially 169. Cf. Hugo Mantel, *Studies in the History of the Sanhedrin* (Cambridge: 1965), pp. 225-27; Lee Levine, "The Jewish Patriarch (Nasi) in Third-Century Palestine," *ANRW* 2.19 (1979) 2:665; especially Leibson, who recognizes the overall shift but in assuming the historicity of the several accounts and in not recognizing (in n. 76) the amoraic increased intolerance to even appearing to eat holy things, imposes an explanation on the threatened ban which is not hinted at in the text; and idem, "The Ban and Those Under It: Tannaitic and Amoraic Perspectives," *Shenaton ha-Mishpat ha-Ivri* 6-7 (1979-80):177-202, which presents an analytical comparison of Babylonian and Palestinian notions of the ban. For models how critically and historically to assess the evidence, see David Goodblatt, "The Story of the Plot Against R. Simeon b. Gamaliel II" [Hebrew], *Zion* 49 (1984):349-74, especially p. 359; Green, especially pp. 636-37 (and n. 69); and Anthony J. Saldarini, "The Adoption of a Dissident: Akabya ben Mahaleleel in Rabbinic Tradition,"*JJS* 33 (1982):547-56.

believed or imagined that a person like Todos had been a member of the rabbinic group or subservient to it or, like all Jews, under its influence and authority.[32]

I therefore propose that we have a *literary model* suggesting a new way of looking at Todos and a *historical context* making people receptive to that new perspective. As the rabbinic group increased in size and influence or desired influence, it could imagine that it had wielded a stick in earlier days. Hence, just as it could cast a Roman Jewish leader such as Todos as the model of the rich community official who supports the rabbis, so it could make him serve as a warning that such an individual should not exhibit too much independence. To be sure, all the sources assume that Todos addressed religious issues and did not represent an alternative power base competing with the rabbis. But while those whom the Tosefta projects as responding to Yose can simply discount the precedent of Todos' practice – whether because they did not perceive Todos as totally under rabbinic authority or because variations were tolerated to a greater degree, in particular regarding the kind of practice which he advocated – amoraic circles prefer to speak of sages actually confronting Todos! Moreover, it is possible that the new image of Todos may be correlated with amoraic wishful thinking regarding rich community leaders in Palestine, who in their own eyes may have been religiously sensitive and guided by positive motives, but who were yet criticized by rabbis for lack of commitment to the Torah.[33]

Finally, our suggestion that a revision has taken place in the depiction of Todos should not be considered unusual. First, the transformation may be part of a larger pattern in which amoraic sources describe masters responding to opposing opinions in a manner significantly more confrontational than do tannaitic accounts of such interchanges.[34] Second, b. Berakhot 19a may actually mention the point that tannaitic disputes between an individual and the majority may later have been recast so as to portray the individual as liable to the ban for adhering to a position opposed by the majority. Clarifying how R. Yehoshua ben Levi was able to find twenty-four cases of the ban in the Mishnah but R. Eleazar only three cases, the Bavli states, "R. Yehoshua ben Levi compares one

---

[32]Peter Brown, "The Rise and Function of the Holy Man in Late Antiquity,"*JRS* 61 (1972):80-101; and Shalom Albeck, *Law Courts in Talmudic Times* [Hebrew] (Ramat Gan: 1980), pp. 23-33. See in general: Martin Goodman,*State and Society in Roman Galilee* (Totowa, NJ, 1983); Jacob Neusner, *History of the Jews in Babylonia*, 5 vols. (Leiden: 1966-70); and idem, *Judaism in Society* (Chicago: 1983), pp. 115-97.

[33]Gedalyahu Alon, "Those Appointed for Money," in idem, *Jews, Judaism and the Classical World* (Jerusalem: 1977), pp. 374-457, identifies such individuals.

[34]See, e.g., the R. Aqiba and R. Yohanan ben Nuri dispute in M. Bekhorot 6:6, which T. Bekhorot 4:8 expands with a comment by R. Yohanan, and which, as David Pardo (in *Hasde David* to *Qodashim* [Reprint. Jerusalem: 1970], p. 74d) observes, b. Bekhorot 40a recasts by supplying Aqiba, as well, with a comment and by making the two additions into a confrontational "debate." Cf. Baruch M. Bokser, "Wonder-Working and the Rabbinic Tradition," *JSJPHRP* 16 (1985): 42-92; and Joel Gereboff, "To Speak, How to Speak, and When Not to Speak," *Semeia* 34 (1985):29-51, and Jack Lightstone, "When Speech is No Speech," ibid., pp. 53-57.

thing to another" (מדמה מילחא למילחא). On this Rashi explains: "Wherever he saw in the Mishnah that an individual disputes with the majority a great dispute or that one of the sages speaks harshly against his superior, he says, 'Here *niddui* was appropriate.'"

We can now summarize our findings. The Todos tradition treats the proper response to the destruction of the foundations for the Holiday of the Passover Offering. According to tannaitic sources, Todos and Gamaliel share in employing imitative acts through which a person replaces and continues what has been lost. In this approach, diaspora and Palestinian Jewry alike would have expressed their high regard for Temple symbolism and institutions. Another approach aimed at restructuring the rite so as to emphasize extra-sacrificial acts that were to be independent of the sacrifice. We cannot know to what degree the latter may have originally been conceived of as a supplement to the former; indeed some tannaitic sources suggest that Gamaliel himself may have advocated an early version of the latter as well. But as the restructuring approach developed and became dominant in the early rabbinic period, it became antipathetic to blind imitation of cultic practices. Enabling people to accept such an approach as religiously viable and meaningful required time and creative effort, an early stage of which may be reflected in the Mishnah. Rabbis then made up a rather small elite group that had little authority outside its own ranks and could only express its displeasure at what it opposed. As the restructuring gained in popularity, it was supplemented – in amoraic times – by symbolic reminders of the lost cultic features. Such symbols by their nature consciously acknowledge that the practice that is performed represents but does not comprise the original protocol. Hence, in moving further away from blind substitutions and in seeing themselves addressing larger numbers of Jews, rabbis took greater steps to distinguish between the reminders and the original – now lost – ritual objects and actions. In not wanting to vitiate the restructured celebration with imitations of what could not be, they even tried to restrict the roasting of any meat, not merely the lambs.

Consequently, the several rabbinic sources employ accounts of Todos for divergent purposes. Projected as a leader of late first- or early second-century Roman Jews, a mid second-century master could still consider his action viable. While late second-century circles believed that he acted independently of rabbis and not in accord with the emerging dominant approach to the loss of the temple cult, third- and fourth-century circles assumed that he had been under rabbinic supervision (and a supporter of rabbis) and thus could be reprimanded by rabbinic authorities. Although the later versions illuminate trends in post-mishnaic Judaism, the earliest version accords with Greco-Roman literary and epigraphical sources that indicate that tannaitic rabbis exerted little, if any, significant or sustained authority in Rome.[35]

---

[35]For their comments on this study, I thank Professor David Goodblatt, who read an earlier version of the paper, and those who heard its oral presentation at the Jewish Theological Seminary of America, February 27, 1986.

Chapter Nine

Constantine, Shapur II and The Jewish-Christian Confrontation in Fourth Century Iran

Jacob Neusner

Brown University

In the fourth century, beginning with the legalization of Christianity by Constantine in 312 and ending with the recognition of Christianity as the established religion of the Roman Empire in the Theodosian Code of 387, Christianity reached that position of political and cultural dominance that it would enjoy until the twentieth. In that same fourth century, in response to the triumph of Christianity in the Roman Empire, Judaism as shaped by sages in the Land of Israel defined its doctrines of history, Messiah, and who is Israel. Those doctrines successfully countered the challenge of Christianity from then to the point at which Christianity lost its status as self-evident truth in the West. So the age of Constantine was marked by the interplay of issues as defined in the same way by Judaism and Christianity. What we shall see in the present instance is that, on the Iranian side of the frontier, in the empire of Shapur II (309-379), the confrontation between Judaism and Christianity in the aftermath of the legalization of Christianity in Rome went forward along precisely the lines that guided discourse within Rome itself. When we recall that Constantine had written to Shapur II and had declared himself the protector of Christians within the Sasanian empire, we understand why the Christian party to the debate, represented by Aphrahat, should have taken his place comfortably within the position outlined on the Roman side of the frontier.

Constantine told Shapur II that it is with "joy" that he heard "tidings so in accordance with my desire, that the fairest districts of Persia are filled with those men on whose behalf alone I am at present speaking, I mean the Christians. I pray therefore that both you and they may enjoy prosperity, and that your blessings and theirs may be in equal measure...I commend these persons to your protection....Cherish them with your wonted humanity...."[1] No wonder, then, that from the viewpoint of Christians in Iran, events in Rome were seen to mark that caesura in time, that validation of the faith, that Christians in Rome itself perceived. In Homily 23, Aphrahat, for his part, despairs of seeing an Iranian Constantine. Seeing Rome as Esau, Aphrahat identified that kingdom with Jesus: "The kingedom of the children of Esau is being kept safe for its giver, doubt not about it, that that kingdom will not be conquered. For a mighty champion whose name is Jesus shall come with power, and bearing as his armor all the power of the kingdom...." When in 337 Shapur II decreed that the Christians pay double the normal head tax, it marked the beginning of a systematic persecution of Christians, which lasted for nearly a half century.

In our setting, we ask whether living in Iran, rather than in Rome, persuaded Aphrahat that the issues separating Judaism from Christianity were to be read in some way other than that of Christian theologians represented, in the time of Constantine, by Eusebius, who found in the conversion of the emperor, then the Roman state, proof for the validity of Christianity. The answer, as we shall now see, is negative. While in Iran, Aphrahat saw things precisely as did his counterparts in Rome, and that is shown, as I shall now demonstrate, by his framing of the issues in the received terms of Christianity in Rome, without the slightest revision of matters to accommodate the condition of Christianity in Iran. Since, when Aphrahat took up other questions than those in the Judaic-Christian confrontation, he found reason to revise the received viewpoint to accommodate the facts of his own time and place, the persistence of the received formulation of the debate becomes suggestive. Specifically, it tells us that once matters had reached theological definition, political circumstances would not greatly affect the framing of issues. Where Aphrahat stood in a line beginning, as we shall see, with Paul, there he repeated, in Iran, viewpoints far more pertinent to the Christian situation in now-Christian Rome than in anti-Christian Zoroastrian Iran.

I

The Issues of the Confrontation in the Age of Constantine and Shapur II

We find in the Judaism of the sages who redacted the principal documents of Judaism that reached closure in the century beyond the conversion of Constantine both a doctrine and an apologetic remarkably relevant to the issues presented to Christianity and Judaism by the crisis of Christianity's worldly triumph. A shared program brought the two religions into protracted confrontation on an

---

[1]A bibliography is given at the end of this article. The reference at hand derives from the following: Trans. Ernest Cushing Richardson in *Select Library of Nicene and Post-nicene Fathers. Second Series* (Grand Rapids: Reprint 1961), 1:543-544; see also Georg Bert, *Aphrahat's des persischen Weisen Homilien* (Lepizig: 1888), pp. 69-88, and my *History of the Jews in Babylonia* (Leiden: 1969) 4:21-2.

intersecting set of questions, a struggle that has continued until our own time – originated in the fact that, to begin with, both religions agreed on almost everything that mattered. They differed on little, so made much of that little. Scripture taught them both that vast changes in the affairs of empires came about because of God's will. History proved principles of theology. In that same Torah prophets promised the coming of the Messiah, who would bring salvation. Who was, and is, that Messiah, and how shall we know? And that same Torah addressed a particular people, Israel, promising that people the expression of God's favor and love. But who is Israel, and who is not Israel? In this way Scripture defined the categories shared in common, enabling Judaism and Christianity to engage, if not in dialogue, then in two monologues on the same topics. The terms of this confrontation continued for centuries because the conditions that precipitated it, – the rise to political dominance of Christianity and the subordination of Judaism – remained constant for fifteen hundred years.

We know the fourth century as the decisive age in the beginning of the West as Christian. But to people of the time, the outcome uncertain. The vigorous repression of paganism after Julian's apostasy expressed the quite natural fear of Christians that such a thing might happen again. Bickerman states matters in a powerful way:

> Julian was yesterday, the persecutors the day before yesterday. Ambrose knew some magistrates who could boast of having spared Christians. At Antioch the Catholics had just endured the persecution of Valens...and unbelievers of every sort dominated the capital of Syria. The army, composed of peasants and barbarians, could acclaim tomorrow another Julian, another Valens, even another Diocletian. One could not yet, as Chrysostom says somewhere, force [people] to accept the Christian truth; one had to convince them of it.[2]

Although matters remained in doubt, the main fact remains: In the beginning of the fourth century Rome was pagan, in the end, Christian. In the beginning Jews in the Land of Israel administered their own affairs. In the end their institution of self-administration lost the recognition it had formerly enjoyed. In the beginning Judaism enjoyed entirely licit status, and the Jews, the protection of the state. In the end Judaism suffered abridgement of its former liberties, and the Jews of theirs.

From the viewpoint of the Jews, the shift signified by the conversion of Constantine marked, as I said, a *caesura* in history. The meaning of history commencing at Creation pointed for Christians toward Christ's triumph in the person of the Emperor and the institution of the Christian state. To Israel, the Jewish people, what can these same events have meant? The received Scriptures of ancient and recent Israel – both Judaic and Christian – now awaited that same sort of sifting and selection that had followed earlier turnings of a notable order,

---

[2]Cited by Wilken, pp. 32-33.

in 586 B.C., and after 70, for example: which writing had now been proved right, which irrelevant? So Christians asked themselves, as they framed the canon of the Bible, both Old and New Testaments. Then to Israel, the Jewish people, what role and what place for the received Torah of Sinai, in its diversity of scrolls? The dogged faith that Jesus really was Christ, Messiah and King of the world, now found vindication in the events of the hour. What hope endured for the salvation of Israel in the future. In the hour of vindication the new Israel confronted the old, the one after the spirit calling into question the legitimacy of the one after the flesh: what now do you say of Christ? For Israel, the Jewish people, what was there to say in reply, not to Christ but to Christians? These three issues frame our principal concerns: the meaning of history, the realization of salvation, definition one's own group in the encounter with the other. In the case of Aphrahat, it was the matter of the definition of "Israel" that comes to the fore. Elsewhere I present all of the three issues in a systematic way.[3]

II
The Issue: Who Is Israel?

The legacy of ancient Israel consisted not only of Scriptures but also of a paramount social category, Israel, God's people and first love. The Church from its origins in the first century confronted the task of situating itself in relationship to "Israel," and Paul's profound reflections in Romans constitute only one among many exercises in responding to that question. For the society of the Church, like the society of the Jews, required a metaphor by which to account for itself. And revering the Scriptures, each group found in "Israel" the metaphor to account for its existence as a distinct social entity. It follows that within the issue Who is Israel? we discern how two competing groups framed theories, each both of itself and also of the other. We therefore confront issues of the identity of a given corporate society as these were spelled out in debates about salvation. The salvific framing of the issue of social definition – who is Israel today (for Judaism)? what sort of social group is the Church (for Christianity)? – served both parties. We deal with a debate on a single issue. It finds its cogency in the common premise of the debate on who is Israel. The shared supposition concerned God's favor and choice of a given entity, one that was *sui generis*, among the social groups of humanity. Specifically, both parties concurred that God did favor and therefore make use of one group and not another. So they could undertake a meaningful debate on the identity of that group.

The debate gained intensity because of a further peculiarity of the discourse between these two groups but no others of the day. Both concurred that the group chosen by God will bear the name, Israel. God's choice among human

---

[3]See my *Judaism and Christianity in the Age of Constantine. Issues in the Initial Confrontation* (Chicago: University of Chicago Press, 1987).

societies would settle the question, which nation does God love and favor. Jews, who saw themselves as the Israel today joined in the flesh to the Israel of the scriptural record. Christians explained themselves as the Israel formed just now, in recent memory, even in the personal experience of the living, among those saved by faith in God's salvation afforded by the resurrection of Jesus Christ. We therefore must not miss the powerful social and political message conveyed by what appear to be statements of a narrowly theological character about salvation and society. In these statements on who is Israel, the parties to the debate chose to affirm each its own unique legitimacy and to deny the other's right to endure at all as a social and national entity.

But both parties shared common premises as to definitions of issues and facts to settle the question. They could mount a sustained argument between themselves because they talked about the same thing, invoked principles of logic in common, shared the definition of the pertinent facts. They differed only as to the outcome. Let us turn to the articulation of the question at hand. The issue of who is Israel articulated in theological, not political, terms covers several topics: are the Jews today "Israel" of ancient times? Was, and is, Jesus Christ? If so, who are the Christians, both on their own and also in relationship to ancient Israel? These questions scarcely can be kept distinct from one another. And all of them cover the ground we have already traversed concerning the meaning of history and the identity of the Messiah. First, was, and is, Jesus Christ? If so, then the Jews who rejected him enjoyed no share in the salvation at hand. If not, then they do. The Christian challenge comes first. If Jesus was and is Christ, then Israel "after the flesh" no longer enjoys the status of the people who bear salvation. Salvation has come, and Israel "after the flesh" has denied it. If he is Christ, then what is the status of those – whether Jews or gentiles – who did accept him? They have received the promises of salvation and their fulfillment. The promises to Israel have been kept for them. Then there is a new Israel, one that is formed of the saved, as the prophets had said in ancient times that Israel would be saved. A further issue that flowed from the first – the rejection of Jesus as Christ – concerns the status of Israel, the Jewish people, now and in time to come. Israel after the flesh, represented from the Gospels forward as the people that rejected Jesus as Christ and participated in his crucifixion, claims to be the family of Abraham, Isaac, Jacob. Then further questions arise. First, does Israel today continue the Israel of ancient times? Israel maintains that Israel now continues in a physical and spiritual way the life of Israel then. Second, will the promises of the prophets to Israel afford salvation for Israel in time to come? Israel "after the flesh" awaits the fulfillment of the prophetic promise of salvation. Clearly, a broad range of questions demanded sorting out. But the questions flow together into a single issue, faced in common. The Christian position on all these questions came to expression in a single negative: no, Israel today does not continue the Israel of old, no, the ancient promises will not again bear salvation, because they have already been kept, so, no, the Israel that declines to accept Jesus' claim to be the Christ is a no-people.

The response of Israel's sages to these same questions proves equally unequivocal. Yes, the Messiah will come in time to come, and yes, he will come to Israel of today, which indeed continues the Israel of old. So the issue is squarely and fairly joined. Who is Israel raises a question that stands second in line to the Messianic one, with which we have already dealt. And, it must follow, the further question of who are the Christians requires close attention to that same messianic question. So, as is clear, the initial confrontation generated a genuine argument on the status and standing, before God, of Israel "after the flesh," the Jewish people. And that argument took on urgency because of the worldly, political triumph of Christianity in Rome, joined, as the fourth century wore on, by the worldly, political decline in the rights and standing of Israel, the Jewish people.

Before Christianity had addressed the issue of who the Christians were, Paul had already asked what the Jews were not. Christians formed the true people of God.[4] So the old and lasting Israel, the Jewish people, did not. Paul had called into question "Israel's status as God's chosen people," because (in Ruether's words) "Israel had failed in its pursuit of righteousness based on the Torah...had been disobedient...[so that] the privileged relation to God provided by the Mosaic covenant has been permanently revoked." So from its origins, Christianity had called into question Israel's former status, and, as Gager says, held that "Israel's disobedience is not only not accidental to God's plan of salvation, it has become an essential part of its fulfillment." The Christian position on one side of ,the matter of who is Israel, namely, who is not Israel, had reached a conclusion before the other aspect of the matter – the Christians' status as a New Israel – came to full expression.[5]

That matter of status closely follows the issue of salvation, as we have already noted. As soon as Christians coalesced into groups, they asked themselves what *sort* of groups they formed. They in fact maintained several positions. First, they held that they were a people, enjoying the status of the Jewish people, and that, as Harnack says, "furnished adherents of the new faith with a political and historical self-consciousness." So they were part of Israel and continued the Israel of ancient times, not a new group but a very old one. But the further defined themselves as not only a new people, but a new *type* of group, recognizing no taxonomic counterpart in the existing spectrum of human societies, peoples or nations. The claims of the Christians varied according to circumstance, so Harnack summarizes matters in a passage of stunning acuity:

> Was the cry raised, "You are renegade Jews" – the answer came, "We are the community of the Messiah, and therefore the true Israelites." If

---

[4]Ruether, pp. 64ff.

[5]Ruether, pp. 64ff., Gager, pp. 256-8.

people said, "You are simply Jews," the reply was, "We are a new creation and a new people." If again they were taxed with their recent origin and told that they were but of yesterday, they retorted, "We only seem to be the younger People; from the beginning we have been latent; we have always existed, previous to any other people; we are the original people of God." If they were told, "You do not deserve to live" the answer ran, "We would die to live, for we are citizens of the world to come, and sure that we shall rise again."[6]

These reflections on the classification of the new group – superior to the old, *sui generis*, and whatever the occasion of polemic requires the group to be – fill the early Christian writings. In general there were three: Greeks or gentiles, Jews, and the Christians as the new People.

When Christians asked themselves what sort of group they formed, they answered that they constituted a new group, and a group of a new type altogether. They identified with the succession to Israel after the flesh, with Israel after the spirit, with a group lacking all parallel or precedent, with God-fearers and law-keepers before Judaism was given at Sinai. The dilemma comes to expression in Eusebius:

In the oracles directed to Abraham, Moses himself writes prophetically how in the times to come the descendants of Abraham, not only his Jewish seed but all the tribes and all the nations of the earth, will be deemed worthy of divine praise because of a common manner of worship like that of Abraham.... How could all the nations and tribes of the earth be blessed in Abraham if no relationship of either a spiritual or a physical nature existed between them?...How therefore could men reared amid an animal existence...be able to share in the blessings of the godly, unless they abandoned their savage ways and sought to participate in a life of piety like that of Abraham?...Now Moses lived after Abraham, and he gave the Jewish race a certain corporate status which was based upon the laws provided by him. If the laws he established were the same as those by which godly men were guided before his time, if they were capable of being adopted by all peoples so that all the tribes and nations of the earth could worship God in accordance with the Mosaic enactments, one could say that the oracles had foretold that because of Mosaic laws men of every nation would worship God and live according to Judaism....However since the Mosaic enactments did not apply to other peoples but to the Jews alone..., a different way, a way distinct from the law of Moses, needed to be established, one by which the nations of all the earth might live as Abraham had so that they could receive an equal share of blessing with him.[7]

Since, with the advent of Constantine, a political dimension served to take the measure of the Christian polity, we have to ask about the political consciousness of the Church in its original formulation. In this matter Harnack

---

[6]Harnack, pp. 241, 244.

[7]*The Proof of the Gospel* I 2:, cited by Luibheid, p. 41.

points out that the political consciousness of the Church rests on three premises, first, the political element in the Jewish apocalyptic, second, the movement of the gospel to the Greeks, and third, the ruin of Jerusalem and the end of the Jewish state. He says, "The first of these elements stood in antithesis to the to others, so that in this way the political consciousness of the church came to be defined in opposite directions and had to work itself out of initial contradictions."[8] From early times, Harnack says, the Christians saw Christianity as "the central point of humanity as the field of political history as well as its determining factor." That had been the Jews' view of themselves. With Constantine the corresponding Christian conception matched reality.

Now the Christians formed a new People, a third race. When the change came, with the Christianization of the Empire at the highest levels of government, the new people, the third race, had to frame a position and policy about the old people, enduring Israel "after the flesh." And, for its part, the Jewish people, faced with the Christian *défi* found the necessity to reaffirm its enduring view of itself, now, however, in response to a pressure without precedent in its long past. The claim of the no-people that the now and enduring Israel is the no-people knew no prior equivalent. The age of Constantine marked the turning of the world: all things were upside down. How to deal with a world that (from the perspective of Israel, the Jewish people) had gone mad? Israel's answer, which we shall reach in due course, proves stunningly a propos: right to the issue, in precisely the terms of the issue. But first let us see how a substantial Christian theologian phrases the matter in the polemic at hand.

III

Aphrahat

To show us how a fourth century Christian theologian addressed the question at hand, namely, who is Israel in the light of the salvation of Jesus Christ, we turn to Aphrahat, a Christian monk in Mesopotamia, ca. 300-350, who wrote, in Syriac, a sustained treatise on the relationship of Christianity and Judaism. His demonstrations, written in 337-344, take up issues facing the Syriac speaking Church in the Iranian Empire. The church then was suffering severe persecution on the part of the Government, for the monks and nuns, maintaining they had no property, could not pay taxes. Since at that time Jews enjoyed stable and peaceful relationships with the Iranian government while Christians did not, the contrast between weak Christianity and secure Judaism required attention as well. Aphrahat presents his case on the base of historical facts shared in common by both parties to the debate, Judaism and Christianity, that is, facts of Scripture. He rarely cites the New Testament in his demonstrations on Judaism. Moreover, when he cites the Hebrew Scriptures, he

---

[8]Harnack, p. 256-7.

ordinarily refrains from fanciful or allegoristic reading of them, but, like the rabbis with whom Jerome dealt, stressed that his interpretation rested solely on the plain and obvious, factual meaning at hand. His arguments thus invoked rational arguments and historical facts: this is what happened, this is what it means. Scriptures therefore present facts, on which all parties concur. Then the argument goes forward on a common ground of shared reason and mutually-agreed-upon facts. Still more important, the program of argument – is Israel, the Jewish people, going to be saved in the future, along with the issue of the standing and status of the Christian people – likewise follows points important to both parties.

Here, as I claimed at the outset, we find Judaic and Christian thinkers disagreeing on a common set of propositions: who is Israel? Will Israel be saved in the future, or have the prophetic promises already been kept. We take up Aphrahat's explanation of "the people which is of the peoples,"the people "which is no people," and then proceed to his address to Israel after the flesh. The two issues complement one another. Once the new people formed out of the peoples enters the status of Israel, then the old Israel loses that status. And how to express that judgment? By denying the premise of the life of Israel after the flesh, that salvation for the people of God would come in future time. If enduring Israel would never enjoy salvation, then Israel had no reason to exist: that is the premise of the argument framed ion behalf of the people that had found its reason to exist (from its perspective) solely in its salvation by Jesus Christ. So what explained to the Christian community how that community had come into being also accounted, for that same community, for the (anticipated) disappearance of the nation that had rejected that very same nation-creating event.

Let me point to Aphrahat's *Demonstration Sixteen, "On the Peoples which are in the Place of the People."* Aphrahat's message is this: "The people Israel was rejected, and the peoples took their place. Israel repeatedly was warned by the prophets, but to no avail, so God abandoned them and replaced them with the gentiles. Scripture frequently referred to the gentiles as "Israel." The vocation of the peoples was prior to that of the people of Israel, and from of old, whoever from among the people was pleasing to God was more justified than Israel: Jethro, the Gibeonites, Rahab, Ebedmelech the Ethiopian, Uriah the Hittite. By means of the gentiles God provoked Israel."

First, Aphrahat maintains, "The peoples which were of all languages were called first, before Israel, to the inheritance of the Most High, as God said to Abraham, 'I have made you the father of a multitude of peoples' (Gen. 17:5). Moses proclaimed, saying, 'The peoples will call to the mountain, and there will they offer sacrifices of righteousness' (Deut. 33:19)." Not only so, but God further rejected Israel: "To his people Jeremiah preached, saying to them, 'Stand by the ways and ask the wayfarers, and see which is the good way. Walk in it.' But they in their stubbornness answered, saying to him, 'We shall not go.'

Again he said to them, 'I established over you watchmen, that you might listen for the sound of the trumpet.' But they said to him again, 'We shall not hearken.' And this openly, publicly did they do in the days of Jeremiah when he preached to them the word of the Lord, and they answered him, saying,'To the word which you have spoken to us in the name of the Lord we shall not hearken. But we shall do our own will and every word which goes out of our mouths, to offer up incense-offerings to other gods'" (Jer. 44:16-17). That is why God turned to the peoples: "When he saw that they would not listen to him, he turned to the peoples, saying to them, 'Hear O peoples, and know, O church which is among them, and hearken, O land, in its fullness' (Jer. 6:18-19)." So who is now Israel? It is the peoples, no longer the old Israel: "By the name of Jacob [now] are called the people which is of the peoples." That is the key to Aphrahat's case. The people that was a no people, that people that had assembled out of the people, has now replaced Israel.

Like Eusebius, Aphrahat maintained that the peoples had been called to God before the people of Israel: "See, my beloved, that the vocation of the peoples was recorded before the vocation of the people. But because the time of the peoples had not come, and another was [to be] their redeemer, Moses was not persuaded that a redeemer and a teacher would come for the people which was of the peoples, which was greater and more worthy than the people of Israel." The people that was a no-people should not regard itself as alien to God: "If they should say, 'Us has he called alien children,' they have not been called alien children, but sons and heirs...But the peoples are those who hearken to God and were lamed and kept back from the ways of their sins." Indeed, the peoples produced believers who were superior in every respect to Israel: "Even from the old, whoever from among the peoples was pleasing to God was more greatly justified than Israel. Jethro the priest who was of the peoples and his seed were blessed: 'Enduring is his dwelling place, and his nest is set on a rock' (Num. 24:21)." Aphrahat here refers to the Gibeonites, Rahab, and various other gentiles mentioned in the scriptural narrative.

Addressing his Christian hearers, Aphrahat then concludes, "By us they are provoked. On our account they do not worship idols, so that they will not be shamed by us, for we have abandoned idols and call lies the thing which our fathers left us. They are angry, their hearts are broken, for we have entered and have become heirs in their place. For theirs was this covenant which they had, not to worship other gods, but they did not accept it. By means of us he provoked them, and ours was the light and the life, as he preached, saying when he taught, 'I am the light of the world' (John 8:12)." So he concludes, "This brief memorial I have written to you concerning the peoples, because the Jews take pride and say, 'We are the people of God and the children of Abraham. ' But we shall listen to John [the Baptist] who, when they took pride [saying], 'We are the children of Abraham,' then said to them, 'You should not boast and say,

Abraham is father unto us, for from these very rocks can God raise up children for Abraham' (Matthew 3:9)."

In *Demonstration Nineteen, "Against the Jews, on account of their saying that they are destined to be gathered together,"* Aphrahat proceeds to the corollary argument, that the Israel after the flesh has lost its reason to endure as a nation. Why? Because no salvation awaits them in the future. The prophetic promises of salvation have all come to fulfillment in the past, and the climactic salvation for Israel, through the act of Jesus Christ, brought the salvific drama to its conclusion. Hence the Jews' not having a hope of "joining together" at the end of their exile forms a critical part of the entire picture. Here is a summary of the argument: "The Jews expect to be gathered together by the Messiah, but this expectation is in vain. God was never reconciled to them but has rejected them. The prophetic promises of restoration were all fulfilled in the return from Babylonia. Daniel's prayer was answered, and his vision was realized in the time of Jesus and in the destruction of Jerusalem. It will never be rebuilt."

Aphrahat thus stresses that the Jews's sins caused their own condition, a position which sages accepted: "On account of their sins, which were many, he uprooted and scattered them among every nation, for they did not listen to his prophets, whom he had sent to them." The Jews now maintain that they will see salvation in the future, but they are wrong: "I have written this to you because even today they hope an empty hope, saying, 'It is still certain for Israel to be gathered together,' for the prophet thus spoke, 'I shall leave none of them among the nations' (Ex. 39:28). But if all of our people is to be gathered together, why are we today scattered among every people?" But, Aphrahat states, "Israel never is going to be gathered together." The reason is that God was never reconciled to Israel: "I shall write and show you that never did God accept their repentance [through] either Moses or all of the prophets .... Further, Jeremiah said, 'They are called rejected silver, for the Lord has rejected them' (Jer. 6:30). ... See, then, they have never accepted correction in their lives."

Aphrahat presents an array of prophetic proof-texts for the same proposition. Then he turns to the peoples and declares that they have taken the place of the people: "Concerning the vocation of the peoples Isaiah said, 'It shall come to be in the last days that the mountain of the House of the Lord will be established at the head of the mountains and high above the heights. Peoples will come together to it, and many peoples will go and say, Come, let us go up to the mountain of the Lord, to the House of the God of Jacob. He will teach us his ways, and we shall walk in his paths. For from Zion the law will go forth, and the word of the Lord from Jerusalem' (Is. 2:2, 3)." Does Israel not hope for redemption in the future? Indeed so, but they are wrong: "Two times only did God save Israel: Once from Egypt, the second time from Babylonia; from Egypt by Moses, and from Babylonia by Ezra and by the prophecy of Haggai and Zechariah. Haggai said, 'Build this house, and I shall have pleasure in it, and in it I shall be glorified, says the Lord' (Hag. 1:8) ... All of these things were said in the days of Zerubbabel, Haggai, and Zechariah. They were exhorting concerning the building of the house." The house was built – and then destroyed, and it will not be rebuilt. (Aphrahat wrote before Julian's proposed rebuilding of the temple, so he could not have derived further proof from that disaster.)

So much for the challenge of those who held such views as Aphrahat expresses. The case is complete: the people which is no-people, the people which is of the peoples, have taken the place of the people which claims to carry forward the salvific history of ancient Israel. The reason is in two complementary parts. First, Israel has rejected salvation, so lost its reason to exist, and, second, the no-people have accepted salvation, so gained its reason to exist. So the threads of the dispute link into a tight fabric: the shift in the character of politics, marked by the epochal triumph of Christianity in the state, bears profound meaning for the messianic mission of the Church, and, further, imparts a final judgment on the salvific claim of the competing nations of God: the Church and Israel. What possible answer can sages have proposed to this indictment? Since at the heart of the matter lies the claim that Israel persists in the salvific heritage that has passed to the Christians, sages reaffirm that Israel persists – just as Paul had framed matters – after the flesh, an unconditional and permanent status. For one never ceases to be the son of his mother and his father, and the daughter is always the daughter of her father and her mother. So Israel after the flesh constitutes the family, in the most physical form, of Abraham, Isaac, and Jacob. And, moreover, as that family, Israel inherits the heritage of salvation hand on by the patriarchs and matriarchs. The spiritualization of "Israel" here finds its opposite and counterpart: the utter and complete "genealogization" of Israel.

IV

The Judaic Response in Leviticus Rabbah

Just as nothing in Aphrahat's case would have struck as alien his Roman-Christian counterparts, so we shall now see that, on the Roman side of the border, the Judaic sages responded just as their counterparts in Iran framed matters. The Judaic position vis-a-vis Christianity was not affected by political frontiers, even as the Judaic-Christian confrontation had been precipitated by a political event in the conversion of Constantine. Briefly to examine the Judaic side of the issue, we turn to a document framed in what Jews know as the Land of Israel, in the Christian Roman empire of the fifth century, a century beyond the crisis at hand. A cogent and propositional commentary to the book of Leviticus, Leviticus Rabbah, ca. 400-450, reads the laws of the on-going sanctification in nature of the life of Israel as an account of the rules of the one-time salvation in history of the polity of Israel.

To the framers of Leviticus Rabbah, one point of emphasis proved critical: Israel remains Israel, the Jewish people, after the flesh, because Israel today continues the family begun by Abraham, Isaac, Jacob, Joseph and the other tribal founders, and bears the heritage bequeathed by them. That conviction of who is Israel never required articulation. The contrary possibility fell wholly outside of sages' (and all Jews') imagination. To state matters negatively, the people could no more conceive that they were not the daughters and sons of their fathers and mothers than that they were not one large family, that is, the family of Abraham, Isaac, and Jacob: Israel after the flesh. That is what "after the flesh" meant. The powerful stress on the enduring merit of the patriarchs and matriarchs, the social theory that treated Israel as one large, extended family, the actual children of Abraham, Isaac, and Jacob – these metaphors for the fleshly continuity surely met head on the contrary position framed by Paul and restated by Christian theologians from his time onward. In this respect, while Aphrahat did not deny the Israel-ness of Israel, the Jewish people, he did underline the futility of enduring as Israel. Maintaining that Israel would see no future salvation amounted to declaring that Israel, the Jewish people, pursued no worthwhile purpose in continuing to endure. Still, the argument is head-on and concrete: who is Israel? who enjoys salvation? To sages, as we shall see, the nations of the world serve God's purpose in ruling Israel, just as the prophets had said, and Israel, for its part, looks forward to a certain salvation.

The position of the framers of Leviticus Rabbah on the issues at hand emerges in both positive and negative formulation. On the positive side, Israel, the Jewish people, the people of whom Scriptures spoke and to whom, today, sages now speak, is God's first love. That position of course presents no surprises and can have been stated with equal relevance in any circumstances. We in no way can imagine that the authors of Leviticus Rabbah stress the points that they stress in particular because Christians have called them into question. I doubt that that was the case. In fact when we survey the verses important to Aphrahat's case and ask what, in the counterpart writings of sages in all of late antiquity, people say about those same verses, we find remarkably little attention to the florilegium of proof-texts adduced by Aphrahat.[9] While the argument on who is Israel did not take shape on the foundation of a shared program of verses, on which each party entered its position, the issue was one and the same. And the occasion – the political crisis of the fourth century – faced both parties.

Sages delivered a message particular to their system. The political context imparted to that message urgency for Israel beyond their small circle. As to confronting the other side, no sage would concede what to us is self-evident. This was the urgency of the issue. For the definition of what was at issue derived from the common argument of the age: Who is the Messiah? Christ or someone else? Here too, while the argument between Christian theologians and

---

[9]See my *Aphrahat and Judaism* (Leiden: E. J. Brill, 1970), pp. 150-195.

Judaic sages on the present status of Israel, the Jewish people, went forward on
the same basic issues, it ran along parallel lines. True, lines of argument never
intersected at all, just as, in our review of sage's doctrine of the Messiah, we
could not find a point of intersection with the Christian position on the
Christhood of Jesus. The issue in both topics, however, is what was the same,
even though the exposition of arguments on one side's proposition in no way
intersected with the other side's.

When Aphrahat denied that God loves Israel any more, and contemporary
sages affirmed that God yet loves Israel and always will, we come to a clearcut
exchange of views on a common topic. Parallel to Aphrahat's sustained
demonstrations on a given theme, the framers of Leviticus Rabbah laid forth
thematic exercises, each one serving in a cumulative way to make a given point
on a single theme. Therefore in order to describe sages' position, we do well to
follow their ideas in their own chosen medium of expression. I can find no more
suitable way of recapitulating their reply to the question, Who is Israel? than by
a brief survey of one of the sustained essays they present on the subject in
Leviticus Rabbah.[10] We proceed to the unfolding, in Leviticus Rabbah
Parashah Two, of the theme: Israel is precious. At Lev. R. II:III.2.B, we find an
invocation of the genealogical justification for the election of Israel: "He said to
him, 'Ephraim, head of the tribe, head of the session, one who is beautiful and
exalted above all of my sons will be called by your name: [Samuel, the son of
Elkanah, the son of Jeroham,] the son of Tohu, the son of Zuph, an Ephraimite'
[1 Sam. 1:1]; 'Jerobaom son of Nabat, an Ephraimite' [1 Sam. 11:26]. 'And
David was an Ephraimite, of Bethlehem in Judah' (1 Sam. 17:12)." Since
Ephraim, that is, Israel, had been exiled, the deeper message cannot escape our
attention. Whatever happens, God loves Ephraim. However Israel suffers, God's
love endures, and God cares. In context, that message brings powerful
reassurance. Facing a Rome gone Christian, sages had to begin with to state the
obvious – which no longer seemed self-evident at all. What follows spells out
this very point: God is especially concerned with Israel.

II:IV

1. A. Returning to the matter (GWPH): "Speak to the children of Israel" (Lev.
      1:2).
   B. R. Yudan in the name of R. Samuel b. R. Nehemiah: "The matter may be
      compared to the case of a king who had an undergarment, concerning
      which he instructed his servant, saying to him, 'Fold it, shake it out, and
      be careful about it!'
   C. "He said to him, 'My lord, O king, among all the undergarments that you
      have, [why] do you give me such instructions only about this one?'
   D. "He said to him, 'It is because this is the one that I keep closest to my
      body.'

---

[10]The complete texts are in the Appendix to my *Judaism and Christianity in the Age of
Constantine*.

E. "So too did Moses say before the Holy One, blessed be He, Lord of the
    Universe: 'Among the seventy distinct nations that you have in your
    world, [why] do you give me instructions only concerning Israel? [For
    instance,] "Command the children of Israel" [Num. 28:2], "Say to the
    children of Israel" [Ex. 33:5], "Speak to the children of Israel" [Lev.
    1:2].'

F. "He said to him, 'The reason is that they stick close to me, in line with
    the following verse of Scripture: "For as the undergarment cleaves to the
    loins of a man, so have I caused to cleave unto me the whole house of
    Israel" (Jer. 13:11).'"

G. Said R. Abin, "[The matter may be compared] to a king who had a purple
    cloak, concerning which he instructed his servant, saying, 'Fold it, shake
    it out, and be careful about it!'

H. "He said to him, 'My Lord, O king, among all the purple cloaks that you
    have, [why] do you give me such instructions only about this one?'

I. "He said to him, 'That is the one that I wore on my coronation day.'

J. "So too did Moses say before the Holy One, blessed be He, Lord of the
    Universe: 'Among the seventy distinct nations that you have in your
    world, [why] do you give instructions to me only concerning Israel?
    [For instance,] "Say to the children of Israel," "Command the children
    of Israel," "Speak to the children of Israel."'

K. "He said to him, 'They are the ones who at the [Red] Sea declared me to
    be king, saying, "The Lord will be king" (Ex. 15:18).'"

The point of the passage has to do with Israel's particular relationship to God:
Israel cleaves to God, declares God to be king, and accepts God's dominion.
Further evidence of God's love for Israel derives from the commandments
themselves. God watches over every little thing that Jews do, even caring what
they eat for breakfast. The familiar stress on the keeping of the laws of the
Torah as a mark of hope finds fulfillment here: the laws testify to God's deep
concern for Israel. So there is sound reason for high hope, expressed in
particular in keeping the laws of the Torah. Making the matter explicit, Simeon
b. Yohai (Lev. R. II:V.1.A-B) translates this fact into a sign of divine favor:

II:V

1. A. Said R. Simeon b. Yohai, "[The matter may be compared] to a king who
        had an only son. Every day he would give instructions to his steward,
        saying to him, 'Make sure my son eats, make sure my son drinks, make
        sure my son goes to school, make sure my son comes home from
        school.'

    B. "So every day the Holy One, blessed be He, gave instructions to Moses,
        saying, 'Command the children of Israel,' 'Say to the children of Israel,'
        'Speak to the children of Israel.'"

We now come to the statement of how Israel wins and retains God's favor. The
issue at hand concerns Israel's relationship to the nations before God, which is
corollary to what has gone before. It is in two parts. First of all, Israel knows
how to serve God in the right way. Second, the nations, though they do what

Israel does, do things wrong. First, Israel does things right. Why then is Israel beloved? The following answers that question.

V:VIII

1. A. R. Simeon b. Yohai taught, "How masterful are the Israelites, for they know how to find favor with their creator."

    E. Said R. Hunia [in Aramaic:], "There is a tenant farmer who knows how to borrow things, and there is a tenant farmer who does not know how to borrow. The one who knows how to borrow combs his hair, brushes off his clothes, puts on a good face, and then goes over to the overseer of his work to borrow from him. [The overseer] says to him, 'How's the land doing?' He says to him, 'May you have the merit of being fully satisfied with its [wonderful] produce.' 'How are the oxen doing?' He says to him, 'May you have the merit of being fully satisfied with their fat.' 'How are the goats doing?' 'May you have the merit of being fully satisfied with their young.' 'And what would you like?' Then he says, 'Now if you might have an extra ten denars, would you give them to me?' The overseer replies, 'If you want, take twenty.'

    F. "But the one who does not know how to borrow leaves his hair a mess, his clothes filthy, his face gloomy. He too goes over to the overseer to borrow from him. The overseer says to him, 'How's the land doing?' He replies, 'I hope it will produce at least what [in seed] we put into it.' 'How are the oxen doing?' 'They're scrawny.' 'How are the goats doing?' 'They're scrawny too.' 'And what do you want?' 'Now if you might have an extra ten denars, would you give them to me?' The overseer replies, 'Go, pay me back what you already owe me!'"

If Aphrahat had demanded a direct answer, he could not have received a more explicit one. He claims Israel does nothing right. Sages counter, speaking in their own setting of course, that they do everything right. Sages then turn the tables on the position of Aphrahat – again addressing it head-on. While the nations may do everything Israel does, they do it wrong.

Sages recognized in the world only one counterpart to Israel, and that was Rome. Rome's history formed the counterweight to Israel's. So Rome as a social entity weighed in the balance against Israel. That is why we return to the corollary question: who is Rome? For we can know who is Israel only if we can also explain who is Rome. And, I should maintain, explaining who is Rome takes on urgency at the moment at which Rome presents to Israel problems of an unprecedented character. The matter belongs in any picture of who is Israel. Sages' doctrine of Rome forms the counterpart to Christian theologians' theory on who is Israel. Just as Aphrahat explains both who are the Christians and also who is Israel today, so sages in Leviticus Rabbah develop an important theory on who is Rome. They too propose to account for the way things are, and that means, they have to explain who is this counterpart to Israel. And sages' theory does respond directly to the question raised by the triumph of Christianity in the Roman Empire. For, as we shall see, the characterization of Rome in Leviticus Rabbah bears the burden of their judgment on the definition of the Christian people, as much as the sages' characterization of Rome in Leviticus Rabbah expressed their judgment of the place of Rome in the history of Israel.

To understand that position on the character of Rome, we have to note that it constitutes a radical shift in the characterization of Rome in the unfolding canon of the sages' Judaism. For the treatment of Rome shifts in a remarkable way from the earlier approach to the subject. Rome in the prior writings, the Mishnah (ca. A.D. 200) and the Tosefta (ca. A.D. 300-400), stood for a particular place. We begin, once more, with the view of the Mishnah. For matters show a substantial shift in the characterization of Rome from the earlier to the later writings. Had matters remained pretty much the same from earlier, late second century, to later, fourth and early fifth century, writings, we could not maintain that what is said in the fourth century documents testifies in particular to intellectual events of the fourth century. We should have to hold that, overall, the doctrine was set and endured in its original version. What happened later on would then have no bearing upon the doctrine at hand, and my claim of a confrontation on a vivid issue would not find validation. But the doctrine of Rome does shift from the Mishnah to the fourth century sages' writings, Leviticus Rabbah, Genesis Rabbah, and the Talmud of the Land of Israel. That fact proves the consequence, in the interpretation of ideas held in the fourth century, of the venue of documents in that time.

We have already seen the adumbration of the position that, in Leviticus Rabbah, would come to remarkably rich expression. Rome now stood for much more than merely a place among other places. Rome took up a place in the unfolding of the empires – Babylonia, Media, Greece, then Rome. Still more important Rome is the penultimate empire on earth. Israel will constitute the ultimate one. That message, seeing the shifts in world history in a pattern and placing at the apex of the shift Israel itself, directly and precisely takes up the issue made urgent just now: the advent of the Christian emperors. Why do I maintain, as I do, that in the characterization of Rome as the fourth and penultimate empire/animal, sages address issues of their own day? Because Rome, among the successive empires, bears special traits, most of which derive from the distinctively Christian character of Rome.

Rome is represented as only Christian Rome can have been represented: it looks kosher but it is unkosher. Pagan Rome cannot ever have looked kosher, but Christian Rome, with its appeal to ancient Israel, could and did and moreover claimed to. It bore some traits that validate, but lacked others that validate – just as Jerome said of Israel. It would be difficult to find a more direct confrontation between two parties to an argument. Now the issue is the same – who is the true Israel? and the proof-texts are the same, and, moreover, the proof-texts are read in precisely the same way. Only the conclusions differ!

The polemic represented in Leviticus Rabbah by the symbolization of Christian Rome makes the simple point that, first, Christians are no different from, and no better than, pagans; they are essentially the same. Christians' claim to form part of Israel then requires no serious attention. Since Christians came to Jews with precisely that claim, the sages' response – they are another Babylonia – bears a powerful polemic charge. But that is not the whole story, as we see. Second, just as Israel had survived Babylonia, Media, Greece, so would they endure to see the end of Rome (whether pagan, whether Christian). But there is a third point. Rome really does differ from the earlier, pagan empires, and that polemic shifts the entire discourse, once we hear its symbolic vocabulary properly. For the new Rome really did differ from the old. Christianity was not merely part of a succession of undifferentiated modes of paganism. The symbols assigned to Rome attributed worse, more dangerous traits than those assigned to the earlier empires. The pig pretends to be clean, just as the Christians give the signs of adherence to the God of Abraham, Isaac, and Jacob. That much the passage concedes. For the pig is not clean, exhibiting some, but not all, of the required indications, and Rome is not Israel, even though it shares Israel's Scripture. That position, denying to Rome, in its Christian form, a place in the family of Israel, forms the counterpart to the view of Aphrahat that Israel today is no longer Israel – again, a confrontation on issues. I present only the critical passage at which the animals that are invoked include one that places Rome at the interstices, partly kosher, partly not, therefore more dangerous than anyone else.

XIII:V

9. A. Moses foresaw what the evil kingdoms would do [to Israel].
   B. "The camel, rock badger, and hare" (Deut. 14:7). [Compare: "Nevertheless, among those that chew the cud or part the hoof, you shall not eat these: the camel, because it chews the cud but does not part the hoof, is unclean to you. The rock badger, because it chews the cud but does not part the hoof, is unclean to you. And the hare, because it chews the cud but does not part the hoof, is unclean to you, and the pig, because it parts the hoof and is cloven-footed, but does not chew the cud, is unclean to you" (Lev. 11:4-8).]
   C. The camel (GML) refers to Babylonia, [in line with the following verse of Scripture: "O daughter of Babylonia, you who are to be devastated!] Happy will be he who requites (GML) you, with what you have done to us" (Ps. 147:8).
   D. "The rock badger" (Deut. 14:7) – this refers to Media.
   E. Rabbis and R. Judah b. R. Simon.
   F. Rabbis say, "Just as the rock badger exhibits traits of uncleanness and traits of cleanness, so the kingdom of Media produced both a righteous man and a wicked one."
   G. Said R. Judah b. R. Simon, "The last Darius was Esther's son. He was clean on his mother's side and unclean on his father's side."
   H. "The hare" (Deut 14:7) – this refers to Greece. The mother of King Ptolemy was named "Hare" [in Greek: lagos].
   I. "The pig" (Deut. 14:7) – this refers to Edom [Rome].
   J. Moses made mention of the first three in a single verse and the final one in a verse by itself [(Deut. 14:7, 8)]. Why so?

K. R. Yohanan and R. Simeon b. Laqish.

L. R. Yohanan said, "It is because [the pig] is equivalent to the other three."

M. And R. Simeon b. Laqish said, "It is because it outweighs them."

N. R. Yohanan objected to R. Simeon b. Laqish, "'Prophesy, therefore, son of man, clap your hands [and let the sword come down twice, yea thrice]' (Ez. 21:14)."

O. And how does R. Simeon b. Laqish interpret the same passage? He notes that [the threefold sword] is doubled (Ez. 21:14).

In the apocalypticizing of the animals of Lev. 11:4-8/Deut. 14:7, the camel, rock badger, hare, and pig, the pig, standing for Rome, again emerges as different from the others and more threatening than the rest. Just as the pig pretends to be a clean beast by showing the cloven hoof, but in fact is an unclean one, so Rome pretends to be just but in fact governs by thuggery. Edom does not pretend to praise God but only blasphemes. It does not exalt the righteous but kills them. These symbols concede nothing to Christian monotheism and veneration of the Torah of Moses (in its written medium). Of greatest importance, while all the other beasts bring further ones in their wake, the pig does not: "It does not bring another kingdom after it." It will restore the crown to the one who will truly deserve it, Israel. Esau will be judged by Zion, so Obadiah 1:21. Now how has the symbolization delivered an implicit message? It is in the treatment of Rome as distinct, but essentially equivalent to the former kingdoms. This seems to me a stunning way of saying that the now-Christian empire in no way requires differentiation from its pagan predecessors. Nothing has changed, except matters have gotten worse. Beyond Rome, standing in a straight line with the others, lies the true shift in history, the rule of Israel and the cessation of the dominion of the (pagan) nations. To conclude, Leviticus Rabbah came to closure, it is generally agreed, around A.D. 400-450, that is, approximately a century after the Roman Empire in the east had begun to become Christian, and half a century after the last attempt to rebuild the Temple in Jerusalem had failed – a tumultuous age indeed. Accordingly, we have had the chance to see how distinctive and striking are the ways in which, in the text at hand, the symbols of animals that stand for the four successive empires of humanity and point towards the messianic time, serve for the framers' message. Rome in the fourth century became Christian. Sages responded by facing that fact quite squarely and saying, "Indeed, it is as you say, a kind of Israel, an heir of Abraham as your texts explicitly claim. But we remain the sole legitimate Israel, the bearer of the birthright – we and not you. So you are our brother: Esau, Ishmael, Edom." And the rest follows.

Sages framed their political ideas within the metaphor of genealogy, because to begin with they appealed to the fleshly connection, the family, as the rationale for Israel's social existence. A family beginning with Abraham, Isaac, and Jacob, Israel today could best sort out its relationships by drawing into the family other social entities with which it found it had to relate. So Rome became the brother. That affinity came to light only when Rome had turned Christian, and that point marked the need for the extension of the genealogical net. But the conversion to Christianity also justified sages' extending membership in the family to Rome, for Christian Rome shared with Israel the common patrimony of Scripture – and said so. The two facts, the one of the social and political metaphor by which sages interpreted events, the other of the very character of Christianity – account for the striking shift in the treatment of Rome that does appear to have taken place in the formative century represented by work on Leviticus Rabbah.

IV

Aphrahat in Iran, Sages in Rome: The Single Issue

The issue is joined, fully, completely, head-on. And well it was. For the stakes, for both sides, were very high. Aphrahat alerts us to the Christians' human problem. They saw themselves as a people without a past, a no-people, a people gathered from the peoples. Then who they can claim to be hardly derives from who they have been. Identifying with ancient Israel – a perfectly natural and correct initiative – admirably accounted for the Christian presence in humanity, provided a past, explained to diverse people what they had in common. One problem from Christians theologians' perspective demanded solution: the existing Israel, the Jewish people, which revered the same Scriptures and claimed descent, after the flesh, from ancient Israel. These – the Jews – traced their connection to ancient Israel, seeing it as natural, and also, supernatural. The family tie, through Abraham, Isaac, Jacob, formed a powerful apologetic indeed. The Jews furthermore pointed to their family record, the Scriptures, to explain whence they come and who they are. So long as the two parties to the debate shared the same subordinated political circumstance, Jewry could quite nicely hold its own in the debate; the pleading tone of Aphrahat's writing opens a window onto the heart of the historical newcomers to salvation, as Christians saw themselves. But with the shift in the politics of the Empire, the terms of debate changed. The parvenu become paramount, the Christian party to the debate invoked its familiar position now with the power of the state in support. Aphrahat's framing of the issue reflects that political fact – even though Aphrahat, living in Shapur II's Iran, did not himself live in a Christian empire. The sages represented by Leviticus Rabbah answered the issues set forth on the agenda represented by Aphrahat, because wherever they lived, they too followed the inner logic of the issue, not the dictates of an ephemeral circumstance, in reflecting on the confrontation with the other Israel.

For Israel what was there to say, but what, in Israel's view, God had said to Israel in the Torah's record of the very beginnings of the world. What now makes that old message matter is simple: the specific context to which, at just this moment, the old words were spoken. That milieu is what imparts meaning to the message: the rise to state recognition and favor of one of the two parties to the dispute of the godly genealogy. And what gives that fact weight for us is the further, equally simple fact that, in the unfolding of the canon of the sages' Judaism, the documents before us contain the first explicit and emphatic statement of the age-old genealogy of God's people. So while the framers of Leviticus Rabbah may have stated in their own medium a familiar and routine message, still, the setting turns out to supply the catalyst of significance. Content, out of political context, is mere theology. But in political context, the theological issues, fully understood in all their awful urgency, focus on matters of social life or death. The doctrines of history and merit, of Israel's identity, selection and grace – these turn out to deal with the very life and identity of a people and its society.

Bibliography

General

N. H. Baynes, *Constantine the Great and the Christian Church* (New York: Oxford University Press, 1972). Second ed., preface by Henry Chadwick.

Erwin R. Goodenough, *The Church in the Roman Empire* (New York: Henry Holt, 1931. Reprint New York: Cooper Square Publishers, Inc., 1970), pp. 41-61.

Adolf Harnack, *The Mission and Expansion of Christianity in the First Three Centuries*. Translated and edited by James Moffatt (London: 1908. Reprint Gloucester: Peter Smith, 1972).

J. R. Palanque, G. Bardy, P. de Labriolle, G. de Plinval, and Louis Brehier, *The Church in the Christian Roman Empire. I. The Church and the Arian Crisis* (New York: Macmillan, 1953). With special reference to Pierre de Labriolle, "Christianity and Paganism in the Middle of the Fourth Century," p. 220-257.

Rosemary Radford Ruether, *Faith and Fratricide. The Theological Roots of Anti-Semitism* (New York: Seabury Press, 1979).

Rosemary Radford Ruether, "Judaism and Christianity. Two Fourth-Century Religions," *Sciences Religieuses Studies in Religion* 1972, 2:1-10.

Marcel Simon, *Verus Israel. Etude sur les relations entre chrétiens et juifs dans l'empire romain* (135-425) (Paris: Editions E. de Boccard, 1964).

Judaism in the Land of Israel and in Babylonia

Jacob Neusner, *A History of the Jews in Babylonia* (Leiden: 1969) III. *The Age of Shapur II.*

Jacob Neusner, *Judaism in Society. The Evidence of the Yerushalmi. Toward the Natural History of a Religion* (Chicago: University of Chicago Press,

1983). I have made use of materials in that work for the description given in this section, cf. pp. 117-121, 196-197, 247-253.

Aphrahat and Judaism

John G. Gager, *The Origins of Anti-Semitism. Attitudes toward Judaism in Pagan and Christian Antiquity* (New York: Oxford University Press, 1983), pp. 247-264.

Adolf Harnack, *The Mission and Expansion of Christianity in the First Three Centuries.* Translated and edited by James Moffatt (London: 1908. Reprint Gloucester: Peter Smith, 1972), pp. 240-278.

Colm Luibheid, *The Essential Eusebius* (New York: Mentor Omega, 1966), p. 41

Rosemary Radford Ruether, *Faith and Fratricide. The Theological Roots of Anti-Semitism* (New York: Seabury Press, 1979).

Marcel Simon, *Verus Israel. Etude sur les relations entre chrétiens et juifs dans l'empire romain* (135-425) (Paris: Editions E. de Boccard, 1964), on Christians as a third type of people, pp. 135-139; on the *Adversus Judaeos* literature in general, pp. 166-176.

Aphrahat and the People Which Is No People

Robert Murray, *Symbols of Church and Kingdom. A Study in Early Syriac Tradition* (Cambridge: Cambridge University Press, 1975).

Jacob Neusner, *Aphrahat and Judaism. The Christian-Jewish Argument in Fourth-Century Iran* (Leiden: E. J. Brill, 1971).

Index

www.ingramcontent.com/pod-product-compliance
Lightning Source LLC
Chambersburg PA
CBHW022023090426
42739CB00006BA/265